APART from a few outstanding personalities of the calibre of Bishop Challoner or Bishop Milner not much is generally known about the Vicars Apostolic under whose guidance the Faith was kept alive in England during a period when the persecution of Catholics took the form of continual and heavy fines, political and social disabilities, and much else which was in many ways far harder to bear than had been the bloodier persecution of the preceding generation. Dom Basil is an authority on this period and his book is the fruit of much research in the Westminster Archives and elsewhere. The first part gives a most useful picture of the general background and brings out many things in the Catholic life of the 18th century which are as fascinating as they are unfamiliar. The second part deals with each of the bishops personally, including two of James I's reign, and all the major crises in ecclesiastical politics, scandalous and otherwise, are dealt with. Another interesting feature is the first emergence of modern landmarks such as Prior Park, Old Hall, Stonyhurst, Downside, Oscott, and so forth. In short this is an exceedingly interesting and readable book which will appeal to both specialists and the ordinary reader.

THE EARLY VICARS APOSTOLIC
OF ENGLAND

Bonaventure Giffard.

1687

Aux

Bishop.

Bp. of Madura.

THE
EARLY VICARS APOSTOLIC
OF ENGLAND

1685—1750

by

DOM BASIL HEMPHILL, O.S.B., M.A.

*"A period in which men were called on to endure,
rather than to achieve."*—POLLARD AND BURTON.

LONDON
BURNS & OATES

PERMISSV SVPERIORVM O.S.B.

NIHIL OBSTAT : EDWARDVS MAHONEY, S.T.D.
CENSOR DEPVTATVS
IMPRIMATVR : E. MORROGH BERNARD
VICARIVS GENERALIS
WESTMONASTERII : DIE XVI OCTOBRIS MCMLIII

MADE AND PRINTED IN GREAT BRITAIN AT THE CHAPEL RIVER PRESS,
ANDOVER, HANTS, FOR BURNS OATES AND WASHBOURNE LTD.
28 ASHLEY PLACE, LONDON, S.W.1

First published 1954

CONTENTS

v

ILLUSTRATIONS

*The above illustrations are reproduced by kind
permission of the Librarian, Ushaw College.*

MAP

INTRODUCTION

THIS book is intended as a small contribution towards helping to bridge a gap that has long existed in our Catholic historical studies. The first half of the eighteenth century has been strangely neglected by our writers. From the time of Bishop Challoner, i.e. from roughly 1750, the ground has been more than adequately covered, but the earlier period is largely a *terra incognita*. Thus Dr. Burton[1] could write of the period 1688-1740: 'There has been no epoch in the history of the Church in this land about which so little has yet been written. From 1690 to 1740 there is almost a blank in our annals . . . a dim twilight in which we have only a blurred outline with occasional glimpses . . . of men and things.' And in the Introduction written in 1909 by Pollen and Burton to Kirk's *Biographies* we read: 'There is no period of Catholic history which is at present more obscure than the 18th century. We know more, far more, about the thirty years that succeeded the landing of Fr. Campion in England than we do about the 140 years that passed between King James's flight from Whitehall and the Emancipation Bill . . . The inconspicuous church in the catacombs of the 18th century has hitherto enkindled but little enthusiasm. But the period of neglect is passing away. It is recognized that we are allied more closely to the latter period than to the former.'

These pages seek to give some picture of the men who were in control of Catholic affairs in England during that largely ignored or forgotten period, with special reference to the manner and circumstances of their appointment. These men, the Catholic bishops in England, were called ' Vicars Apostolic ', because they were not ordinary diocesan bishops, since in those days of persecution it was impossible to set up the normal ecclesiastical hierarchy. England was thus considered a ' missionary ' country, and so was ruled ecclesiastically by Vicars Apostolic—just as the foreign missions are to-day. Thus it is with the Vicars Apostolic of England, the ' emergency bishops ' who ruled the Church in this country in those abnormal circumstances, that this volume is concerned. That that picture is in some respects not altogether

[1] *The Life and Times of Bishop Challoner.*

what one would have liked is merely the consequence of the fact that the clergy, then as now, were humans, and therefore, like the rest of us, they possessed their individual failings. We must expect, then, to find the usual human weaknesses, including such things as personal ambitions, jealousies, uncharitableness, and the like. That is inevitable. And partly for that reason the characters in these pages have been allowed very largely to tell the story in their own words, with a minimum of comment. The picture that emerges is the product of their own letters.

In this connection it is necessary to realize that most unfortunate jealousies persisted between the secular and the regular clergy throughout the seventeenth and eighteenth centuries, and with an intensity which seems incredible to us to-day. Any picture of the times which ignored this factor would be completely misleading. Indeed so great was this friction over a very long period that Mgr. Bernard Ward did not hesitate to say that

> When all allowance has been made for the natural and inevitable friction, when we view the period as a whole, without apportioning the blame between one side or the other, we cannot escape the conclusion that the grumbling was carried to a degree which was even scandalous; and it was this more than anything else which led to the loss of the Faith in this country.[1]

And he goes on to quote the Jesuit Father Morris to the effect that the blood of the martyrs was shed in vain because of ' the awful dissensions that prevailed between seculars and regulars . . . God's blessing could not rest on the work of men amongst whom such animosity was found '. No one wants to perpetuate such memories, but history if it be truthful must necessarily include abuses and scandals, and if it be not truthful it is of no use at all. Pope Leo XIII urged the Catholic historian never to shrink from telling such things, and said he should never fear to relate what is true, appealing to the example of Scripture which did not gloss over the fall of St. Peter. Lingard, too, was of the same opinion, and in other of his works Bishop Ward wrote :

> Now that the unfortunate disputes . . . which have disfigured our English Catholic history are happily a thing of the past, there is nothing to gain by refusing to face the mistakes committed on both sides in the heat of the fray; and anything

[1] MS. of Ward's *The English Secular Clergy*, in Westminster Archives.

which helps towards a dispassionate and impartial narrative of events is a point gained.[1]

If the lessons of history are to be learnt, it is necessary that we should be willing to face such matters [dissensions], provided that sufficient time has elapsed to prevent the recital from being the source of a revival of party feelings now happily long extinct. Milner expressed his opinion that 30 years ought to elapse.[2]

But while there is inevitably this less attractive side, it should never be lost sight of that all these men were deeply spiritual and zealous priests, that their virtues greatly outweighed their failings, that they lived in circumstances of the greatest difficulty, discomfort, and often danger, and that only a burning faith and indomitable courage, fed by the grace of God, could have kept them going in those discouraging days. When all is said and done there stands out ever in our memory the steadfastness and long-suffering patience of Bishop Giffard, the gentleness and humility of Bishop Petre, the charity and self-sacrificing zeal of Bishop Smith, the truly apostolic labours of Bishop Prichard, and the inspiring vigour and leadership of Bishop Stonor. In face of these things we can forget and condone whatever was petty, whatever was 'of the earth, earthy'; it is the spirituality and the courage and the unflagging zeal for God and for souls that matters and that will inspire posterity.

Finally, this book was originally designed, and written, as a history of all the Vicars Apostolic (1685-1850), but in that form it proved too cumbrous, and it has therefore been re-written and cut down to its present limits (1685-1750), thus affording space for a considerable amount of material that had had to be excluded from the original work. Many documents and letters (now in various archives) are here published, it is believed, for the first time; and the author desires to express his warm thanks to those in charge of these archives for the cordial help they have so kindly afforded him. He also humbly acknowledges particular indebtedness to His Eminence Cardinal Griffin for permission to make use of the Westminster Archives, and to the late President of Ushaw, Mgr. Corbishley, for so kindly placing the archives of that College at his disposal.

[1] Ward, *The Eve of Catholic Emancipation*, I, xii.
[2] Ward, *The Sequel to Catholic Emancipation*, I, ix.

THE VICARS APOSTOLIC

ALL ENGLAND AND WALES

1685-1688. John Leyburn, Bishop of Adrumetum.

THE LONDON DISTRICT

1688-1702. John Leyburn.
1703-1734. Bonaventure Giffard, Bishop of Madaura.
1734-1758. Benjamin Petre, Bishop of Prusa.

THE MIDLAND DISTRICT

1688-1703. Bonaventure Giffard.
1703-1716. George Witham, Bishop of Marcopolis.
1716-1756. John Stonor, Bishop of Thespia.

THE NORTHERN DISTRICT

1688-1711. James Smith, Bishop of Callipolis.
1716-1725. George Witham.
1726-1740. Dominic Williams, O.P., Bishop of Tiberiopolis.
1740-1752. Edward Dicconson, Bishop of Malla.

THE WESTERN DISTRICT

1688-1705. Michael Ellis, O.S.B., Bishop of Aureliopolis.
1713-1750. Matthew Prichard, O.S.F., Bishop of Myra.

CHART SHOWING THE FOUR CONTEMPORARY
BISHOPS AT ANY GIVEN TIME.

	LONDON	MIDLAND	NORTHERN	WESTERN
1688				
1695	LEYBURN	GIFFARD		ELLIS
1700			SMITH	
1705				
1710	GIFFARD	WITHAM		Vacant
1715			Vacant	
1720			WITHAM	
1725		STONOR		PRICHARD
1730				
1735			WILLIAMS	
1740	PETRE			
1745			DICCONSON	
1750				

CHAPTER I

VICARS APOSTOLIC, OR BISHOPS-IN-ORDINARY?

WHEN James II ascended the throne in 1685 England, after a lapse of one hundred and twenty-seven years, had a Catholic ruler once again. This fact might have had truly momentous consequences had James been a prudent, wise and discreet man; though even then it is probable that he came too late to have a reasonable chance of succeeding in restoring the Faith to England, which was his dearest aim. For five generations had been systematically imbued with Protestant propaganda and prejudice, and if the task of Queen Mary Tudor in the previous century had been a formidable one, the mere lapse of time had made that of James inestimably more difficult. Still, much might have been done gradually and cautiously, and at least James himself might have held his throne until his death. But unhappily he, as all the world knows, had none of the qualities called for in his very delicate position, and even his undoubted courage and piety, his extreme devoutness and enthusiasm for the Faith, did but exacerbate the situation. It is not to our purpose to weigh up here the forces, motives and circumstances which were arrayed against him, for the formidable nature of the opposition which he had to encounter is not in dispute. Had it been very much less formidable he would still have failed by reason of the methods which he adopted.

But one thing he did do for which the long and sorely persecuted Catholics of that time, and even many successive generations in the succeeding two centuries, might well be grateful to him : he did succeed in setting up a regular (though not the normal) system of Catholic church government in this country. This was the one lasting benefit that English Catholics derived from his brief reign, but for this much may be forgiven him. Since the suppression of Catholicism by Elizabeth I the country had not always been without a Catholic bishop : but it was only for a very brief period (1623-1631) that there had been one. Thus in addition to the civil, political and social disabilities under which Catholics had so long lain, there was also for them the grave handicap of a lack of pastors. Not only had the vast

1

majority of the Catholic laity throughout this century no opportunity of ever even seeing a priest, they were also deprived of their bishops. Save for the above-mentioned short period of eight years there had been no Catholic bishop in England for over a century. Queen Mary Tudor had, of course, restored the Catholic Hierarchy on her accession to the throne in 1553, but at the end of her short reign of five years her work had been completely undone by her sister Elizabeth, and soon after the latter had become Queen there was no Catholic bishop exercising his office in England. The Marian bishops were cast into prison or else driven into exile overseas, and the last of these had died in Rome in 1585. This was Bishop Goldwell of St. Asaph, and he had been predeceased the previous year by the last Catholic bishop in England, Thomas Watson, Bishop of Lincoln, who died in prison.

Thus exactly a century before the date that we are considering the English Catholic Hierarchy became extinct, and for a quarter of a century before that it had ceased to function, its members being either in prison or in exile. A century and a quarter, then, had elapsed, for one hundred and twenty years disastrous Protestant error had been hammered into the English people, perverse distorted propaganda sponsored by the Government had been poured out unceasingly to give a false picture of Catholicism and its teachings, when James II came to the throne and attempted to reverse the process. And during those critical one hundred and twenty years there was (save for the brief period already noted) no Catholic bishop in the land, no one to give the sacrament of Confirmation, no one to direct the missionary efforts of the pitifully few, and fiercely hunted, priests who risked their lives and very often shed their blood to preserve the faith of their dwindling flocks. In that dark period it was to Cardinal William Allen more than to any other single man that, humanly speaking, the preservation of the Faith in England was due. From the seminary which he founded in France at Douay in 1572 there came at first a trickle and then a steady stream of priests who, knowing full well the awful risks they ran and the dread penalty if they were caught, landed secretly in England to minister in secret to the faithful. And in their devoted labours they were joined by the equally courageous regulars: the Jesuits, Benedictines, Franciscans, Dominicans and others. What a saga is the tale of their heroic toil! What a drama was that which was enacted in England throughout the seventeenth century with the immortal welfare of countless souls as the prize, and the lives of hundreds of clergy as the cost! And yet how little attention has been given to this drama by the mass of our countrymen, and how few Englishmen to-day have ever even heard of it! For most of the period between the accession of Elizabeth in 1558 and that of James II in 1685 the chances of survival for any priest in England were slim indeed. Sooner or later the rack and the gallows awaited him if he did not escape into exile overseas, for quite apart from the ' crime ' of exercising the functions of his sacred priesthood, it was, by the Statute of Q. Eliz., 27, c.2, ' high treason ', punishable by death, for a priest merely ' to breathe the air of England.' But even without these extreme dangers the lot of a missionary priest was extremely hard in those years. If actual death or confinement for life were escaped by the clergy ' there yet remained hardships enough to enable them with truth to echo the words of the Apostle : " Even unto this hour we both hunger and thirst and are naked, and are buffeted, and have no fixed abode, and we labour working with our own hands : we are reviled, and we bless : we are persecuted, and we suffer it." '[1] And what was true of the clergy in general was to a great extent true also of the bishops.

But for many a long year England had no Catholic bishop, though repeated efforts were made to procure one. The authorities in Rome feared that such an appointment would increase the hostility of the English Government, and lead to an intensification of the persecution of Catholics in England. But at last, in 1623, the Holy See reluctantly decided to accede to the repeated requests for a bishop, though even now it was not a ' Bishop in Ordinary ' that was sent, but a ' Vicar Apostolic '. The precise distinction between these two types of bishop will be discussed below, but briefly the former is one with full jurisdiction, governing a diocese and assisted by a Chapter of Canons, in accordance with the normal forms of church government, while the latter is a ' titular ' bishop without a diocese or Chapter, and with restricted powers. He is, in fact, the type of bishop that is given to a missionary country in which normal church government does not exist. As it was, the decision to send a bishop at all to

[1] Dr. Burton, C.T.S. pamphlet, *Bishop Challoner*.

England was taken only after very prolonged discussions in Rome, and was the personal decision of Pope Gregory XV, against the advice of his Cardinals. The man chosen for this onerous task was Dr. William Bishop, who was given episcopal jurisdiction over the whole of England, as well as over Scotland and Wales : a herculean task, as well as a highly dangerous one. Dr. Bishop was a very well-known English Catholic, and he had signed the famous Protestation of loyalty to Queen Elizabeth in 1602, which was in such sharp contrast with the now reversed policy of Pope Pius V. He landed secretly in England at midnight on July 31, 1623, but died only nine months later. He was succeeded by Dr. Richard Smith, who eventually resigned in 1631, and there ensued another period of over fifty years during which the country was without a bishop.

Dr. Bishop, during his short rule, had set up a Chapter (subsequently always known as the Old Chapter) consisting of twenty Canons, to advise and assist him, and to preserve jurisdiction in case of his death. He applied for Roman confirmation of his act, but this was never forthcoming, although Propaganda[1] recognized the existence of the Chapter and allowed it to exercise certain jurisdiction. The second Vicar Apostolic, Richard Smith, not only continued it, but gave it the privilege of electing its own Canons and Dean, if the Vicariate should remain vacant after his death; and in fact during the long vacancy that followed until 1685 it did exercise jurisdiction, reporting to Propaganda and issuing faculties to the clergy. Throughout this period of the vacant Vicariate the Chapter repeatedly tried to procure the appointment of a bishop from Rome, but the difficulty was to find a suitable man. Several envoys came privately from Rome to investigate the position, and the Internuncio in Paris recommended Philip Howard, the chaplain of Charles II's Queen. He had the qualifications of illustrious birth, influence with the King, exemplary life, and the fact that he was neither a Jesuit nor a secular priest, but a Dominican friar. The main stipulation

---

[1] The Sacred Congregation for the Propagation of the Faith (commonly known as ' Propaganda '), i.e. the body of Cardinals in Rome charged with conducting the affairs of the Church in non-Catholic countries. Throughout the period covered by this work, and right down to very recent times, English Catholics came under Propaganda, and the Vicars Apostolic therefore transacted their business in Rome through the Cardinal Prefect of that Congregation.

made by the Chapter was that, whoever was appointed, he should be a ' Bishop in Ordinary' and not a mere Vicar Apostolic. Actually the views of the Internuncio prevailed and Howard was appointed, but only as Vicar Apostolic. The briefs of his appointment, however, never got beyond Paris, because Charles II objected to it.[1] This was a great disappointment because, as early as 1656, Mr. Leyburn[2] (later Vicar Apostolic) had written to the Chapter from Rome to the effect that the Pope had promised them a bishop within seven months, and desired the Chapter to propose names of suitable candidates.[3] Later on, in 1667, the Chapter ordered a letter ' to be written to Mr. Lesley in Rome (the Agent of the English clergy) expressing the great desire they had of a Superior from His Holiness, but that to receive an Apostolical Vicar is displeasing to the State and against the ancient laws of the kingdom. Resolved to move for an absolute Ordinary, but if that cannot be had, for a Bishop on the same tenor as the Bishop of Chalcedon[4] was; that each member propose three for that dignity and that the five who have the majority of votes be proposed at Rome.'[5] Similarly at the Assembly of the Chapter in 1684 the chief business in hand was the procuring of a bishop, and again a list of names was put forward. Of the six names which then headed the poll it is interesting to note that three of them (Bonaventure Giffard, John Leyburn, and James Smith) were future Vicars Apostolic. These six names were sent to Cardinal Howard in Rome, but at the same time the Dean and Chapter asked for the Cardinal himself as their bishop, and since he would not be able to leave Rome they asked him to choose one of the six as his suffragan or coadjutor in England.[6] But in April of the following year they received an answer from the Cardinal to the effect that their desire for an Ordinary was not likely to be granted; and soon afterwards Dr. Leyburn arrived in England with

[1] Eventually Howard became a Cardinal in May, 1675.
[2] The priests were in those days always called ' Mister '.
[3] Ushaw Archives: 5 Ch.
[4] Bishop Richard Smith, who had resigned in 1631.
[5] Kirk, *Biographies of English Catholics*, p. 84, quoting the Minutes of the Assembly. The five chosen were Dr. Godden, Dr. Ellice (the Dean), Mr. John Leyburn, Dr. Gage, and Mr. Manley.
[6] In the previous year (1683) the Dean and Chapter had written to the Cardinal ' to acquaint him with their ardent desire for a bishop, and to desire His Eminence's judgment and direction, whether it might be proper at that time to move in order to the obtaining of one '. (Kirk, *Op. cit.*)

B

the title of Vicar Apostolic.   Thus it is plain that for very many years the clergy had desired to have a bishop (and the laity shared this wish), but it is also clear that they were very averse to having another Vicar Apostolic, and in this they were supported by James II.

The above-mentioned Chapter of 1684 had declared that the appointment of a Vicar Apostolic would be ' directly against the King's command; very offensive to the State; provided against by our ancient Laws; and extremely dangerous to the Catholics of England.'[1]   And in the following year, when explaining to King James the difference between a Bishop in Ordinary and a Vicar Apostolic they took the opportunity of setting out further reasons why they objected to having a Vicar Apostolic.   They argued (1) that if England were given a Vicar Apostolic she would be governed ecclesiastically in a manner different to other countries; (2) the power of a Vicar Apostolic is revocable, and so Catholics might be left with no one to govern them; (3) his rule would be arbitrary and uncertain, as he would not be bound by the Canons of the Church, but by the will of the Pope; (4) a Bishop in Ordinary would be bound to espouse the King's interests, whereas a Vicar Apostolic would be bound to the Pope, and would have to obey instructions which might be contrary to English law, e.g. on the recovery of the confiscated church lands; and this would greatly prejudice the King's Protestant subjects; (5) the mere name of Vicar Apostolic would make Protestants think that Catholics were subject to foreign jurisdiction.[2]   ' A true bishop is one who governs his clergy and flock under him and them by the known laws of the Church, the Canons; and not arbitrarily; no such Church government being instituted by Christ; and to be free from any such kind of slavish government is and has ever been claimed by the secular clergy as their peculiar right.'   Any other form of government would be ' new and unepiscopal in reality, whatever it is in name, and utterly destructive of their interest and influence over the laity.'[3]   Over fifty years later the then Dean of the Chapter (Dr. Day), writing to Bishop Stonor in 1738, mentions ' the unhappy acceptation of Vicars Apostolic

---

[1] MS. of Kirk's *Church History* in the Westminster Archives, Misc. I, 116.
[2] Westminster Archives, XXXIV, 236: Memorial of Dean and Chapter to James II, June 23, 1685.
[3] *Id.*, 248.

instead of Bishops (in 1685); for Vicars are not to be called our Bishops, because they still remain the Ordinaries of other sees,[1] and their jurisdiction here is but for a short and unlimited time, to be renewed ad beneplacitum Sancti Sedis.'[2]

In their objection to having a Vicar Apostolic given to them, the clergy, as already stated, were entirely supported by King James, whose accession to the throne had brought the whole matter to the fore. He, in fact, flatly refused to receive a Vicar Apostolic in the kingdom, and on the appointment of John Leyburn in this capacity in September 1685 he promised in reply to a protest from the Chapter that Leyburn would not be received with that title. ' But a certain party prevailed with the King to receive him as such ', and the King told the Dean (Dr. Parret) that ' we must be content with what the Pope has ordained.' Thus were the clergy forced to acquiesce ' though they never freely consented thereunto.'[3] This reluctance on the part of the King to receive Leyburn in this capacity is the more remarkable in that it was James himself who had selected Leyburn in preference to Cardinal Howard to be the new bishop, and on his representation the Pope had appointed him.

It is probable that the distaste shown by James for the office of Vicar Apostolic was due to the Chapter's influence on him, for he had asked that body for a clear explanation of the difference between a Vicar Apostolic and a Bishop in Ordinary, and several replies made by the Chapter are extant. An extract from one of these has already been given above, and to that may be added the following rather curious statement of the difference offered to the King by the Dean and Chapter :

By a Bishop who is an Ordinary is meant one who hath power in Himselfe to govern the flock over which he is sett, according to the common received Rules or Canons of the Church, and is not revocable at pleasure. On the contrary a Vicar is one who hath no power in himself, but only the Use or Exercise of the power of the Person whose substitute he is (e.g. an Ambassador or the like); so that what he does, he does not by his own power, but by the Power of the Person he represents, to whom therefore he is at all times accountable as

---

[1] I.e. of their titular Asiatic sees.
[2] The faculties of Vicars Apostolic had to be renewed every five years.
[3] MS. of Kirk's *Church History* in Westminster Archives.

using purely his Power, and both that and himselfe revocable att pleasure. Whence it followeth that a Vicar need not be a Bishop at all, but in certain cases, and although he be consecrated, and so hath the title and character of a Bishop, yet acting only in and by the power of another according to the Orders and Instructions given by him, he is not properly bishop of the flock to which he is sent, but Officer or Delegate of the person who sends him.[1]

A further document from the Dean and Chapter on the same subject contained this passage :

Ordinary power is that which is exercised by the Bishop as his own, making use of his own prudence, his own proper authority when he acts, responsible to none as long as he acts conformably to the Canons of the Universal Church, nor revocable by any Person or Power whatsoever. Whereas all other persons[2] make noe use of the power which is theirs, are directed by the persons from whom they receive their power, are responsible to them at all times for what they doe, and may have their power either limited, altered or revoked at their will and pleasure.[3]

And this same paper went on to petition the King not to allow a Vicar Apostolic to be appointed, and asking for a Bishop in Ordinary. It is hardly necessary to add that Vicars Apostolic, since they were not the 'Ordinaries' of the territory they governed, did not take their titles from that territory but were given sees *in partibus infidelium* (mostly in Asia Minor), and had neither cathedrals nor Chapters of Canons. It is clear, however, that the King's objections to them were of a political nature, and that the Chapter played upon this in their petitions. Thus we find in the above-mentioned document the objection put forward that if a Vicar Apostolic were appointed ' the King's spiritual and ecclesiastical concerns would lie exposed to the will of a foreign court; his plans might be revealed and his will thwarted; and he would be ill-served, as a Vicar Apostolic would be chiefly devoted to the Pope.' And this brings to light the curious fact that whereas the Chapter wanted a Bishop in Ordinary for nationalist reasons (it was indeed generally considered to be strongly Gallican in its

---

[1] Westm. Archives, XXXIV, 236.
[2] E.g. Vicars Apostolic.
[3] Westm. Archives, XXXIV, 247.

ideas, a belief that is given colour by the above extracts), and because such a bishop would (so it thought) be less dependent on the Holy See and more amenable to the King,[1] yet when such bishops were eventually given to England at the restoration of the Hierarchy in 1850 it was a precisely contrary reason that lay behind that restoration.   Both Dr. Wiseman and the Cardinals in Rome hoped thereby to bring England into closer relations with Rome and to help the bishops thereby to work in closer harmony with the Papal Court.   The 'Old Chapter' of the seventeenth century had nationalist (almost anti-Papal) motives, while their successors two centuries later had ultramontane motives; yet both looked to the same means for bringing about their ends.

But, as we have seen, all the efforts of both King and Chapter to procure a Bishop in Ordinary failed, as Cardinal Howard had foretold would be the case; for the Holy See considered that it would be highly imprudent to appoint such a bishop so long as the penal laws remained in force.   It was therefore determined to revive the office of Vicar Apostolic which had been unfilled since the resignation of Bishop Richard Smith fifty-four years earlier, and the man 'pitched upon' (to use the quaint phraseology of the period) was Dr. John Leyburn, a former President of Douay College, of whom it has been said that he was 'so remarkable for prudence and conduct that he was judged fit for a mitre when he was scarce old enough to receive the order of priesthood.'   This alludes to the fact that he was mentioned as early as 1669 as being worthy of a bishopric.   He came of a Protestant Westmorland family and his brother was a prominent Puritan, but it would seem that he was a nephew of the martyred James Leyburn.   Educated at Douay, where his uncle, John Leyburn, was President of the College, he took his doctorate at the Sorbonne, and himself became President of Douay in May 1670.   But this position he relinquished five years later in order to accompany Cardinal Howard to Rome as his secretary and auditor.   The Cardinal held a very high opinion of him and had supported the King's recommendation of him for the post of Vicar Apostolic of England in preference to the other five named

---

[1] Such also was the motive which lay behind the demand of the 'Catholic Committee' at the end of the eighteenth century for the abolition of Vicars Apostolic and the appointment of territorial Bishops in Ordinary.

by the Chapter, most of whom were senior to him and had received more votes. He was duly consecrated in Rome with the title of Bishop of Adrumetum on September 9, 1685 (the date is sometimes given as September 13), and a month later he came to England in the company of the Papal Nuncio, Archbishop d'Adda.

It has already been seen that the arrival of a Vicar Apostolic was not welcomed by the secular clergy, and within a few weeks of his landing the Chapter requested him to declare his exact title and the nature of his jurisdiction over the clergy, as well as his attitude to the Chapter itself. The position was a delicate one, and Leyburn replied that while his title was not ' Ordinary ' his power was that of an Ordinary. As regards his attitude to the Chapter, of which he himself had been a member since 1667, he answered that ' if he should proceed according to his inclinations he knew what he would say; but according to what his circumstances required he could not acknowledge our Chapter, but should carry himself abstractedly : meaning, as both he and the rest of the Bishops frequently afterwards declared and promised, that they would leave it as they found it. As to the clergy : he showed his Ordinary authority, excepting in extraordinary occasions.'[1] The anxiety of the Chapter on the question of its own position in view of the appointment of a Vicar Apostolic, and of its future relations with that prelate, was natural, even though Dr. Leyburn in his long membership of the Chapter had been a fervent supporter of its authority and had maintained that it had the approval of Rome.[2] Ever since the resignation of the former Vicar Apostolic, Bishop Richard Smith, in 1631, the Chapter had in effect ruled the Church in England, and though never officially and formally recognized by Rome it had yet been tolerated by the Papal Curia.[3] But now, after an interval of fifty-four years, there was once more a bishop in the land, and what was to become of the Chapter? In point of fact it ceased from now on to have any effective power and its position became purely honorary. Election to the Chapter continued to be a high honour amongst the secular clergy, but gradually its functions became entirely philanthropic, an organization for the

---

[1] Statement by the Chapter, quoted by Kirk, MS. of his *Church History* in Westm. Archives.

[2] See Appendix I.

[3] Documents on this subject will be found in Appendix I.

relief of financial distress, and as such it continues in existence at the present day. Clearly the new situation brought about by the appointment of Dr. Leyburn had made the Old Chapter otiose, and in fact Rome decreed that its authority, hitherto tolerated *sede vacante,* must now cease with the coming of a Vicar Apostolic. Kirk indeed states[1] that Leyburn was bound by a solemn promise and an oath exacted by Propaganda that he would never acknowledge the Dean and Chapter to be a lawful or canonical body of men possessed of any spiritual power, or approve of any Act that might give authority to the Chapter. But Leyburn himself was not actuated by any feeling of hostility to it, despite its opposition to the appointment of any Vicar Apostolic. He had many intimate friends amongst its members, and in fact, less than three years after his coming, two of the Chapter were, on his recommendation, raised to episcopal rank.[2]

On beginning his duties in England Bishop Leyburn made a small change in the organization that he found in existence. The first Vicar Apostolic, Dr. William Bishop, had divided the country in 1623 into six districts over each of which he placed a Vicar General as his deputy, and this system had continued under the Chapter. But now Leyburn reduced these areas to four, and the Vicars General whom he chose for these were Drs. Parret, Giffard, Godden and Betham, who were the four most prominent of the secular clergy of the day. Dr. Parret was the Dean of the Chapter, Dr. Giffard was soon to become Vicar Apostolic (and we will have much to say of him in this book), and Dr. Betham later on became chaplain to the Queen during the years of exile at St. Germains, and as such he possessed much influence in ecclesiastical politics. All the above names were on the *terna* of six names drawn up by the Chapter in the previous year (1684) for the vacant bishopric that had eventually been given to Leyburn. To assist these Vicars General Leyburn also appointed Rural Deans for each district. But there was much work which the new bishop could not delegate to others, and one of these tasks was the carrying out of innumerable confirmations up and down the country. As there had been no bishop available for over fifty years the urgency of this will be obvious, and in illustra-

[1] *Op. cit.*
[2] Drs. James Smith and Bonaventure Giffard, who were made Vicars Apostolic of the Northern and Midland Districts respectively.

tion of Bishop Leyburn's energy in this matter it may be mentioned that in his tour of the North in 1687 he confirmed no less than 20,859 persons. Nor were his cares confined to England and Wales, for he also had charge of the Catholics in the British possessions in the West Indies and those in North America, and strangely enough those countries continued to be in the charge of the Vicar Apostolic of the London District until the consecration of the first North American bishop, Dr. John Carroll of Baltimore, by Bishop Charles Walmesley, O.S.B., Vicar Apostolic of the Western District of England, a century later.

And through all these activities one of the bishop's chief anxieties was the imprudent ardour of the King to restore Catholicism as the official religion of the country, and above all to remove the many disabilities and penalties under which Catholics groaned. Time and again Dr. Leyburn sought to exercise a restraining influence, as also did many other leading Catholics, including Cardinal Howard and even the Pope himself, but with scanty success. For prudence and moderation were qualities entirely lacking in James, though one cannot but admire the single-mindedness and courage shown by him in this matter. For he well knew that he was risking his crown, but he scorned to let worldly considerations weigh when all-important spiritual matters were at stake; and in later years he never regretted the loss of his kingdom in such a cause. None the less the results for Catholics were disastrous. The only minor success which the bishop had in this respect was that he eventually induced the king to restore the Protestant Fellows of Magdalen College, Oxford, whom he had dispossessed in favour of a number of Catholics with Dr. Giffard (the future Vicar Apostolic) at their head as President of the College. But this was not until the very eve of the Revolution of 1688, and by then it was much too late for this retraction to have any good effect.

Meanwhile, however, there was a brief spell of wonderful liberty for the long-oppressed Catholics. Religious houses were re-established even in London itself : the Benedictines set up a monastery in St. James's Palace in addition to the one at Somerset House which had been established in Charles II's reign, while the Franciscans and the Jesuits also established houses, and the religious openly walked the streets in their habits. The Mass was celebrated in public and in the King's presence with great pomp,

and it seemed as though the great days of the past had indeed
returned.   In short the faithful were once again free, and it
remained to be seen how they would comport themselves in these
novel circumstances.   This was a matter which caused the bishop
great concern, and on June 27, 1687, he issued to his four Vicars
General the following letter which, while of the utmost interest,
is at the same time pathetic reading in view of the tragic sequel
which was so swiftly to befall.[1]

Sir,
    It having pleased God, by meanes of the King's late
Declaration[2] to put the Catholics of this Kingdom in a
capacitie of exercising theyr religion without fear of being
persecuted or molested by theyr adversaries, it is justly
expected on theyr parts that they endeavour to make of this
Indulgence the best advantage theyr circumstances will permitt;
everyone contributing thereunto, in such manner and in such
proportion as his calling and condition inableth him to doe.
The Clergie is to contribute their labour in a more than
ordinary measure, and the Laytie must inlarge theyr charityes
so far as may be necessary for a decent maintenance of those
that undergoe it.   We have before our eyes the Examples of
sectaries who spare neither cost nor pains to improve theyr
share of the common indulgence : what will the world say of
Catholics if they only be found slow in this occasion?   What
scandalous Reflexions will they not draw upon themselves and
their Religion if after complaints continued more than a
hundred years against the severitie of penall Laws, whereby
the exercise of theyr religion hath been obstructed; now that
the execution of such Laws is suspended and the obstruction
removed, they make it not theyr principall buysiness to promote
and propagate the long-wished for blessing, whereof they are
made partakers.   This is a point which I esteemed my selfe
obliged to inculcate to all my Brethren, and more particularly
unto those whom I have trusted with some superioritie over the
rest.   It is upon this account that I direct this present letter
unto you.   My desire is that the contents of it may be
frequently called to mind, and considered with much attention
to the end that your harts being inflamed with a Holy Zeall,
may kindle the like in the laytie under your direction in order
to a propagation of the Catholic Faith.

[1] Westm. Archives, MSS., XXXV, 66.
[2] The Declaration of Indulgence.

The readiest way of affecting this will be to procure your chappels be opened in places proper for that purpose, and that choice be made of such Preists to officiate in them as are powerfull *opere et sermone*, Preists that are able to instruct by their doctrine, and to edifie by theyr examples. From discourses had with several qualified persons, I have good reason to hope that the laytie in generall will not be backward in theyr cooperation to so pious and necessary a work. But if among them there be some in whom this good disposition doth not appear, you and your Brethren must labour by seasonable exhortations and remonstrances to bring them up to it, representing strongly to them the importance of complying faithfully with theyr obligations in this point, as they will answer to God whose mercy hath placed them in advantageous circumstances for promoting the Catholic Religion; as they will answer His Majesty, who by his gracious declaration hath removed the obstacles which hitherto we have complained of; as they will answer the Catholic world which expects an inlargement of its Communion from a harvest to be gathered in this nation; and finally, as they will answer and stop the reproches of theyr own consciences for not concurring in a work which themselves and theyr posterity are highly concerned in.

The Church, in its beginning and Infancie, was nourished by collections made amongst the first Professors of her Faith. It hath subsisted ever since upon the stock raised by the charitie of true believers. Our Catholic Ancestors have not been inferiour to those of other nations for provisions of this kind; but these Provisions by an unfortunate Revolution being fallen into other hands than those they were intended for, the Church in our nation is reduced as to this point unto its prime condition, and accordingly may by the rules of justice, as well as pietie, require to be maintained after the Prime method.

This I hope will be sufficient for the design I have in writing it, which is to excite in you and the rest of my Brethren within your district, a religious zeal for the glory of God, and gaining of souls to Him; as also to dispose the Laytie by your exhortations and example to a cheerfull contribution on theyr parts of what is necessary in order to the compassing so great an end.

This is a moving and a historic document. To read it to-day brings alive for us the actuality of those momentous days. The need for making converts on a large scale was obvious, the more

so since none could feel any assurance that the favourable circumstances then existing would be of long duration, though probably
none thought that the breathing space accorded by the reign of
King James would be as brief as it proved to be.   But Leyburn
himself was not very sanguine as to the prospect of making
converts, for he realized how well a century of Protestant propaganda and misrepresentation had done its work; and writing
this same year to William Lesley[1] in Rome he said :

Men's mindes heere are not so plyable as in Scotland, nor
like to be, without extraordinary touches of God's grace; theyr
animosityes against us being at present verie high.   But we
hope the blessings of heaven upon His Majestie which have
alreadie been so visible to the world, will by theyr continuance
and increase effect what remains to be desired by
Your most affectionate friend and servant,
Jo. Bp. of Adramite.[2]

The bishop himself was indefatigable in his labours and in his
constant journeyings up and down the country, and he must have
found it a remarkable experience to be able thus to travel openly
and to perform his sacred functions without fear of arrest.[3]   But
it was an overwhelming task that faced him, and after some two
years both he and the King realized that the whole country was
too large a diocese for one man, despite the small number of
Catholics.   It was therefore decided that Rome must be
petitioned to appoint more bishops.

[1] The Agent in Rome for the Scottish and English clergy.
[2] Westm. Archives, *Id.*
[3] He is said to have always refused to carry out mixed marriages ' because
concurring to profane a Sacrament ' (Kirk).   The same is also reported of
Andrew Giffard, brother of Bishop Giffard.

CHAPTER II

THE FOUR DISTRICTS ARE SET UP

T HE vast task of organizing the shattered Church in England, of nursing the flickering flame of Catholicism, of sowing the seed that would bring a worthy harvest of converts : this task was far too much for one man, and the King and his solitary bishop, Dr. Leyburn, therefore petitioned the Holy See for the appointment of more bishops. The upshot was that in 1688 England and Wales were divided up into four ' Districts,' each of which was given its own Vicar Apostolic,[1] and they were known respectively as the London District, the Midland District, the Northern District, and the Western District. The actual extent of each of these Districts can be seen on the map, but it may be noted that the London District included all the Home Counties and also stretched as far afield as Bedfordshire and Berkshire. The Northern District comprised all England between the Humber and the Tweed; the Western District stretched from the west coast of Wales to Wiltshire inclusive; and all the rest was in the Midland District. Dr. Leyburn was henceforth to be in charge of the London District, and three new bishops were appointed for the remaining three Districts. Of these, the Northern District was given to James Smith, the Midland to Bonaventure Giffard, and the Western to Dom Michael Ellis, O.S.B. These three men were all very well known to English Catholics, for Dr. Smith was President of the famous Douay College, and Giffard had long been one of the most prominent of the clergy, while Ellis was celebrated as a special preacher before the King in the Savoy Chapel. Naturally the creation of three new bishops was a sensational event in those days and the King was determined to make the most of it. Accordingly he arranged for their consecrations to be carried out with the utmost publicity and splendour. Bishop Giffard was therefore consecrated in the Banquetting Hall at Whitehall on April 22, 1688, Bishop Ellis in St. James's Palace on May 6, and Bishop Smith at Somerset

---

[1] The decree by Propaganda, granting the King's request for the three new bishops, was dated January 12, 1688, and it received the approval of Pope Innocent XI on January 30.

THE FOUR DISTRICTS

House (then a Palace) on May 13. It was arranged that all four bishops should receive an annual salary of £1,000, but of course this was prevented by the outbreak of the Revolution a few months later.

The new prelate of the North was not himself a Northerner for he came from Winchester, where he was born in 1646, and according to Bishop Giffard Dr. Smith was 'heir to a great estate' and had a comfortable patrimony, though in fact he passed most of it on to a younger brother. Up to the time of his consecration he had spent nearly all his life at Douay where, like most of the clergy, he was educated, and where he lived as student and professor for some thirty years, becoming the college's tenth President in 1683. One year later, as has already been mentioned, his name was put forward by the Chapter as worthy of the episcopate, but he continued to rule Douay until his appointment as Vicar Apostolic of the North in 1688. After his consecration the new bishop proceeded to his District and reached York on August 2, where he was received with a military guard of honour, and sang High Mass.[1]

> He was received [says Kirk] with great ceremony by the Clergy and Regulars of those parts, who sang Te Deum publicly upon the occasion. On the Sunday following he appeared in the Chapel belonging to the Clergy[2] in his Episcopal habit, and was present at a sermon preached by Mr. Parkinson, his Lordship's chaplain. In the afternoon he attended at the service performed in the Friar's Chapel, where a sermon was also preached. The Commanding Officer of Lord Dumbarton's Regiment, which then lay in York, complimented him with the offer of a sentinel to stand at the door of his lodgings, but this honour Bishop Smith declined.

There, for the moment, we will leave him, and turn to his episcopal colleague, Dr. Giffard of the Midlands. Of the three new bishops, he was much the most notable. One of the most outstanding of all the long line of Vicars Apostolic between 1685 and 1850, he was for very many years the leading representative

---

[1] The antependium used on that occasion has been preserved at Hazlewood, the Yorkshire home of the Vavasours for centuries. There the Blessed Sacrament was uninterruptedly reserved from Norman times until a few years ago, and Mass is still said there regularly.

[2] I.e. to the secular clergy. The word 'clergy' was always applied to the seculars, as distinct from the regulars.

of the Church in England. Born away back in the reign of
Charles I (the date is said to have been 1642, and the place
Wolverhampton),[1] he survived into that of George II, having
during his long life of 92 years lived in the reigns of eight rulers
and the pontificates of twelve Popes. His home was Chillington
in Staffordshire where his family had lived since two generations
before the Norman Conquest without failure of heirs male, and
had long been the mainstay of Catholicism in the southern half
of Staffordshire. This famous house near Brewood (where two
of the Vicars Apostolic, Drs. Hornyold and Berington, are buried)
became specially prominent in the latter half of the eighteenth
century because on the estate stands the house known as Long
Birch which was from 1753 to 1804 the home of the Vicars
Apostolic of the Midland District. There also Bishop Dicconson
had been chaplain round about 1720, and a little later Bishop
Hornyold was also chaplain there, in each case, of course, before
their consecration. It is surprising, then, to find that such a
staunch and ancient Catholic family produced the notorious
Gilbert Giffard, Government spy in Queen Elizabeth's time, who
did such immense harm to Catholics and was the betrayer of
Mary, Queen of Scots, as well as the revealer of the Babington
Plot. He was the great-uncle of our bishop.

Dr. Giffard himself was educated at Douay, and went on to
complete his studies at St. Gregory's College in Paris,[2] of which
he was the first student, and where, after twelve years, he took
his doctorate in 1678. Coming over to England, he soon became
prominent amongst the clergy, notably in his desire for the
appointment of a Bishop in Ordinary rather than a Vicar
Apostolic, and his own name was among those selected by the
Chapter in 1684 as worthy of the episcopate. It was to James II
that he owed one of the strangest episodes of his long career : his
appointment as President of Magdalen College, Oxford, when
James expelled the Protestant Fellows and installed Catholics
(including Giffard's brother, Andrew) in their place. As regards
his consecration as Vicar Apostolic, it has sometimes been thought

---

[1] His father was killed during the Civil War.
[2] The English college set up to enable English priests to pursue advanced
studies and to take their doctorate at the Sorbonne. The course was a very
long and arduous one, lasting some twelve years, but amongst those who took
the doctorate there were five future Vicars Apostolic: Giffard, Smith, Witham,
Stonor, and Berington.

that this took place in 1687, a year before that of the other two bishops, but most authorities agree that it was in 1688.   On this point it is worth quoting a remark by Dr. Kirk : [1]

> Dodd says Bishop Giffard was consecrated on April 22, 1687. This must be a mistake, or error of the press. The Bull [of appointment] is dated 1688, and I find from the Minutes of the Chapter that he assisted at the General Assembly on April 22, 1687, and signed the resolutions in quality of *Secretary*. No mention is made of his being Bishop Elect. . . . He assisted again at the Meeting held on March 5, 1688 in the capacity of Secretary. Bishop Witham expressly says it [the consecration] was on April 22, 1688.

The third of the new bishops, Michael Ellis, was a Benedictine monk, and he had perhaps the strangest career of all the forty-six Vicars Apostolic in England.   Born in 1652, Philip (in religion, Michael) Ellis was the third son of a Protestant clergyman, the Rev. John Ellis of Waddesdon, Bucks, and the six sons of this gentleman had strangely varied careers.   The eldest son, John, became Under Secretary of State to William III, while the second son, Sir William Ellis, was Secretary of State to William's rival, James II, in exile in France.   And to this lack of political harmony in the family were added religious differences; for the third son, Philip, the subject of these pages, while a schoolboy at Westminster School, became a Catholic (a remarkable achievement in the circumstances of those days), and followed this up by becoming a monk, and eventually a Catholic bishop.   Meanwhile the fourth son in due course became Protestant Bishop of Killala and later Bishop of Meath, while the fifth son, Samuel, was appointed Marshal of the King's Bench, and the sixth, Charles, was a Protestant clergyman.   Altogether a distinguished, if disunited, family; but Philip had the most varied career of them all.

On becoming a Catholic the boy left Westminster School and escaped overseas where he became a Benedictine at St. Gregory's Priory, Douay,[2] taking his vows there in 1670.   At school he had been generally known as ' Jolly Phil,' and this nickname followed him through life.   But he also seems soon to have made a name for ability and eloquence, and on being sent on the English Mission he attracted the attention of the Duke of York (later

---

[1] Westm. Archives, MS. of Kirk's *Church History*, Misc. I, 116.
[2] The modern Downside.

James II) who appointed him one of his chaplains and preachers. A number of his sermons preached before the Royal Family in the Savoy Chapel are still extant. It was to the high opinion entertained of him by James II that he owed his selection as one of the three new bishops in 1688, and he was allotted the Western District. Of course the Revolution a few months later put an end to all his plans in England, and he was in fact imprisoned in Newgate. On his release he left the country and went first to St. Germains where he was kindly received by the exiled monarch, and then to Rome. There he became a friend of Cardinal Howard and was made an Assistant Prelate at the Pontifical Throne by Pope Innocent XII.

But the bishop wanted to get back to England and to govern his Vicariate (which was meanwhile being cared for by Dr. Giffard of the Midland District), and he made repeated efforts to be allowed by Rome to return. Writing to Giffard in 1702 he said he had made so many efforts that he was even blamed for it. Meanwhile he declared that he could and would do much for English Catholics by his influence in Rome, and he personally thought that there should always be an English bishop in that city. But by 1705 he had despaired of ever being permitted to return and therefore he resigned his Vicariate altogether. He continued to live in Rome until suddenly in 1708 (when he had been twenty years a bishop without ever having been able to visit his Vicariate) there came the strangest twist in his career. For in that year the new Pope, Clement XI, nominated him to the Italian see of Segni, and so the one-time English Protestant schoolboy ended up as bishop of an Italian diocese. There, despite his English origin, he proved both popular and successful, and there he is still remembered both for the seminary which he founded and fostered there, and for the Synod which he held in 1710 in his cathedral, and of which the Acts were ordered to be published by the Pope. The seminary had been attempted in vain by several of his predecessors, but he established it at his own expense by rebuilding an abandoned monastery. For eighteen years he governed that diocese until stricken by dropsy which caused his death on November 16, 1726.

But we must return to the England of that summer of 1688 which made the long-downtrodden Catholics rub their eyes. Those must have been marvellous days for those who had hidden themselves away in dark corners for so long, who had for years paid their crushing fines for their fidelity to their Faith, who had seen their fathers or sons carried off to prison, and who were ostracized from all society and from all public employment. Now they came out, at first unbelievingly, into the light of day. They witnessed the magnificent spectacle of the public consecration of the three new bishops, they saw everywhere the clergy openly fulfilling their religious duties and ministering to the faithful. Did any of them suspect for how short a period that state of affairs was to last? But while it lasted all seemed to be well, and the prospects for religion truly seemed to be rosy. It was in such circumstances that in 1688, but a few short months before the whole dream was to be swept away and the Church to be again outlawed, the four Vicars Apostolic issued a joint Pastoral Letter to all the faithful of England. Evidently they thought that the days of persecution were over, and in view of the sequel and the storm so very soon to break with fury upon them the document makes poignant reading.

Episcopal Authority, dear Brethren, of which you and your Catholic ancestors have been long deprived, being lately, by a merciful providence of God, and the Piety of His Majestie, restored unto you; and our Persons, though unworthy of such a dignity, made choice of to bear the weight, and undergo the solicitude annexed to it: We have judged it proper, before we separated Ourselves in order to a discharge of Our Duties in the respective Counties committed to our Care, to join in a Common Address unto you all, hoping that what comes thus directed by an united Application, will make a deeper impression on your Minds, and dispose you to an easier compliance with the Fatherly admonitions which every one in his particular District shall think fit to be made unto you.

Your condition for many years past hath been such, as enabled you to manifest a steadfastness in your Religion, rather by suffering for it in your own Persons, than by contributing actively towards the planting it in the Minds and Hearts of your fellow-subjects. The Exercise of it hath been private and precarious, tending rather towards the Preservation of it in yourselves, than a Propagation of it in others. But now you are in Circumstances of letting it appear abroad, and of edifying your Neighbours by professing it publicly, and living up to the Rules prescribed by it.

The Pastoral then warned Catholics of the necessity of setting a good example to Protestants, and of having charity towards them, even to those who had persecuted them. This would bring union of hearts and peace with God and men. They must love Protestants, so that ' as they profess themselves to be Christians, they may become members of the Catholic Church.' And Catholics must show this love by an inoffensiveness in their behaviour.

The memory of past hardships which you have suffered from some among them, may be apt to create provoking animosities, and the Liberty you now enjoy may possibly tempt you to insult over those who formerly abridged you of it; but it must be your care to prevent or suppress all such irregular Motions. . . . You are indulged a public Exercise of your Religion; a great part of the Nation, whose Persuasion in point of Religion doth differ most from yours, and which in time past hath been severe upon your Persons, is willing to enter into a friendly Correspondence with you; and if some others do repine at your being sharers in the Liberty which themselves enjoy with much greater Advantage, the most effective means to convince them of their Error, is to edifie them by your good Example.

You live under a Prince of your own Religion, to whom next under God, you owe this Felicity. You have his Power to protect you in the free Exercise of your Religion, and his Example to encourage your discharge of this Duty in a most edifying Manner. His Majesty's assiduousness at the Divine Service and other Functions performed in his Chappel, notwithstanding the multitude of weighty Affairs, which might frequently excuse him from such Attendance; the respectful Posture in which he performs this Religious Duty, and which argues a Presence of Mind no less than of his Body, cannot but invite you, both as good Catholics and as good Subjects, to a Conformity with so Eminent a Pattern. What business can dispense you from discharging these Obligations, when you see His Majestie under the weight of the whole Government so punctual in his compliance with them?

It may seem needless to suggest unto you another Obligation you lie under, not only of passive Obedience to His Majestie's Orders relating to the Government, but also of an active and cheerful Concurrence with Him therein. Your own safety and interest being concerned in this, and depending on it, are

sufficient inducements for your endeavouring to give full satisfaction in this Point.

His Majestie hath been graciously pleased not only to favour
you with his Royal Protection, but moreover to honor many
amongst you with a Share of the Government under him. He
hath admitted you to Employments both Civil and Military,
from which by the severitie of our Laws you have formerly
been excluded; he hath placed you in circumstances of mani-
festing to the World that it was neither want of Loyalty nor
Ability that occasioned your former exclusion; he hath capaci-
tated you hereby to remove the Prejudices which in former
Reigns your Religion and Persons have lain under. So that
henceforth there will be no reason to apprehend your being
sufferers, or that your Fellow-Subjects will be preferred before
you in management of public Trusts on these accounts, since
Religion is no Longer a Bar to your Preferment.

We therefore earnestly desire those amongst you who are
already in Offices, so to behave themselves in them, that neither
His Majestie may have occasion to repent, nor His other subjects to repine at the Choice he hath made of them. We
exhort those who are not yet in public Employment to bear
their Lots with Modesty and Patience, without Murmuring or
Envy. We conjure you all to abstain from speaking or acting
any thing that may seem to have the least indecent reflection
upon the Government. The Councils of Kings are sacred, as
well as their Persons; and it is a kind of Sacrilege in Subjects
to be too bold with either: Their Duty is, not to approach
their Persons but with respect, not discourse of their Councils
without submission.

The Pastoral concludes by adding that this respect is due pro-
portionately to subordinate officers of state as representing the
King, and that detailed instructions on their duties will be given
the faithful by each Bishop in his own District. The document
is signed:

> Your most affect. Servants in Christ,
> John Bishop of Adramite, V.A.
> Bonaventure Bishop of Madaura, V.A.
> Philip Bishop of Aureliople, V.A.
> James Bishop of Callipoli, V.A.[1]

[1] Westm. Archives, XXXV, 88. The four signatories are, of course, John
Leyburn of the London District, Bonaventure Giffard of the Midland District,
Philip Ellis of the Western District, and James Smith of the Northern District.

The concluding paragraph will read strangely to many people to-day, so far has the world fallen away from Catholic teaching; but the whole document is of special interest as showing what the attitude of the Church and of Catholics in general would have been, had toleration continued to be extended to them, and as illustrating their complete lack of intolerance or of hostility as regards Protestants, despite all they had so sorely suffered at their hands. And not the least interesting part of it is that section which portrays the very genuine devoutness of King James which was so marked a feature of his later years.

But hardly had this Pastoral Letter been issued when the storm broke. The vested interests of many, and the blind and fanatical hatred and prejudice of many more, imperatively demanded that Catholicism should not thus be allowed to come out into the open. The Revolution of 1688 broke out, William of Orange with his Dutch soldiers invaded these shores, and, betrayed and forsaken, James was driven out of the country. With him vanished the dreams and hopes of Catholics, and they were driven back into the Catacombs for another hundred years. Bishop Leyburn himself, in company with Bishop Giffard of the Midland District, tried to leave the country, but both bishops were captured at Faversham and were taken back to London. There each of them lay in prison for twenty months, Leyburn in the Tower, and Giffard in Newgate, where, as already stated, Bishop Ellis was also confined. The fourth bishop, Dr. Smith of the Northern District, was more fortunate, for he was not arrested. But he had to retire into obscurity, and took refuge at Wycliffe Hall in Yorkshire, the home of his old friend, Francis Tunstall, and there he remained for the rest of his life carrying out his episcopal duties in secrecy and disguise and in constant danger of betrayal. So ended ' the flash in the pan ' of the Catholic revival of 1685-1688 : a brief glimpse of sun-light between two long stretches of darkness, persecution, and dogged endurance. Apart from the Faith, one thing alone remained amidst the ruin of all the Catholic hopes and plans : the establishment of the four Vicariates. This endured through all the difficulties and dangers of the coming eighteenth century, and without this foundation, without this organization, it is difficult to see how the flickering flame of Catholicism could have been kept alive at all through those long weary years. And so we arrive at the second period of what we call the 'Penal Times,' which was to last until Catholic Emancipation in 1829, the first sixty years of which, in so far as they affected the Catholic bishops, is to be the subject of this book.

CHAPTER III

THE VACANCIES IN THE WEST AND THE NORTH

AFTER Dr. Leyburn's release from prison in 1690 he continued to live in London and to govern the London District, and the Government refrained from molesting him; but his life henceforth was one of great poverty and hardship (as was that of his episcopal colleagues), till at length he passed away at the advanced age of 86 on June 20, 1702. He had lived through many vicissitudes and had seen the brief ephemeral blossoming of Catholic liberty wither away and the rigour of the penal laws again clamped down on his fellow-Catholics; but he had the satisfaction of having laid the foundations of episcopal government for them, and those foundations endured through all the agony and despair of the years of persecution to come.

On his death it was suggested that he should be succeeded in the London Vicariate by Bishop Smith of the Northern District, but Dr. Smith was most unwilling that his name should go forward. He was a modest, retiring man, and he had no desire to be thrust into the limelight. The prospect of the London Vicariate, which would make him *ex officio,* though quite unofficially, leader of the English Catholics, horrified him. Already in previous years he had vehemently and successfully struggled to avoid promotion several times. Thus twice he had been suggested for the Cardinalate and the office of ' Protector ' of England vacant by the death of Cardinal Howard in 1694. According to Kirk[1] the letters of Dr. Witham, the English Clergy Agent in Rome, make it clear that he had instructions from the Court of St. Germains (i.e. from the exiled James II), if not from Bishops Leyburn and Giffard, to solicit from the Pope the Cardinal's hat for Bishop Smith and the office of Protector, and that the Duke of Berwick had the same commission. This matter was twice put forward, the second time in 1699, and in 1701 Dr. Witham reported that he thought the King's recommendation would make the application successful, though some were praising Leyburn and Giffard in an attempt to stop the

[1] *Op. cit.*

promotion of Smith.   But the whole matter remained something
of a mystery, though in July the Holy Father told Dr. Witham
that as regards the office of Protector ' one had refused, and the
other did not please ', and Witham assumed that the one who
had refused was Bishop Smith.   As a matter of fact there is in
the Westminster Archives a letter written by Smith the previous
April (1701) in the characteristically obscure language of the
period (adopted by Catholics for security reasons), which displays
the feelings and tastes which were typical of him all his life.   In
it he declares :

> I am well pleased with what you write of Mr. Harper.[1]   He
> is verie easy in his present service, as most conformable to the
> will and ways of God : [he] would have great difficulties in
> leaving his poor dear wife and children[2] and is better contented
> to go on in his little way, than be put in circumstances quite out
> of his talents and education.   He has a deep sense of the
> honour and kindness designed him.   Contrary to his own judg-
> ment he submitted himself to the acceptance of the proposal;
> and he will allwaies be ready to comply with that or anything
> else more in the compasse of his parts.   One great comfort of
> his life is to have been more under the direction of others than
> his own.   He fears he has been easie in that particular, in
> yielding to what he is; in resigning to what was proposed him
> to be.   He begs you . . . to joyn him in the prayer that
> nothing but the will and honour of God may be consulted and
> followed by him, and those that are to determine his post and
> service.[3]

He was not forced to become a Cardinal and was able to
remain in peace in his Vicariate, but only a few years later came
the further alarm when Bishop Leyburn of London died.   Shortly
before Leyburn's death Rome had already agreed that Dr.
Witham, the Agent in Rome of the English Clergy, should be
consecrated bishop as coadjutor to Leyburn, but by the time he
was consecrated Leyburn was already dead, and it was therefore
arranged that Witham should succeed him in London.   But this
was not at all to Witham's taste, partly because he shrank from
so great a responsibility, and partly because he was a North-

---

[1] I.e. himself.   All prominent Catholics used aliases for safety, and often
wrote of themselves in the third person.

[2] His District and flock.

[3] Westm. Archives, Par. Sem. Col., I, 153.

countryman and wished to live in the North. He therefore suggested that Bishop Smith of the North was a much more suitable man for London, and the post was accordingly offered to Smith. Let us see his reaction to this in a letter to Dr. Betham (now tutor to the young son of James II at St. Germains) dated January 5, 1703 :

I have yours of Dec. 16, which from a hint given in your former letter was answered before in my reply to the said letter. Tarlton[1] has all possible deferences and respect and obedience to his father Abraham;[2] to be disposed of as the common good and the will of God shall direct. He humbly begs leave to represent that his little talents are best, and of most service where he is known and loved by his wife and children,[3] and where these mutual communications make everything more practicable and easie. He looks upon it as a great violence upon him and his family to be separated after so long and so loving communications not only without any considerable prospects, but even contrary to all prospects, of a more common good. He wonders that anyone should be thought on for the vacancie of Wortlie[4] but cosen Bona,[5] who has been, and is like to be allwaies upon the place, acquainted with people and business, and therefore in every respect most fit for the administration and management of both. George[6] then may be in Cosen Bona's station,[7] and so every place will be best filled and the common good best carried on.

These are my little thoughts. They appear to me so evident and convincing, that tis a wonder to me how any other measures should be preferred. But these thoughts are entirely submitted to better judgments; and whatever be the final resolve of matters, Tarlton is resolved not only to be patient but also as easie as he possibly can, in the orders of Superiors and the will of God. This is his spirit, and will alwais be his obedience to what God and authority shall ordain. He will suffer a great violence in being torn away from what is most dear to him in the very thought of, as it were, beginning the

---

[1] Himself. This was the alias most often used by him.

[2] The Pope. The code-name frequently used for him in the penal times.

[3] The Northern District.

[4] The London District.

[5] Bishop Bonaventure Giffard. Letters of the period often give him this name.

[6] Bishop Witham.

[7] The Midland District.

world again, amongst strangers, and without any interest.   He recommends this affair to your kindness and management, that if possible, and without offense, it may be otherwise determined, and he left to end his life and labours where he is : but still with a humble and I hope chierfull submission to what may be sweetened and sanctified by the will of God, and most conducing to his honour.   He will be in tears and fears expecting the last determination, praying that the will of God may be done, and submitting all inclinations of nature to that divine standard.   This is all he can say, and what he hopes will be in every respect the disposition and comfort of his heart.[1]

To his vast relief he was left in peace, and his very sensible suggestion that Dr. Giffard should be moved from the Midlands to the London District, and the newly-consecrated Dr. Witham be given the Midland District, was adopted and carried out.

With Dr. Witham we reach a new character, the first to be added to the original list of four Vicars Apostolic, and it is necessary to see something of his career.   He was in fact one of the most prominent Catholic figures even before he was consecrated, for as missioner (i.e. priest-in-charge) at Newcastle-on-Tyne he had been Vicar General to Bishop Smith until he was sent to Rome in 1694 to be Agent there for the English Bishops, which post he held until his own consecration in 1703.   He had been born in Cliffe Hall, Yorkshire in 1655, and he died in the same house seventy years later.   His final promotion to the Episcopate he owed to Queen Mary of Modena (widow of James II) who wrote to Pope Clement XI suggesting that he might be made coadjutor to Bishop Leyburn in London.   He had taken his doctorate at the Sorbonne from St. Gregory's College, Paris in 1688, and had then been Professor of Theology at Douay for four years before going on the mission at Newcastle.   His reluctance to accept the Episcopate as shown in his letter of April 15, 1702, to Dr. Betham, is typical of the attitude of most of the Vicars Apostolic when appointed.   Acknowledging his indebtedness to the Queen, he writes :

. . . Indeed I cannot hartily write a letter of thanks on this subject, having much more reason for trouble and fear than joy, and if after a serious consultation with my confessor here

[1] Westm. Archives, Par. Sem. Col., I, 191; and Anne, II, 29.

[Rome], and others, I had not been told it was God's will, I should never have accepted it.[1]

In his capacity as Agent of the English bishops he had several audiences at this time with the Pope, just before his own consecration, and he reported on these to Dr. Betham at St. Germains. A few extracts from these will be of interest. In February, 1703, reporting one such audience, he says :

> . . . Then he [the Pope] spoke to me and Don Gulielmo[2] about Bishop Ellis,[3] but we were silent, having had no orders about him, but the Pope seemed resolved to make another Vicar Apostolic in his place, and may be it is for this he sent for him of late. . . . I presume the Bishop, if he can, will gett in one of his own Order. He discoursed also about my busynesse,[4] and whereas I protested my indignity, especially in comparison of others more worthy, he would not give the least ear to any such excuses, and asked me if I had the Breves [sc. of appointment]; and when I told him I had not, he bid me go to Mgr. Fabroni,[5] and tell him from him to gett them despatched. Then he turned to Don Gulielmo and asked him when and where it were best to performe the ceremony of Consecration. The Pope told me he must have me to come to audience before I parted from Rome, because he would say something to me by way of exhortation or instruction, telling me by way of compliment that I needed it not.[6]

A month later this final audience took place and the bishop reported :

> Yesterday I had my last audience of the Pope, it being the Feast of St. Gregory, Apostle of our Island . . . and for this reason, maybe, His Holiness made choyce of that day, on which to give me my Mission and last instructions, as he did, with a particular advise, or rather command, not to intermeddle with politick concerns or intrigues of state, but to attend to my functions, which order, he says, he will give in writing. He discoursed also upon some other points, and in

---

[1] Westm. Archives, Anne, II, 25.

[2] William Lesley, Agent in Rome of the Scottish bishops.

[3] The Benedictine Vicar Apostolic of the Western District, who had then been 14 years in exile from his Vicariate.

[4] I.e. his elevation to the episcopate.

[5] Secretary of the Congregation of Propaganda.

[6] Westm. Archives, *Idem.*, p. 203.

particular declared that absolutions given by Regulars in England without approbation of the Vicars Apostolic were invalid,
extra articulum necess.[1] . . . He talked also of substituting
me in place of Bishop Ellis,[2] and sayd that a Congregation
must be held on it. And I perceive that Fabroni has much the
same thoughts; for he required of me lately an account of the
ablest of our Clergy, which indeed I gave him, but desyred at
the same time that regard might be had to the recommendation
of our King and Queen,[3] and the presentation of our Clergy;
and because, maybe, they here will be more hasty than is
expected, I wish you would please to be vigilant in it, and that
none be nominated but such as will be justly acceptable. The
Pope also sent the two bishops[4] each a little gold medal, and
gave me one. The Propaganda has also offered to give me
300 Crowns for my Viaticum,[5] which indeed I may well stand
in need of, being likely to have either a very long journey to
England through Germany, or be forced to stay maybe a great
while in the Spanish Flanders before I can gett into Holland.[6]
Friends here rather advise me to take the way to Flanders,
which if I do, I must not only avoid coming at your neighbourhood, but even at Paris, for fear of people's talking, and
making that publickly known which ought to be kept secreat
as possible.

In due course his consecration took place in the chapel of the
seminary at Montefiascone at the hands of Cardinal Barberigo,
and describing the scene in a letter to Mr. Lesley, Witham said
that the Cardinal would not let him pay for his board at the
seminary, and

made a sumptuous dinner after the consecration which might

[1] This was a matter that had long been in dispute in England and continued
to be for many more years.
[2] I.e. in the Western District.
[3] The young James (son of James II), and his mother Mary of Modena. In
Catholic eyes he was the rightful king. The list of the most able clergy in
England which Dr. Witham gave to Rome contained twelve names, of which the
best known were Parret (Dean of the Chapter), whom he thought too old for
the episcopate; Betham, whom he thought was doing more good as tutor to
Prince James than he would do in England; Paston (President of Douay);
Thomas Witham, his own cousin, who was Superior of the Paris Seminary;
and Andrew Giffard, brother of Bp. Giffard. None of these ever became
a bishop.
[4] Drs. Giffard and Smith, the only two in England.
[5] The expenses of his return journey.
[6] This because of the War of the Spanish Succession then raging.

be fitt to entertain a Prince, and this upon the occasion of the consecration only of a poor Missionary Priest.[1]

Writing in March to Dr. Betham about the plans for his consecration, he had described how he proposed to travel to England, and this part of his letter is worth reproducing for the picture it gives of the difficulties of such a journey in those days :

. . . From [Montefiascone] I think I shall goe forward to Besancon in Burgundy, or Lyons, and so to Flanders; very sorry that I cannot performe my duties to their Majesties,[2] and wait on you and receive your commands, which would be a great comfort to me; but I hope to send one from Rheims who will supply my place and who may follow me after to Flanders, where I think to ly hid till I find an opportunitie to steale into Holland.[3]

I was much inclined to go through Germany, but generally friends have dissuaded me from taking that way, and indeed since the Duke of Bavaria and Marquis de Villars have brought the war into Germany it will be hard to gett through by that way, and the greatest danger will be from stragglers, deserters, etc. . . . so that it seems best to gett first to Flanders, and there by help of letters to the Envoy of Portugall in Holland, and the Nuncio at Brussells, which will be writ from hence, strive to passe, or go on foote like a country Curate from one village to another, till I get to Liege, or some Catholick town under the Hollanders, or Emperour : or, in fine, if it be God's will that I may not passe so soon, live retired and hid till such time as I may; which retirement may be of great help to me to prepare still more and more for what I am going about.

And in the interim we have two Bishops in England, who will look to that poor flock of the Catholics so well that they will suffer little by my absence, though it should be for some months or even years. . . . And I suppose Bp. Smith and my Father, when they advised me to the way of Germany had not heard of the wars there, as on the contrary I believe Bp. Giffard had not known of the late prohibition of all commerce betwixt France and Holland, which much increases the difficulty of passing that way, yet, it is hoped, not insuperable. . . .[4]

---

[1] Westm. Archives, Kirk's MS. *Records of the Vicars Apostolic*, III, 11.
[2] ' James III ' (the ' Old Pretender ') and his mother.
[3] He had to beware of falling into the hands of the English Protestant soldiery.
[4] Westm. Archives, Par. Sem. Col., 205.

Such were the delights of travelling in those days. Eventually the bishop got safely through to England towards the end of June, as appears by the following report from Gordon (Witham's successor as Agent in Rome) to Betham, dated August 14, 1703; but he did not after all travel by France and Flanders, but by Venice, Vienna, Prague, Hanover and Amsterdam, as appears from another source.[1] Gordon's letter runs :

> On the 9th current I received a letter from Bishop Witham dated London, June 23, O.S., in which he writes that the day before, after a long and expensive journey, he had arrived there in very good health. He had discoursed with Bishop Giffard, and was to go quickly to the North. He was in hopes to persuade Bishop Smith to leave those north parts to him.[2] Things were then pretty quiet in England for Catholics, although not long before there had been some little trouble.[3]

Before leaving Italy Bishop Witham had written to his friend, William Lesley, a letter which illustrates his warm-heartedness as well as his spirituality :

> Honoured and dear Don Gulielmo,
> It is impossible for me to express in this short letter all my obligations to you, or sufficiently to thank you for them : nor is this any compliment but the bare truth. And yet after all your favours, I have two more petitions to make to you; to wit that you would still have an eye towards our Mission,[4] and with your advice and credit help Mr. Gordon, who has the goodness to supply the place of an Agent for us, and is so well qualifyed for that and greater employments. Secondly, that you would help me with your devout prayers and sacrifices at the altar to comply with my duty. I doubt not but your goodnesse will move you to this act of charity; to which you seem to have some kind of obligation, both by reason of my particular need, and because I conceive you had some hand in laying on me this burden, which I have reason to fear will be too heavy for me. I despair of ever having the satisfaction of seeing you in this world, but I trust in the mercy and grace of God to see you again *in patria nostra, in terra viventium,*

---

[1] *Idem.*, Ep. Var., I, 85.

[2] This is of interest as showing that right from the start Dr. Witham hoped to get the Northern District. But it was not until 1716 that he succeeded in procuring his transfer.

[3] Westm. Archives, Par. Sem. Col., 205.

[4] I.e. the Church in England.

if I, by my demerits, doe not render myselfe unworthy of so great a happynesse.   Once more therefore adieu, my dear old good worthy friend and benefactor, and pray for

yr humble obliged servant and friend,

George Witham.

There had long been uncertainty as to which Vicariate Dr. Witham was to rule.   He himself wanted the North, he had been originally chosen to fill the vacancy in the London District, then, as we have seen, Rome talked of sending him to fill the vacant Western District, and by the time he left Rome it seemed probable that he was destined for the Midland District!   For it had been decided not to force the reluctant Dr. Smith into the London District, but to try to induce Dr. Giffard to go there instead, thus leaving the Midlands vacant.   To this course Dr. Giffard agreed and moved to London.   Dr. Witham therefore took over the Midland District.   Incidentally Bishop Giffard had been looking after the Western District (in addition to his own Midlands) ever since 1688, as Bishop Ellis could not return to England; and since the death of Dr. Leyburn in 1702 he had also cared for the vacant London District, so that his hands were full.   But now he became Vicar Apostolic of the London District, and he held this post until his death thirty years later.

Meanwhile there was still that long-standing vacancy in the West, and incredible though it may seem, it was to remain vacant for a further ten years.   This was largely because the secular clergy, despite their utmost efforts and although they put forward a considerable number of names, could not produce a really satisfactory candidate.   The position was also complicated by the fact that the first Vicar Apostolic of the West had been a Benedictine, and there were strong influences in favour of keeping this Vicariate in the hands of regulars.   In the actual event, it always remained in regular hands (with one exception) right up to the restoration of the Hierarchy in 1850, when all the Vicariates came to an end.   Some account of the efforts made to fill this vacancy must now be given.

In this same year (1703) Dr. Betham at the Jacobite Court in France made tentative efforts to get the Queen-Mother at St. Germains to move in the matter, but she wished to wait until informed of the views of the English clergy.   Writing to Gordon, the new Agent in Rome, Betham declared on June 8 :

The Queen does not claim a right of naming Apostolical Vicars, but expects none should be promoted but whom she approves of.

As Tutor to her son, Dr. Betham acted as liaison between the Queen and the bishops, and as such he had considerable influence on the appointment of bishops. He was violently opposed to the regulars and his references to them in his many letters are extremely outspoken. Naturally he keenly desired to see a secular priest get the Western Vicariate. On September 15, 1704, he told Gordon that the Pope had ordered the bishops to propose names in strict secrecy for the Western District, and that these had suggested Thomas Witham (superior of the Paris Seminary) and John Goter[1] (who died soon afterwards). He went on :

> Should there be any motion made for any of another body,[2] it would cause confusion . . . and the Clergy [sc. the seculars] would have reason to complain to see poor insignificant men put over them, when they are, God be praised, so plentifully supplied with eminent subjects of their own . . . I need not recommend the matter to your prudence, both as to secrecy and conduct. Fish out enough rather to act upon your own knowledge than by any information from hence.[3]

Betham had always been a strong supporter of the Queen's ' rights ' in such matters, and was her mouthpiece, which makes it surprising to find him writing to Gordon in December to tell him that neither Gordon nor himself need stretch matters too far in this matter of keeping the Queen informed, because she has no strict right to nominate bishops, and still less mere Vicars Apostolic. The reason for this striking change of front is that meanwhile he has discovered to his horror that the Queen desires a regular to be appointed, as he admits.

> . . . But since we have on all sides most dutifully desired nothing should be concluded without her Majesty's knowledge, I cannot think we are bound further to obstruct, upon her account, the proceedings at Rome, to the end the matter should

[1] Who received Bp. Challoner, as a boy, into the Church, and sent him to Douay.

[2] I.e. in clear English: ' Should a regular be proposed.'

[3] Westm. Archives, Epistolae Variorum (henceforth referred to as ' Ep. Var.'), I, 115.

be put wholly into her hands, since we know she designs none but a Regular to fill up the vacant place; therefore I cannot think tis any failure in our duty to let our Superiors at Rome doe as they think fit. And as I would not advise an un-mannerly opposition to her Majesty's proposals, yet I think wee may without overheating ourselves for carrying on her designs (since Rome both by the Queen and us is fully informed of what she designs) let things for the future take their natural course, and if they are resolved to make a Clergyman[1] let them doe it. Tis decent, if they at Rome are of the same mind, that the Queen should be informed of the person to be promoted, to know if she hath any just exception against him, besides his not being a Regular.

He first suggested Thomas Witham for the post, and then a certain Mr. Jones. Six months later he had discovered that the Queen had suggested to Rome two names, one that of a monk, the other that of a Franciscan friar, and he commented to Gordon on June 15, 1705, when telling him that the monk in question was Dom Bernard Gregson :[2]

> . . . a man of good common sense, and that's all; no epis-copal parts either for scholarship, preaching, or anything else : as to his person, though that be no crime, he is of an exorbitant bulk, with a carbuncled face which would not recommend his exterior to our English Catholics. As to his life and manners I know nothing against him. The other was a friar, but I know nothing of him.[3]

He added that he thought neither could compare with Andrew Giffard (brother of Bishop Giffard), who had lately come to the fore as the favourite candidate of the seculars. But still nothing definite happened, and in September Betham was wondering what was holding up Andrew Giffard's appointment. He told Gordon[4] that the three bishops in England were of one heart and soul and in entire unanimity, and were dreading the possible appointment of ' one of a different coat ' (i.e. a regular) which might disturb this harmony. They would ' much rather remain

---

[1] I.e. to appoint a secular priest.

[2] Bernard Gregson was President of the English Benedictine Congregation from 1697 to 1701, and again from 1705 to 1710. He had been Prior (i.e. Superior) of St. Lawrence's monastery (the modern Ampleforth) from 1681 to 1685.

[3] Ep. Var., I, 145.

[4] Ep. Var., I, 149.

D

as they are, with their present good understanding, than have their number increased, and by it this peace diminished.' Next month he wrote :

> . . . We will hope the affair of Mr. Andrew Giffard is not so desperate as we feared. The Queen assured me she had never made any opposition against him, since he was chose; only she had lett that Court [sc. Rome] know she thought herselfe hardly used, and that she disapproved the expedient fallen upon to save her right.[1]

Suddenly, in October, 1705, the news at last came. Andrew Giffard[2] had been definitely appointed by Rome and the Briefs had been made out naming him Bishop of Cantusiensis and Vicar Apostolic of the Western District. Dr. Betham on November 2 acknowledged receipt of them ' with much satisfaction ', and arrangements were put in train for Giffard's consecration in great secrecy, lest the British Parliament should get to hear of it and start a new persecution. But then arose an unexpected difficulty. To the dismay and annoyance of his colleagues, Andrew Giffard flatly refused to accept his appointment, and nothing that anyone could say would induce him to alter his decision. Thereupon more lengthy negotiations, and no fewer than eight secular priests were proposed. But to none of them did Rome offer the vacant bishopric, and as late as ten months after this (September 10, 1706) Bishop Smith of the North wrote to Betham :

> . . . Old Andrew is stiff and not to be moved from his resolution. He is hardened against all that was offered, and gives no other answere but that he cannot, will not agree to what is desired; and as it appears to me, required by God and his friends. This peremptory refusal puts us hard to it to find out an excuse for the good man, for he will not write himself [sc. to Rome], and, to offer another that may be acceptable to Mr. Clement,[3] has talents, and will accept of the farm.[4] Such is hoped may, in some measure, be Mr. Saltmarsh, who, though in some particulars less qualifyed, yet *omnibus consideratis* is as, or more, fit than any we could pitch on. But in

[1] *Id.*, 153.
[2] Four years earlier, Dr. Witham had suggested Andrew Giffard as coadjutor to Bishop Leyburn.
[3] Pope Clement XI.
[4] The Western District.

all appearance the management of that farm will by Mrs. Grace's interest, and other insinuations, be put into other hands,[1] and provided he be an able, good man and a good neighbour, tis no great matter who he be, or of what coté, or parish.[2]

But if Bishop Smith were ready to acquiesce if necessary in the appointment of a regular, his example was not followed by his two colleagues (Giffard and Witham).   In December Saltmarsh was ' presented ' to Rome by them as their choice, but he proved unacceptable there, and both Betham and Giffard were anxious. Six months later (June 18, 1707) the latter wrote to Lawrence Mayes who had recently taken over the Agency in Rome[3] and who will frequently appear in these pages :

. . . I could be glad some determination were fixed as to the supplying of the vacant Vicariate, the care whereof has lain upon me a long time.   Yet I had rather continue under the burden than to have a person who may take different ways [sc. a regular].   Amongst many miserys and afflictions we have had the happiness of great unity; and I think the consideration thereof ought to influence those masters in their choice.   Besides they have seen with what zeal and constancy we have persevered in the discharge of our duty.   This also should make them relye more confidently on our recommendation.   If they take other measures they will quickly find the ill consequences.   Had we been guilty of any maladministration they might with reason look for one in some other corporation [sc. a regular].   But I hope and am confident they will find nothing to ground a complaint on.   In fine, tis the work of God, and he will order it to his glory.[4]

In August Betham was sure it was the Queen who was causing the delay, and, though her employee and nominally her friend, he was trying to work against her in Rome through Mayes.   In October Bishop Smith told Mayes not to press Saltmarsh's claims too far, but to switch to Paston (President of Douay) or Jones if necessary, either of whom would be acceptable to the secular

---

[1] I.e. the Vicariate will be given to a regular through the influence of the Queen-Mother (' Mrs. Grace ').

[2] Westm. Archives, Par. Sem. Col., I, 257.

[3] His predecessor, Dr. Gordon, had been made Vicar Apostolic of the whole of Scotland, and remained so till his death forty years later.

[4] Par. Sem. Col., I, 331.

clergy.[1] At this time Mr. Saltmarsh offered to stand down altogether, if that would calm the storm; and meanwhile 'James III' and the Queen-Mother were both offended because the bishops, on orders from Rome, had not told them the names they had proposed for the vacancy. But the affair still dragged on, not without a note of comedy at times, and in June, 1708, Dr. Giffard told a correspondent that his brother had at last been induced to write a civil letter to Rome thanking Cardinal Caprara for his favour in nominating him and giving his excuses for declining the bishopric. These were, he stated, advancing age and ill health. By October Betham was convinced that Salt-marsh would never be offered the post, because the Queen would insist on it being given to a regular; and he proceeded to put forward a number of reasons why any regular would be unsuit-able (they would work for their own Order, not for the good of the Mission, they would need financial support from Rome because their Order would give a regular bishop nothing, and so on at considerable length). In January, 1709, Bishop Giffard despairingly proposed John Rivers, who was heir to an Earldom, and gave him a strong recommendation, and at the same time mentioned the names of Jones and a certain Jenks who later crops up again. Still only inscrutable silence from Rome. 1709 and 1710 slipped away, and the Western District remained vacant (which it had been ever since it was set up in 1688), and then in 1711 Bishop Smith of the Northern District died, and this complicated matters more than ever. There were now two Districts vacant, and it may be mentioned now that the Western remained vacant until 1713, and the Northern until 1716; so that for two years, 1711-1713, there were only two bishops in England, Drs. Giffard and Witham.

[1] *Idem.*, 371.

CHAPTER IV

BISHOP GIFFARD AND BISHOP STONOR

THE death of the gentle and much-loved Bishop Smith had resulted from an illness which had befallen him during his Visitation of East Yorkshire during the very hot weather of 1710, for this brought on a fit which was followed by severe nervous attacks for the next ten months, and after dropsy had set in he died on May 13, 1711, which was the twenty-third anniversary of his consecration as bishop. This cast upon the two surviving bishops the task of proposing to Rome a successor to Dr. Smith, and as the Western District was also vacant it may be imagined into what a state of activity the higher clerical circles in England were thrown at this time. Giffard promptly wrote to the Agent in Rome, Lawrence Mayes, instructing him to propose the name of Mr. Savage,[1] adding that Jones, Jenks and Paston were now too old. He said that Mayes himself would do admirably for the post but that he could not be spared from Rome. Yet Giffard himself was hoping soon to retire (actually he ruled the London District for a further twenty years) and he now hinted to Mayes that he (Mayes) might succeed him at London.[2] A few weeks later Dr. Ingleton (who had now succeeded Betham at St. Germains) told Mayes that the Queen had proposed a friar, and he considered that this would cause censure and calumny against the secular clergy. ' Since the fall of religion in England no Religious [i.e. regular] has ever been Bishop there, except Bishop Ellis; and I think his choyce ought to be no encouragement for another such.'

In August the authorities in Rome were impatient for nominations for the Northern vacancy to be sent to them; but Dr. Giffard, after describing Smith's death as ' an inexpressible losse ', explained that they had not sent them because they had

---

[1] This was the Mr. Rivers who has been already mentioned, and who had now taken this *alias*. He succeeded to the title of Earl Rivers in 1712. In view of the fact that he was heir to this title, he had asked for a dispensation to allow him to marry, but this was refused. For some years he was the priest at York, but his closing years were spent in Douay and Louvain, where he died in 1737.

[2] Ep. Var., IV, 75.

not been asked to do so, and also because the King and Queen would take it ill.   Moreover he himself did not know many of the northern clergy, and some that he could recommend would not accept.   In any case, a man of private means was needed.

> This is of great moment.   My brother Smith was heir to a great estate.   Brother Witham has a very considerable annuity; and as my relations are none of the meanest, so I am so far supplyed as to be no burden to the Holy See.   No person can live in that station with less than £100 per annum.   I am sure it costs me £150 one year with another. . . . Brother Smith has left a very large provision for his successors, but with this proviso, that he be of the secular clergy.[1] . . . Besides the four Vicars Apostolic chosen out of the Clergy [i.e., from the Seculars] have, I hope, given satisfaction to the Holy See; *portavimus pondus diei et aestus.*   We have remained firm and constant in the discharge of our duty notwithstanding the continual hardships, difficulties and dangers we have been exposed to.   Some of us allso have been honoured with the mark of St. Paul's election and Apostleship : *in carceribus abundantius.* I think therefore it will be very hard and some undervalueing of the Clergy, if these should be succeeded by persons of another Body.[2]

In September Dr. Dicconson, the Vice-President of Douay (himself to become a bishop 29 years later), told Mayes that the ' Fryar ' nominated by the King was Matthew Prichard (it was he who eventually was appointed), while the two bishops had nominated Saltmarsh and Savage.   Dicconson himself protested against the King having any voice in such appointments, saying that English kings never had had one from the time of King John to that of Henry VIII.   But four days later Giffard himself told Mayes that the bishops had sent up eight names for the two vacancies.   These were Dr. Jones, Saltmarsh, John Savage, Thomas Yaxley, Dr. Simon Rider, Dicconson, Edward Parkinson (assistant and companion to the late Bishop Smith), and Silvester Jenks.   He lamented that Smith, though urged to do so, would never name a coadjutor and had died without one.   And later he told Mayes : ' If our masters would transfer Bishop Witham to the North and make some other for the Midland District, and

---

[1] This told against Bp. Williams, the Dominican appointed in 1725.
[2] Ep. Var., IV, 117.

joyn to it South and North Wales, I could manage the West well enough. But the best will be to have four out of our (secular) Clergy for the four Districts.' The King, for his part, said he had no objections to any of those proposed by the bishops, while the Holy Father in Rome stressed the need of care that no one suspected of Jansenism should be appointed, especially as Douay was accused of being tainted with it. 1712 arrived, and in April Mayes was instructed to press for the one chosen by the King from the first three of those chosen by the bishops, i.e. Jones, Saltmarsh, and Robert Witham;[1] but Cardinal Gualterio (head of Propaganda) said that he had so much pressed the King's earlier recommendation of Prichard that he thought it would succeed. In that case, said Ingleton, Mayes should try to secure that if Prichard must be made a bishop it might be for the Western District (which was remote and poverty-stricken) ' and another chosen to succeed Bishop Smith.' Of course these partisan moves, by both seculars and regulars, left Rome largely unmoved; indeed the Cardinal stated that Propaganda thought it a matter of indifference whether they appointed a secular or a regular ' as long as he was the best man.' His merits must determine it. A doctrine that must have seemed almost heresy to the two contending parties in England.

The year 1712 went its way, and 1713 was ushered in and had travelled half its course when Dicconson reported from Douay that the Jesuits were trying to win over the other Orders to join them in their opposition to the secular clergy, and that they had promised to get mitres for Prichard (Franciscan) and for Father Williams, a Dominican; and he repeated this the following month. And then suddenly Rome at last spoke. In August the Congregation of Propaganda selected Dr. Jenks for the North and Fra Matthew Prichard for the West. It was believed that ten Benedictines, one Dominican, and several Carmelites had also been considered, and the King sardonically remarked that it was very strange that among all the nominations that he had sent to Rome none should proceed but that which he desired should not! Quite typically, Ingleton's comment on the appointments was that since Prichard ' is deputed to the Welsh Diocese, I hope it will bring no great damage to the Mission of England, farther

---

[1] Brother of Bishop Witham and one of the greatest of the Presidents of Douay. He figures largely in these pages.

than being a precedent for choosing Regulars.' Prichard was thus the first regular to rule in England since the Reformation. Jenks, it may be mentioned, was very infirm and was stricken with palsy.

As may well be imagined the Western District was more than ready to have for the first time a resident bishop of its own (twenty-five years after the setting up of the Vicariate), and a most formidable task awaited Dr. Prichard. Born at Graig, between Monmouth and Abergavenny, in 1669, he was thus a native of the District. He had made his noviciate at St. Bonaventure's, the Franciscan monastery at Douay, and after his ordination became a missioner at Perthyre in his native county. Though appointed Vicar Apostolic in 1713, it was not till Whitsun, 1715, that he could be consecrated, and the ceremony took place at Cologne. On reaching his Vicariate he laboured hard, in great poverty, to organize the Church in the West, but caution and moderation and patience were essentials in that time of potential or actual persecution, and no extension of the Faith was then to be expected. For most of his long period in office he lived at Perthyre, and he strove to hold the balance impartially between seculars and regulars. For though, unlike the Dominican Bishop Williams who came to the North a few years later, he took the side of his religious brethren in their conflict with the bishops on the subject of their faculties, and declined to sign the promulgation of the Papal Decree of 1745 which temporarily settled this matter in favour of the bishops (thereby earning a reprimand from Rome), yet at the same time he was always fair and friendly to the secular clergy, as even his bitterest opponents testified. There are several witnesses to this fact, amongst others Dr. Robert Witham, President of Douay, one of the most fervent anti-regulars who seldom had a good word for them. Writing to Mayes on July 5, 1729, he said :

. . . I have a late letter from Bp. Prichard, a very worthy Prelate, and who has shown himself not only just and impartial to the Clergy [sc. seculars], but I have reason to say, he has shown himself a particular friend to me and to this House [Douay] even more than every Bishop has done of our own Body;[1] having a true zeal for the King's service, as I can

---

[1] I.e. ' than any Secular Bishop '.

truly say in this we have been always of the same sentiments. . . . But now Bishop Prichard has so ill-health and
is so poor that he desired me in his last letter to let his Master
[the King] know that he hoped he would not take it amiss that
he desired of the Pope to be freed from his present charge of
his District, not being able to acquit himself of those obligations.[1]

Anyone who is familiar with the great state of (shall we say?)
tension then existing between the seculars and the regulars, will
realize that, coming from such a source, the above letter is high
praise indeed.   Incidentally it shows Prichard's Jacobitism,
which was a characteristic of nearly all the Catholics at that time,
despite the severe political handicap which that imposed on
them.   A year after the above letter was written further testimony
to Bishop Prichard was given by the equally anti-regular Ingleton,
at St. Germains, in a letter to Mayes :

. . . What you say of Bishop Prichard's desire to lay down
his office is surprising.   I am apt to think it may be an artifice,
whereby to obtain a subsidy; and I am glad tis like to be
granted.   For he has a very good character ever since he was
promoted.   I doubt not but that the Congregation [sc.
Propaganda] has likewise petitions from Bishop Williams, who
is as poor as a Mendicant should be.

And these testimonials were the more noteworthy in that the
bishop had incurred much ill-will from the fact that he was
generally reputed to be a close friend of the Jesuits (with whom
the secular clergy were having at this time a long-drawn and
bitter dispute over their attempt to win back control of the
English College in Rome from the Society).

By this time Bishop Giffard was an old man.   He was already
over seventy, and living, as he did, in the Metropolis, he was
immediately under the eye of the Government and therefore
more subject to persecution than were his colleagues in the
Provinces.   Already at the time of the Revolution he had
suffered a term of twenty months' imprisonment in Newgate, and
altogether he had four separate spells of imprisonment for the
Faith.   Moreover the threat of further imprisonment hung constantly over him, and for many years he had to keep constantly

[1] Ep. Var., IX, 217.

on the move to escape the pursuivants and the Government spies.
Thus in 1714 he declared that he had recently had to change his
lodgings fourteen times within five months to escape his pursuers,
and he had only once slept in his own lodging. His age made
these sufferings particularly acute, as we can well gather from the
graphic account in some of his letters preserved at Westminster.
Writing on January 30, 1705, to Thomas Witham (President of
St. Gregory's College, Paris) in the third person for security
reasons, he says :[1]

Your friend B. G.[2] remembers himself very kindly to you,
and bids me tell you that he has had many tryalls of late,
both publicke and private, and has sufficiently experienced
that of the Apostle : *foris pugna, intus timores.* After having
appeared several times before the Judges and at the Old Baily,
on the 8th December [he] was to have had his tryal, and as
he could expect nothing else but to be condemned to Hurst
Castle or some remote prison for his life, so he had prepared
accordingly, having, as he told me, resigned himself entirely
into the hands of Providence, and finding in himself great
comfort to think that he should end his life in a prison. And
thereunto he had settled all his little affairs relating to others.
But the night before the tryal was to be, there came to him
several persons of all states and conditions, who told him that
they having consulted together, twas the unanimous judgment
and advise of all that he should not appear, but rather forfeit
his recognizance. This was a great suprise to him, and filled
his mind with various and very anxious thoughts. But having
no time to consult others, or to reason things within himselfe,
he was forced to yeald to the advise then given. Next morning
therefore he withdrew into a private solitude.

I was with him at his taking leave of some few friends; but
never beheld so much trouble and concern in his countenance,
as then; and he told me [that] all the prisons he had been in,
and hardships he had suffered gave him not the tenth part of
the trouble he then experienced. Since, I understand, he is
better satisfyed, since he finds all people approve of the advise
given him, and thence concludes twas what God required of
him in the present circumstances. He's forced as yet to lye
very private, but hopes in some time to see his friends again.
He . . . bids me tell you if you would understand his present

---

[1] Par. Sem. Col., I, 247.
[2] Himself: Bonaventure Giffard.

condition, you must read the several epistles St. Cyprian writ, whilst he remained much in the same circumstances, after having withdrawn from Carthage into a private retirement.

That the bishop really was in great danger on this occasion is borne out by a letter from Dr. Betham in France to Mr. Gordon,[1] written on June 15 of that same year :

You will have known the great trouble Bp. Giffard has lain under, and is not as yet quite clear. Had he not had great friends, and even among those in the Government, he had certainly been condemned to perpetual imprisonment without any possibility of relief from the Government, either as to the moderating or changing of the penalty. They have been of late more troublesome than ordinary to Priests, and a letter to Rome giving an account of the Mission and Church matters there, if discovered, were more than enough to raise a persecution.

A few further extracts from his own letters will make clearer the picture of his mode of life and the difficulties under which he laboured. Thus, to Mayes three years later :

I have had all your letters, though at present cannot set down the dates, being tossed about into different lodgings, and my papers and other concerns deposited with friends according as I could get admittance for them. I had a poor garret at the Venetian Ambassador's, which served for a lodging, oratory, dining room, kitchen, etc., but the Ambassador being upon his remove, I am forced to seeke another habitation; and having no settled one, twill render me less capable of doing business. If your great men [sc. in Rome] saw my circumstances they would be much surprised. However, such was the life of our Divine Master, and that is my comfort as well as my example. . . .[2]

And this state of affairs persisted for very many years. Six years after writing the above letter, i.e. in 1714, he again writes to Mayes :

. . . At present I can do little, being under a persecution which obliges me to scamper about and often change lodgings and seek hiding-holes. The first occasion of this was a terrible Proclamation which came out at the beginning of May. That

[1] Ep. Var., I, 149.
[2] Ep. Var., II, 85.

was no sooner calmed, but a far greater danger threatens us, viz. warrants for siezing of Mr. Joseph Leveson, me, and several others. This comes from the malice or covetousness of some miscreant Apostate Catholics, who to get the £100[1] informe against us; and if we are taken we are condemned to perpetual imprisonment,[2] so far, that tis not in the Queen's power to deliver us. This . . . fills us full of fears; this obliges us to hide ourselves, and all our concerns . . . as also all papers and writings relating to ecclesiastical affairs, which causes great confusion. . . .[3]

The above are a few amongst very many such references to his troubles and dangers; and it is a striking fact that not only were his provincial colleagues never in these straits, never chased from pillar to post, but also the same applies even to his successors in the London District. None of them had the constant persecution to suffer which was the lot of Bishop Giffard for so many years, though for many of them the threat of it still existed and might materialize at any moment. It happened that he was in the centre of the danger area at the most perilous time. And every now and then Protestant hostility was aroused afresh by his success in making converts. In 1719 he told Mayes:

. . . What I mention of the daily increasing number of persons coming into the Church is so far true that I am persuaded, since the fall of Religion, there was never so great and general a disposition to the Catholic Faith as at present. One reason of this may be the great animosityes and divisions which of late have happened among the chief Protestant Doctors. Our converts are most of the middling sort of people. Such also were they that adhered to our Blessed Saviour . . . [My recent escape from arrest] tells me I must not reckon on any quiet in this world. Had the officers that searched the house found me, you would have heard of me being for the fifth time condemned to prison. Indeed tis often in my thoughts that although I am not worthy of dying a martyr for Religion, yet I may end my life in some miserable jail. In fine I hope the great Father of Mercy will lett me find veryfied the Prophet's saying: *Senectus mea in misericordia uberi* (Ps. 91, 11). . . . I was consecrated [bishop] on the

[1] There was a standing reward of £100 for information leading to the arrest of a priest.
[2] For being priests.
[3] Ep. Var., V, 139.

Feast of St. Athanasius, and a good priest told me even then, by way of prophecy, that I might likely have him for my pattern, and copy him in his persecutions. Oh! that I may find something of his reward in the next world, and let what will happen to me in this. I begg the assistance of your prayers. I hear that you have in your Town a great Lady, to whom I would pay all dutifull respects. Be pleased to tell her the poor old Bishop prays for her. You will apologize to the [Congregation of] Propaganda for my ill writing. I have no Secretary, and my hand is very old. You will help the Secretary [of Propaganda] to read it.

And so throughout his long life Dr. Giffard had persecutions and sufferings to endure, although, as he himself pointed out : ' I have been particularly careful not to interfere in political affairs of State : so that whatever I shall have to suffer will be purely on the score of Religion.'

But now we must get back to the vacant Northern District. We have seen that in August, 1713, Prichard had been appointed to the West and Jenks to the North, but the Briefs of Appointment were not sent to Jenks from Rome because the King at St. Germains ordered his consecration to be postponed for political reasons, and on December 26, 1714, Jenks died. So there was a renewed spate of speculation and of proposals. Both Robert Witham (brother of Bishop Witham) and Mayes were fancied for the North, but the former was also proposed for the Presidency of Douay,[1] and the latter was indispensable in Rome. In fact Witham received the Douay appointment in March, 1715, and then for the first time we find mentioned a man who was to play a very prominent part for the next forty years. This was John Stonor, who was then only 37, and so was thought by many to be too young for the episcopate. He himself, though intensely ambitious, did not desire to go to the North; it was on London that his eyes were fixed. It was Ingleton who had the idea that Bishop Witham might be transferred to the North (where he had always wanted to be) and the Midlands left vacant for a while, and the King also favoured this, but Ingleton himself reported in April that Giffard had told him that he had sent five names to Rome for the North : Mayes, Stonor, Rider, Dicconson,

---

[1] The same alternatives were to face Dr. Challoner in 1738 on the death of Witham, for he too was wanted both as President of Douay and as bishop. But in his case the upshot was the reverse.

and Parkinson, though Ingleton added that some time previously the King had told him that he had recommended *him* for the post, which fact prevented the King from supporting any of the above five.

It is at this point that there occurs the extraordinary intrigue promoted by Stonor and his close friend, the highly eccentric Abbé Strickland. Stonor's career affords a remarkable contrast between his earlier and his later years. In his youthful days he was a storm-centre, and an object of anxiety and dislike to both bishops and clergy alike. But as he grew older he gradually won his way to a position of great influence in the Catholic affairs of the country, and was held in the highest respect by all. Moreover he ruled for the long period of forty years and consequently left behind him a resounding memory in the Midland District, in which his fame was equalled only by that of Bishop Milner a century later. He was of high birth, being the son of Lady Mary Talbot (daughter of the 11th Earl of Shrewsbury), and as such he was a second cousin of the two Bishops Talbot, James and Thomas.[1] As a boy of twelve he entered Douay College, and six years later began to study at St. Gregory's, Paris, for the priesthood and for his Doctorate; but suddenly he gave up his plans for becoming a priest as he wanted to marry. However in the end he changed his mind again, and seven years later resumed his studies in Paris and after his ordination he took his Doctorate in 1714. From then on he was very much to the fore amongst Catholics, and his high birth, great ambition, and undoubted abilities coupled with a forceful personality clearly marked him out for promotion. At this stage, and for some years to come, he was a constant source of trouble and was deeply distrusted by his fellow-clergy, even after he had become a bishop, partly because of his Hanoverian sympathies, but chiefly because of his undisguised ambitions and pushing, intriguing ways which earned him many opponents. He was unwise enough to become a close friend of that queer enigmatic character the Abbé Strickland, who was equally ambitious but more unscrupulous, and who ended his life as Bishop of Namur. For some years these ' two young doctors ', as they were often called, were inseparable, and a constant source of uneasiness to the Vicars

[1] Hon. James Talbot, Vicar Apostolic of the London District, 1781-1790; and Hon. Thomas Talbot, V.A. of the Midland District, 1778-1795.

Apostolic (especially because Strickland had many powerful friends in high places); but as soon as Stonor found that his intimacy with Strickland was harming his own prospects he dropped him completely and without pity, telling him bluntly that he must not look for any help from him henceforth. These two were indeed the *enfants terribles* of the period, and every one knew they were scheming to obtain bishoprics (indeed they openly boasted of it): Stonor to have the London District, and Strickland the North. Stonor, indeed, had become Vicar General to Bishop Giffard, and the plan was that he should be appointed coadjutor-bishop in London. On all this, and on the sequel, these is a great mass of letters in the Westminster Archives, and a selection from some of them will make the situation clear. The first mention of the plot, which included a systematic ' denigration ' of Bishop Giffard to the Roman authorities, occurs in a letter from Dr. Carnaby (the Procurator of the Paris Seminary: St. Gregory's) to Mayes, the Agent in Rome. It is dated April 9, 1715.

> You'll wonder to have a line from me, but I think myself obliged to disclose a certain affair to you, which I had entrusted to me by your old scholar, Dr. Strickland. He is at present in Paris, and has been lately with Santini.[1] . . . He says he is so much esteemed by Santini that he is resolved to have no other [sc. than Strickland] for the Northern Vicariate in Mr. Jenks' place. He pretends to have had no hand in this. . . . Now if such thing should happen, it would be of dangerous consequence. He would be topped over us, against the universal comfort of our Brethren; and though a man of excellent parts, as you well know, his life has not bin so very Apostolicall as to deserve to be elevated to so high a dignity, nor does he seem sober and serious enough for so weighty an office. He tells me that the affair will be very soon done, and that Santini will have his Bulls [of appointment] before Whitsuntide. I hope you will do what you can to obstruct this : for he is not in the list, and by consequence would not be acceptable to the Brethren. But pray let nothing of it be known. I was obliged to keep this secret, but I thought myself more obliged to open it so far as to intrust it to you.
>
> They, i.e. Mr. Stonor and he, are also endeavouring to get Mr. Stonor made Coadjutor to Bp. Giffard; for which reason

[1] The Papal Nuncio in Brussels.

they lessen the good Bishop's credit with the Internunce as
much as they can. I have reason to think that they are also
making their applications that way against Dr. Witham,[1] to
have him removed from hence by order from Rome : whereas
I think his greatest fault was over-indulgence to them while
here. You see what it is to have young men with noysy heads
in a body, of which they think themselves only fit to have the
management and government.[2]

A month later Dr. Ingleton at St. Germains reported that he had
been told by Cardinal Gualterio that Stonor and Strickland had
both been recommended to Rome as possible coadjutors to
Giffard. Ingleton was a friend of Stonor's and always tried to
excuse him. In this letter he goes on :

As for Mr. Stonor, he deserves the character that is given of
him; but I am persuaded they who know Dr. Strickland will
not think him as yet cut out for a Bishop.

On July 23 Carnaby again wrote to Mayes :

. . . I had a letter from Mr. Paston[3] two days agone. He is
for excluding both Strickland and Stonor from mitres, and
with good reason, considering their late conduct;[4] but they are
both of them mightily set upon Episcopacy, which makes me
think neither are fit . . . so I hope you'll do what you can to
hinder their promotion. All people agree that come from
England that Bp. Giffard is more fitt for labour than ever,[5]
and in effect he does more than all about him. However he is
advised to get a Coadjutor by those very persons who have a
mind to have all power taken out of his hands, and placed in
their own.[6]

These intrigues had caused great resentment amongst the clergy,
by whom Giffard was universally beloved and respected, and
Dicconson spoke for all of them when he characterized the

[1] Thomas Witham, President of the Paris Seminary, under whom Stonor
and Strickland had studied for their doctorates. For many years they waged
a campaign against him in Rome, accusing him of Jansenistic tendencies (at
that time a fatal accusation that blasted many a career).

[2] Ep. Var., V, 229.

[3] The alias of Henry Howard, a most saintly priest in London, on whom
see p. 67, *infra*.

[4] See following page.

[5] Strickland and Stonor were telling Rome that Giffard was too old to be
able to work.

[6] Ep. Var., V, 243.

conduct of the two as ' underhand and ungrateful '. Even the gentle Howard deplored what had happened. He said the two had accused Dr. Giffard of being too old, incapable and irresolute, and Bishop Witham of being eaten with scruples and totally incapable of business. But he feared they would have their way, that Strickland would get the North and Stonor be coadjutor in London with all the real power, ' and then what a condition our affairs will be in ! '

As for Mr. Stonor [he went on], I must confess I fear him in some measure still more [sc. than Strickland]. His great desire and endeavours he has used for his promotion, which I have known by his own letters; his beginning so soon after he came over [from France], to undermine his own Superior, to whom he has been so particularly obliged; his accusing one of his own Body of what tends at least to Jansenism, while in his own conscience he thinks him orthodox; his doing all these things, not only without, but knowingly contrary to the will of Superiors; the ill-will he has incurred among all his Brethren by these underhand dealings, joined to that uneasiness of temper he is always under, till he has some project in hand, and to his dislike of all the missionary functions [duties], are reasons I believe most persons would think sufficient to endeavour to hinder his promotion.

And all this was confirmed by Thomas Day, a member of the Chapter in a letter of August 27, in which he said that Giffard had never thought of taking a coadjutor and was naturally indignant at Strickland soliciting one for him from the Nuncio behind his back. His two Vicars General, Saltmarsh and Stonor, were privy to all this in secret, but a certain Mr. Hesqueth informed Giffard of what was afoot, whereupon Giffard called Saltmarsh and Stonor into his room and made Hesqueth repeat his story. He then asked them whether they had told Strickland to do this, and they had to admit it, whereupon ' this being all they had to say, he gave them such a warm and vigorous reprimand that they knew not which way to look.' Giffard flatly refused the suggestion of the Nuncio that he should have Stonor as his coadjutor, said he had no need of any coadjutor, and added that Strickland was totally unfit to be Bishop of the North.

This, whatever I have related that concerns Bp. Giffard, I have from his own mouth, and the rest from Mr. Hesqueth.

E

. . . Thus Mr. Saltmarsh and Dr. Strickland judged Dr. Stonor the fittest person for Coadjutor to Bp. Giffard at present, and for his successor hereafter; and Mr. Saltmarsh and Dr. Stonor judged Dr. Strickland the fittest person for a Bishop in the North. Thus they divided the nation between them; and it may be presumed that Mr. Saltmarsh was not to remain unpreferred, if this design had taken effect. Could an attempt of this nature, in two young inexperienced persons, just stepped into the vineyard, proceed from anything else but an unparalleled ambition, joined with an uncommon degree of blind and headlong presumption? And from a violent desire for revenge.[1]

It should be added that subsequently Stonor denied that he ever judged Strickland to be fit for the Northern District, or that they were reprimanded by Giffard. Bishop Witham, when he heard what had happened, wrote to Mayes in Rome, instructing him to tell the Cardinals that Strickland was entirely unsuitable for promotion, and that Bishop Giffard was as active as ever and needed no coadjutor, and that he was sure they would not force one on such a man: ' a Bishop venerable for his known piety, prudence, zeal, and other talents, and who has spent so considerable a part of his life in promoting the Catholic Religion with so much labour, and in the midst of so many dangers and sufferings for the same.' Actually Witham himself would have liked to have a coadjutor as he was now very infirm, but he was afraid to petition for one lest Rome should give him Strickland. Everyone feared Strickland's extraordinary influence in Rome and with notabilities everywhere, and there are many letters extant full of alarm at the prospect of his promotion and all convinced of his utter unfitness. It was known that he had publicly declared his determination to have Giffard removed from London.

But, to conclude this matter for the present, it will be fitting to give Bishop Giffard's own defence, as written by him to the Agent in Rome, the more so as it includes an interesting picture of the conditions of the time. Writing on October 15, 1715, he says :

[1] Westm. Archives, Chap. Col., 263. Saltmarsh was at this time sixty-four, and had been soured by the cancellation of his appointment to the Western District.

If my letters have not reached you it is not my fault. Our circumstances are such that all our letters are opened and oftentimes stopt. This I have experienced in the various letters I have written to Mgr. Santini. Notwithstanding all the pains I have taken they have been intercepted. . . . I hear that two of our clergy have reported to him [Santini] that it was necessary to give me a Coadjutor; although this ought not to have been done without my knowledge and consent. The reasons alledged by them, as I hear, are these: 1. That I am too old. 2. That I neglect my flock and pastoral duties. 3. That I attend to, and am fit for, nothing else than to say my prayers.

As to the first, it is true that I am now in my 73rd year, but I thank God I am yet strong and enjoy better health than when I was only 30 years old. As to the second, they ought to have specified in what particulars I neglect my duty. I make my Visitations in the country, as far as the circumstances of the time permit, and the houses of Catholics are open to receive me. As to the obligation of preaching, called by the Council of Trent the peculiar duty of a Bishop, it is notorious that I never neglect it on Sundays and Festivals, where circumstances allow me to do it. In London it cannot always be done, but in the country I never omit it. I confirm whenever I am desired, and on these occasions I give them a preparatory discourse; and sometimes I have done this three times in a day and in three different places. In London I have no Chapel of my own, but I am at all times ready to perform this duty where wanted, and when it can be done without exasperating the Government. While I was under the roof and protection of the Venetian Ambassador I gave confirmation once a week, if wanted, and always gave a discourse on that sacrament, which I have also done in the Chapels of other foreign Ministers: and the last time I did this in the house of the Envoy of Florence, Mgr. Bianchini, the domestick Prelate of His Holiness, and Count Bardi, were present, who can testify to the vigour which they may have noticed in my voice and gestures while I preached. Almighty God has given me such strength and such consolation in seeing the fruit produced by my preaching, that I can in truth say with the Apostle: ' Woe to me, if I preach not the Gospel '. The dangers which continually hung over me in London, and which obliged me in the space of nine days to change my lodging *seventeen times,* have forced me to take shelter in the house of a Gentleman in the country where, having more liberty, I expound the Gospel every Sunday, and besides make a discourse to those who receive confirmation. As to my other pastoral duties, hundreds of persons can testify that, not having either carriage or horse, I go on foot from house to house, and to visit the sick and the dying; giving such instructions as the case requires.

As to that part of my duty which regards the Government of my flock, for many years I have been burdened with the care of three parts of this kingdom,[1] and not being able to visit them all in person, I have caused my Vicars General to report to me the state both of the priests and of the People; and have used such diligence in sending back the instructions and directions which were wanted, that without the assistance of a Secretary, I have many times sent off ten letters in a day. [He adds how he has corrected erring priests, and that] the necessary expenses though considerable have been well laid out, notwithstanding that I have been obliged on that account to deprive myselfe not only of the conveniences, but also of some of the necessities of life.

If I be taxed of vain glory in the recital of these good deeds, I will avail myselfe of the Apostle's apology : ' I have become foolish, you have compelled me '. I do not pretend to be free from all fault : God forbid I should be guilty of any such presumption. In the meantime, whenever their Eminences or His Holiness or Mgr. Santini shall make me acquainted with those neglects of my duty of which I have been accused, either I will justify myselfe by a modest reply, as far as truth allows me, or I will submit with all humility to their correction.

If I were not afraid of being taxed with folly for saying so much of myselfe, I might say a great deal of the labour of so many long and painful Visitations, and of the sermons and instructions given to my Flock. Much I might add of my sufferings in divers prisons, and of the prosecutions I have undergone for the space of twenty-seven years, without ever abandoning my flock, to whom I have constantly given all that consolation and assistance which the times and circumstances permitted. . . . But I am now drawing up an account of my pastoral administration from the day of my consecration to the present time, and I have determined to submit it to the Congregation of Propaganda, when I will resign myself entirely to its disposal. And if it be thought of advantage to this poor Church that I be removed from the pastoral charge of it, I

---

[1] It will be remembered that in addition to his own District he had also for many years charge of two of the other three.

shall have more pleasure in being eased of it by Pope
Clement XI, than I had in receiving it from Pope Innocent XI.

P.S. It will probably be some time before you receive this as
I am at present in the country, where few opportunities occur
of sending letters. All by the Post are opened. Before I left
London I was in imminent danger of being apprehended. The
officers had entered the house where I was, so that I was
obliged to effect my escape by a back door. I have been
particularly careful not to interfere in political affairs of State :
so that whatever I shall have to suffer will be purely on the
score of Religion.

A month later Bishop Giffard received a Breve from Propaganda
in highest praise and commendation of himself, his sufferings and
constancy, and his labours for religion, which was signed by
Cardinal Sacriponti, the Prefect of Propaganda.

CHAPTER V

THE LONDON DISTRICT

In September, 1715, the situation was radically altered by the promotion of Dr. Stonor to the Episcopate: an event which greatly upset many. At first his ' breves ' were made out for the Northern District, but this arrangement was soon cancelled, and it was understood he was to go to the Midland District. It was thought well, on account of the recent Jacobite rising, to postpone his consecration until matters had somewhat quietened down, for several priests had lately been arrested, including Fr. Plowden, who was a close friend of Stonor. On hearing of the promotion Dr. Carnaby told Mayes:

> I am much mortified [by the news]. I apprehend Mr. Stonor's promotion will cause great heats amongst the Brethren on account of his late strange proceedings against Bp. Giffard and Dr. Witham [of Paris]. However, we must submit to Providence and adore its appointments. The wishes and hopes of all, both here [Paris] and in England were for you; or someone else, whose integrity one was assured of. . . . I wish Strickland may not come over to take your place [in Rome], by Stonor's solicitations. It is certain they have both of them a spleen against you, and Stonor now will frighten or bully the other two good bishops into what he pleases.[1]

And Mayes had a similar warning from Carnaby's superior, Dr. Witham in Paris: ' If Strickland be promoted, he and Stonor will govern all, and dispose of all posts as they please. *You* may expect to decamp for one.'

These and similar fears appeared to be justified when in March, 1716 (i.e. before his actual consecration) Stonor obtained from Rome a ' Brief of Inspection ' (a cause of much subsequent trouble) empowering him to administer the London District in the case of the absence, illness, or disability of Bishop Giffard, but not otherwise.[2] Naturally this greatly offended the aged

[1] Ep. Var., V, 269.
[2] The document itself will be found in Appendix II.

58

bishop, and it was also hotly resented by most of the clergy. It showed where Stonor's ambitions lay, and though in fact he was never given an opportunity of putting the Brief into execution, yet it was not till some seven years later that his persistent hopes of getting the London District eventually faded away, i.e. after Dr. Giffard had secured first Henry Howard and then (on Howard's death) Benjamin Petre as his coadjutor with right of succession. It is, however, but fair to let Dr. Stonor speak for himself on this matter of the Brief. Here, then, is what he wrote to Dr. Robert Witham of Douay on June 5, 1716, from Paris where he was about to be consecrated :

Hnrd. Sir,
. . . I must begin with what sticks most to my heart. I find that the affair of the Brief of Inspection has taken air. All I know is that this discovery is not come from me. And I cannot believe it is come from you. In all appearance tis now also known to Bp. Giffard and to the Brethren in England. . . . I cannot say that some such thing as this Brief was not necessary, though a very unfit person has been pitched upon for the employment. All who will impartially consider both my temper and the circumstances of my fortune together with the present situation of Catholick affairs in England will easyly be persuaded that neither the inspection nor the Vicariate are agreeable to my inclination, much less that they are the effects of my solicitations and intrigues. But whatever be my own private judgment and inclination, I don't see how I can well decline the burden that is thrown upon me, and tis no less visible that the Holy See will not let a decree which it has been so long a-weighing and considering, be easyly set aside.
On the other side, tis cruel to think of causing a new division, and giving a new Subject of Scandal to the Catholicks of England in these unhappy times. I flatterd myself that I had pitched upon an expedient which would have prevented all such ill effects. But those measures have been beside what now are to be taken. I see no others but what your prudence and public spirit made you to suggest at first, viz. that you yourself would be pleased to intimate this Brief to Lord Bishop Giffard and the Brethren, and use your interest and credit with them to make them satisfyed and pleased with the contents of it. The proposal I made of having it kept a secret amongst us three, and which proposal l lykewise made to the Internunce is a sufficient pledge of my designs of peace and

quiet in regard of the body of Priests and Laity, and respect and tenderness in regard of him whom I look upon as my chief, Bishop Giffard. I shall look upon myself as abundantly satis-fyed, if, as to what relation I shall have to his District, he'l treat me in the same manner as he would do a grand vicar in whom he has confidence, or, if you will, a Suffragan that depends entirely upon his orders.

If the Apologies I can make for my past behaviour can not yet induce him to declare me innocent of ever having injured him, the submissions which I am ready to join to these Apologies ought at least to obtain his favour by way of pardon, and now that everything is settled . . . to forget what's past. I know there are preventions[1] against me, and there will be need of all your zeal and prudence to bring this matter to an amicable composure. These preventions are so strong that it comes from   ?[2] that some persons have entertained a design *quale nec inter gentes auditum est,* viz. to inform against me and cause me to be delivered up to the Government. God Almighty pardon them. I heartyly doe. All I can say is that whatever complyance and condescension charity can prompt to, and verity will allow of, I shall be allways ready to exhibit on my side. And however others may be affected or behave towards me, I shall never but upon the last extremyty and the evident call of my duty make use of high and authoritative means. . . .[3]

This letter might lead one to suppose that Dr. Witham had been privy to the obtaining of the Brief but, in addition to the fact that Witham was a loyal friend of Giffard and a long-standing opponent of Stonor, the letter which he wrote to Dicconson a few days after receiving the above shows that he had discovered the existence of the Brief by accident, and apparently Stonor had then attempted to explain it away to him. That he was in no way placated by the above letter is clear from the aforesaid communication to Dicconson of June 17, in which, after dealing at length with the political question of Stonor's desire that Catholics should renounce the Stuarts and take an oath of allegiance to George I (another matter on which he was at variance with his brethren), he then goes on :

[1] The word in the MS. is not clear, but presumably ' prejudices ' is intended.
[2] Here a word is indecipherable.
[3] Ushaw MSS., I, 44.

. . . Tis evident by Mayes' letters to me that the Secretary of Propaganda sent some time ago briefs to Santini to order my brother George[1] to ye Northern District and Mr. Stonor to the Middle District. These Bulls are and have been for some time in Santini's hands. In all appearance he stops them at the request of Bp. Stonor and Strickland, because Strickland hopes still to get Stonor settled in ye South[2] and to be promoted himself to be Bishop in ye Northern District.

By Stonor's letter to me he seems to have no thought of leaving the south of England, but of making use of that late Brief [of Inspection] which you know fell into my hands. With submission to better judgments, I should think the King might protest against Strickland being promoted to what he aims at, and likewise desire and require that the governing of the southern district remain still to Bp. Giffard, who is still very vigilant, laborious and capable; and that Stonor be not appointed to govern in ye south, but sent to ye middle district, as the Congregation of Propaganda have allready ordered him, though the orders be stopped.

These two points seem of importance to me : to stop the harm they [sc. Stonor and Strickland] may do as to the project they are about in drawing formulas of oaths, abjurations, etc.[3] I'll wait on Mgr. Santini in a day or two and will endeavor to represent to him the inconvenience of such intended oaths. I must also give him a handsome hint that the Secretary de Propaganda told Cardinal Gualberi [that] the Bull for sending Stonor to ye middle district and Bp. Markham[4] to ye North were sent some time ago, so that I hope my brother may have his orders and be gone to ye north, where he is so much wanted. Bp. Stonor will do ye least harm in the middle district both as to the King's interest,[5] and besides his acting in the south would occasion divisions of ye highest nature, our Brethren and all Bishop Giffard's friends being so displeased at his and Strickland's strange proceedings against Bp. Giffard. . . .[6]

And so, in the event, it actually came about. Bishop Witham departed for the North (where the long delay had given rise to

[1] Bishop Witham of the Midland District.

[2] I.e. given the London District.

[3] This refers to the search by Stonor and Strickland for a formula for the oath of allegiance to George I and of abjuration of King James which they wished Catholics to take.

[4] Bishop Witham. He was often given this *alias*.

[5] I.e. the interests of the Jacobite cause.

[6] Ushaw MSS., I, 109.

fears that a regular would be appointed), and Dr. Stonor took his place in the Midlands.   But the storm of indignation raised by the Brief of Inspection caused him to lie low for a time, and he made great promises of peacefulness.   It must now have seemed to Strickland that *his* time had come and that the outlook was rosy for him now that Stonor was firmly settled as a bishop in England.   Actually it was at this juncture that, for prudential reasons, Stonor finally dropped Strickland altogether as mentioned above; so that just as his plans seemed to be coming to fruition Strickland found that his prospects of preferment in England had ended.   Stonor had come to realize that the unpopularity of his associate was doing himself no good, and now that he was a bishop he decided to see no more of him.   In this course he was encouraged by his friend Dr. Ingleton, who was able to report in June that Stonor and Strickland were now at complete variance and that Stonor had told his former associate ' that he must never expect to be employed by him either as Grand Vicar or in any other way '.

> This he thinks absolutely necessary to remove the great preventions and prejudices which many conceived against him.

Ingleton said he had made great efforts to instil into Stonor a love of union and peace and loyalty, and that if he lived up to this he would remain his friend, ' but if he recedes from these dispositions . . . he knows me too well to expect any countenance from me '.[1]   Stonor himself wrote to Mayes criticizing Strickland strongly, but telling him not to let Strickland know he had written, ' lest he suspect '.   Small wonder that the breach steadily widened, and Stonor, fearing the great influence which Strickland still had in Rome, wrote to Mayes in April, 1717, ' because that gentleman may very likely set about playing some of his old tricks . . . I think tis fit I should tell you what I conceive of his character '; and there follows a lengthy and outspoken condemnation of Strickland and all his ways, ending with the devastating and apparently unintended self-revelation : ' My particular fault, who defended him as long as possible, is that I would not continue to doe so and to deal with him as an intimate, when I clearly saw that it would only make myself

[1] Ushaw MSS., I, 110.

odious without any benefit either to myself or to him '.[1] Even
Ingleton commented : ' So that having employed this poor tool
while he wanted him, he now drops him where he found him '.
Strickland in fact realized that he had now no prospects in
England.   According to Ingleton he had actually had a picture
of himself painted in a bishop's robes, and gave it to the nuns
at Louvain.   Perhaps the wisest verdict on Strickland is that of
Bishop Giffard who had been grossly misrepresented by him to
Rome.   Referring to his flashy talents, Giffard wrote to Mayes :

> . . . Had that good gentleman some place in a foreign
> seminary he might doe much better than in such a country as
> this. Tis neither great wit, nor a fine tongue, nor a knack of
> writing letters, that will make a Churchman valued here, much
> less secure him against the innumerable dangers young men
> are continually exposed to. Humility, prudence, a constant
> application to God in prayer, and a watchfulness over our
> words and actions : these are our only security.[2]

Meanwhile Bishop Stonor was settling down in England (though
not in his District, for his interests still lay mostly in London),
and there was an uneasy truce between him and his clerical
brethren who were suspicious as to what he might be hatching.
In reality, apart from his overweening ambition, Dr. Stonor had
many admirable qualities, and his later career as a bishop, after
he had shed his youthful indiscretions, was of great value to the
Church in England.   He had a very clear mind and a firm will,
as well as great energy, so that it is not surprising to find that
for very many years he was the leading spirit amongst the
bishops.   But before leaving this picture of his early years there
is one more extract from the correspondence of the period which
will be helpful for the glimpse it also gives of the other bishops
of the time.   It is from the President of Douay to Lawrence
Mayes in Rome, and is dated September 7, 1717 :

> We were sorry you gave the first notice [of Cardinal
> Gualterio being made Protector of England] to Bp. Stonor,
> whose chief and almost only great talent lies in writing letters.
> And since I've named him I'll let you know how things stand
> betwixt him and our Brethren [sc. the Secular Clergy].

---

[1] Ep. Var., VI, 99.
[2] *Id.*, VI, 127.

Generally speaking, they have not that respect for him nor confidence in him, that they have for the other bishops, not even that they have for Bp. Prichard the Fryer. Two things seem to have occasioned this. First his taking particular ways and measures, particularly in regard to that project of taking oaths [sc. of allegiance] to [King] George; and secondly the more than ordinary attachment he, apparently at least, has to the Politick Padri.[1] . . . I find that the chief of our Brethren fear nothing so much as lest Bishop Stonor should succeed Bp. Giffard in the London District, with whom twill, as things have gone, be very hard for them to have a perfect union; and therefore, to speak my mind to you, I think if ever it lies in your way you would do well rather to obstruct it. Bp. Stonor very seldom or never preaches; his talent, as I told you, is in writing letters. . . . Bp. Giffard is really and truly as hearty and as vigorous as ever I knew him. He often walks from one end of the City to another.[2] He preaches on every occasion with great zeal; confirms, hears confessions. Never Prelate was so wronged as he in those representations made against him to Santini by Stonor, Saltmarsh, and Strickland. . . . Tis on this account that the Testimony[3] of his present, as well as his past, labours is sent to our Protector. . . . I am convinced tis short of what with truth might justly be said of this Apostolic Prelate.

My brother George[4] is also now in better health than he used to be since he came to Cliff.[5] He's not so fat, nor troubled with the gout. He confines himself to the quantity of a Colledge portion. He is now making his visits, nor does he fail to instruct and preach, as tis always necessary for our bishops in England,[6] as you would do well to take notice of that, and not promote men who will not, or cannot, labour in that kind. Bishop Prichard is much commended and keeps in his own District. Bishop Stonor is only in his about six weeks in a year.[7]

[1] The Jesuits. This friendship was for long a frequent cause of distrust of Stonor.

[2] At that time he was seventy-four.

[3] A testimonial to Giffard drawn up and signed by the London Clergy and sent to Rome.

[4] Bishop Witham of the Northern District.

[5] His birthplace and home near Darlington.

[6] Another shaft at Stonor.

[7] This was true of his early years as a bishop, but not later. In those early years he lived in London, until he gave up hope of ever getting the London District. The above letter is in Ep. Var., VI, 153.

But now that Dr. Stonor was established as a bishop in England
it was necessary for the clergy to find some *modus vivendi* in
regard to him, and despite the continuance of some bitter correspondence in the next few years there were those who tried to
heal the breach, if only from motives of policy.   Such a one was
Dr. Dicconson who urged this course upon his brother, the Vice-
President of Douay, who had long been at daggers drawn with
Stonor, for an undated and unsigned fragment which is
apparently from him in the Ushaw Archives is to this effect :

I sent ye letter you writ me, as well as the other, to Dr.
Ingleton, but I must needs say I cannot think it prudent to
breake with Bp. Stonor.   It is manyfest his proceedings have
not been such as could have been wished, his letter concerning Dr. Witham[1] very unsincere, and ye character he underhand gives him very undeserved.   And certainly nothing can
appear more ridiculous (if one may say it) than that two young
men[2] at their first appearance on ye stage should assume an
authority and fancy themselves fully qualified to reform all
abuses and even their Superiors themselves, before they had
almost thrust their hooke into ye harvest.   Yet as I said, notwithstanding all this, I would still say Bp. Stonor need not be
quarrelled with.   His rank is now considerable, his credit at
Rome established, he is a man of learning and sober parts, a
man of good quality and allyd to great familys, and notwithstanding all that has happened I cannot but think him true
to his body,[3] though not so zealous an assertor of its privileges
as some others.   To break with him might (all things considered) be of more consequence to you than to him, for his
good word at Rome and his sollicitations there will go further
than perhaps anyone's now in ye Mission, and to rank such
a help on occasion, not to say to have that power turned against
you, might be no small disadvantage. . . . Dr. Strickland, I
fear, must have still a little more string before he be convinced
that he has taken a wrong course, though I cannot despair
but he will in ye end, and perhaps soon, see his errour.   You
will find Bishop Stonor and he will soon part, and when he
finds himself abandoned by almost all his Brethren it will, or
nothing, bring him to himself.[4]

[1] Thomas Witham, President of the Paris Seminary
[2] Stonor and Strickland.
[3] I.e. to the Secular Clergy.
[4] Ushaw MSS., I, 112.

It has been necessary to dwell at some length on this early aspect of Bishop Stonor, in order to give a true picture of the man as he then was, and also of the time; but it would be grossly unfair to leave it at that.   For, as has already been suggested above, these were but the days in which he may be said to have been sowing his ecclesiastical wild oats, and when he matured he presented a very different picture.   Indeed there is a very remarkable contrast between the young, ambitious, intriguing cleric and prelate of the period 1714-1725 and the dignified, wise, and widely influential bishop of his later years. It is difficult to believe they are the same man.   For at least the last twenty years of his life his was the preponderating influence in English Catholic affairs, and in matters affecting the bishops it was generally he who took the initiative, largely because it happened that none of his episcopal brethren sought the limelight or were anxious to lead.   For (to glance ahead at those years) Bishop Petre of London was extremely retiring by nature, and his coadjutor and successor, Bishop Challoner, was also humble and self-effacing, while Bishop Prichard was too far away in the West and out of touch with affairs, even if he had wanted to act prominently.   In particular Stonor took the lead in the matter of the very long drawn-out dispute between the bishops and the regulars, which was settled first by the Decree of 1745, and then by the Brief *Apostolicum Ministerium* of Benedict XIV.   After quitting London he lived at Heythrop, Oxon., placed at his disposal by the Earl of Shrewsbury (his kinsman), and at his family estate Watlington Park in the same county, and sometimes at Stonor Park, near Henley.   Described by Dr. Burton[1] as 'the indomitable old Vicar Apostolic of the Midlands', and as 'imperious, autocratic, and masterful', he was certainly in his old age an impressive figure.   Born in 1678, he died at Stonor Park[2] on March 29, 1756, and is buried there.

But to return to the second decade of the century: the years were pressing heavily on old Bishop Giffard, and though he had for years protested that he needed no help, and especially that in any case he would not accept that of Stonor, when he reached his 76th year he thought it wise to ask for a coadjutor lest he might suddenly die, thus leaving the Vicariate vacant—with

---

[1] *The Life and Times of Bishop Challoner.*
[2] Kirk says he died at Heythrop.

perhaps unfortunate results. The man for whom he asked from Rome was Henry Howard. This very holy young priest, heir to the Dukedom of Norfolk and thus to one of the highest positions in the land, Dr. Giffard praises over and over again in the most glowing terms in his letters to Rome and to various of the clergy in England. He calls him ' my joy and my admiration . . . especially for the two great virtues of humility and charity ', and describes his amazing devotedness to the sick and the poor in the London slums. As Henry Howard was eventually appointed coadjutor with (as almost always in the penal times) right of succession, though he did not live to be consecrated, he should have some place in these pages, and the best description of him is that given by Dr. Giffard himself :

I say nothing of his ancient birth (according to which, should the present Duke of Norfolk dye without male issue, he's the first nobleman next to the Royal Blood), though that is of great consideration, especially where all other qualifications concur; as indeed they do in this most excellent person. His humility is so great that he applies himself wholely to the poorest sort of people, in so much that the character of Our Blessed Saviour is truly verifyed in him, *Evangelizari pauperibus misit me Dominus*. He frequently visits them in their poor cellars; he instructs them with an incredible zeal, and the poorest and most abandoned by others are the objects of his care. His attendance on them in sickness is wonderfull. No diseases, though never so dangerous, can frighten him. The smallpox is a very fatal distemper in London, and though he never had it, yet he has watched whole nights with severall poor creatures who have dyed under his pastoral care. In fine, his zeal, his diligence, his continual application to these works of a Missioner, is so great and so conspicuous that he's become the admiration of all persons. Tis true he has not been above three years in the Mission, but I can truly say *consummatus in brevi, implevit tempora multa*. . . . He has a very solid judgment, as I find by often discoursing with him. He is also of so sweet and inoffensive temper that he is never engaged in quarrel with anybody. Hence he is generally esteemed and beloved by his own Brethren, and also by the Regulars of all Bodys, who all admire, extol, and magnify him. He has also a good talent in preaching, and as for catechizing and familiar instructions, these are his daily and continual exercises. . . . Hence you will not wonder that I propose him for my Coadjutor, or even to take my place at present. . . . No person can say that I have in the least exceeded in what I have said of him.[1]

Elsewhere he calls him ' *Dilectus Deo et hominibus* ', and in November, 1719, he made formal application to Rome for him as his coadjutor. But this was opposed by Bishop Stonor who claimed to have the first reversion of the London District by reason of the ' Brief of Inspection ' given to him by Rome in 1716, which authorized him to manage the District if Giffard should become incapacitated. But Giffard persisted and made another formal application for Howard in April, 1720, to which ' King James III ' added his recommendation, with the result that eventually Howard was appointed coadjutor with right of succession by a Breve dated September 30, giving him the title of Bishop of Utica. The letter did not reach England until the end of November, and to the great grief of all Henry Howard died on November 22 without ever having heard of his appointment, after having caught ' a great fever . . . taken in running up and down after some poor sick people '. Dr. Giffard was inconsolable at this crushing blow, and the London clergy greatly feared that Dr. Stonor would again try to secure the succession. But Bishop Giffard almost at once chose another coadjutor, putting in an application for Benjamin Petre, the youngest son of a wealthy Essex family; and though the matter was held up by the death of the Pope in June, 1721, it was eventually carried through despite the dismay and vehement protests of Mr. Petre.[2] Thereupon Stonor made vigorous protests to Rome, as he had done on the appointment of Howard, telling Mayes that it was due to his Hanoverian leanings which had offended King James, and also that it was a slur on him on the part of the Pope. He wanted to know the details of the accusations against him, and he wrote to Propaganda protesting that he was still Delegate to

---

[1] Giffard to Mayes, Ep. Var., VI, 223. The glowing terms used by Dr. Giffard remind one forcibly of Bp. Petre's language exactly 20 years later when applying for Challoner as his coadjutor, or that of Bp. Walsh when pleading to be given Wiseman in 1840. Howard was the only coadjutor to die before consecration, though three others died before they could succeed to their Vicariates.

[2] Giffard himself said that he was still perfectly active. ' My only reason therefore for moving for a Coadjutor is to secure the succession to one, who I think is of all others most acceptable to God, and universally to all Bodys ' (sc. to Regulars and Seculars alike). In other words his motive was to prevent Dr. Stonor from getting the London District.

Giffard by virtue of the 'Brief of Inspection', and therefore coadjutor. The reply from the Roman authorities was that his delegation was for the lifetime of Giffard, not for the succession after his death, and therefore the appointment of the coadjutor was not aimed against him, nor a reflection on him. With that he had perforce to be content.

But if Dr. Stonor hankered after the London District the very opposite was the case with the man who actually obtained it. Surely never did anyone receive the Episcopate so unwillingly as did Benjamin Petre (save possibly the two Talbot brothers of the next generation). It has already been mentioned that he strongly protested against his appointment, but both before and after his consecration his agonized protests continued. But before going into that, who and what kind of man was this, and why had he been selected by Giffard as his eventual successor? Like his nephew, Francis Petre, who was to be Vicar Apostolic of the Northern District from 1752 to 1775, Benjamin Petre belonged to that branch of the family which resided at Fidlers in Essex where they owned a large estate. He came, in fact, of a very rich family—a fact which was not altogether unconnected with his appointment. He was the youngest son (hence, perhaps, his Christian name) of John Petre, the holder of the estate, and he was also a relative of the famous Jesuit Father Petre, so prominent at the Court of James II. After his ordination as priest, Benjamin became for a time tutor to the ill-fated Earl of Derwentwater who was eventually executed for his share in the Jacobite Rebellion, but he was in reality never in any sense a learned man. He was a little over forty years of age when Bishop Giffard applied to Rome for him as his coadjutor and news of the appointment came through in a letter from Cardinal Sacriponti that was dated July 1, 1721. His consecration took place on November 11 at the hands of Bishop Giffard, assisted by three priests, no assistant-bishops being available for the ceremony. That is the brief sketch of his life up to that point, and the question arises: why did Giffard select him for such a vitally important post? To that, the general answer may be made that Dr. Giffard had had long experience of judging men and must have highly approved of what he saw in Petre, and it is indeed certain that Benjamin Petre was a deeply spiritual man. He was the antithesis of the worldly, self-seeking, ambitious type, and that also probably

F

made a powerful appeal to Giffard who had suffered not a little
from that very type.   But we can be more precise than that, for
the actual reasons are given in Giffard's letter of application to
Rome.   Therein he gives three reasons, and if those reasons may
appear to us to-day as somewhat naïve, they are those which
had much weight at that time, and which were, in fact, put
forward on several other occasions for other candidates.   These
reasons, given by Giffard, were that Petre was (1) Of ancient
and noble family (in those days this carried very much weight,
for in the eighteenth century, as in those before it, the aristocracy
were given vastly more respect, almost veneration, than they are
given to-day); (2) He had been educated at Douay, both as boy
and student for the priesthood, and that, from the point of view
of the secular clergy, was the hallmark of suitability; (3) He was
wealthy.   Yes, that was a reason too, and a very good one in
those days when there were no endowments and but a scanty
and poverty-stricken flock.   We have ample evidence of the great
difficulties brought upon the bishops by lack of means.   Nothing
was said about learning or ability or experience.   Now the
interesting thing is that when Petre was desperately struggling to
be released from his office, he came to fear that he had been
chosen merely for those very reasons which had in fact influenced
Giffard; and this caused him agonizing scruples.   Furthermore,
fifty years later one of his successors in the London District, James
Talbot, had precisely the same fears, and with equal justification,
for he had the same three qualifications, and the same reluctance
to trade upon them.

The adjectives used by Dr. Burton[1] to describe Bishop Petre
were ' gentle, pious, humble, timorous, and affectionate ', and
this was the man whose lot it was to be to govern the chief
Vicariate in England, to be the nominal head of the English
Catholics, and to have to face all the dangers and complications
of those unruly times.   We cannot be surprised that such a man
shrank from such a task, and yet the further surprising fact is
that though he himself in his letters to Rome touches the very
depths of self-criticism and disparagement, yet strangely enough
everyone else, despite his inactivity and indecisiveness, speaks of
him in terms of highest praise.   Obviously there must have been
real merit in him, and much firmer character than one can

[1] *Op. cit.*

discern at this distance of time. In this respect he remains
something of an enigma.

Be that as it may, having been forced by great moral
pressure to undergo his consecration, he at once set about seeking
his deliverance from a position which he had never desired and
greatly dreaded. As early as November, 1722, he wrote both to
Mayes and to the Pope himself asking to be allowed to resign,
after only one year's experience as a bishop. Already before that
he had repeatedly told his chief, Bishop Giffard, that he wanted
to resign, and the latter's comment to Mayes was that Petre's
' humility is too great, and his courage too little '. Giffard would
not hear of any resignation, for, as he wrote to Mayes in
October, 1722, if Petre be allowed to resign

> the Clergy is ruined. My great age and load of troubles sink
> me down; so that I shall be forced to resign the place to any
> one the Holy See shall appoint; for I shall never more propose
> anybody. So that you see the absolute necessity of your being
> active to prevent the Pope's accepting of his dismission. I
> cannot hear of any one person, but himself, but is highly
> pleased with him and his conduct, especially for his prudent
> management in affairs and his pious exhortations when he
> confirms.

And Mayes soon had occasion to exercise this vigilance to which
he was thus bidden, for it was on November 8 that Petre wrote
the aforesaid letters to Rome. In his appeal to the Holy Father
he pleaded his lack of talents and his lack of theological studies,
pointing out that his predecessors had been Professors or Doctors
of Theology, of which he knew nothing. He said he was tortured
by the contumaciousness of some and the licentiousness of others;
and was terrified of strifes, and by the cases of conscience which
he was called upon to resolve. He was not even fluent in Latin,
and his sole wish was to be a private missioner.[1] In the letter to
Mayes which covered this petition he repeated that he had never
had a proper course of studies, that he cannot write Latin nor
even read it without the help of a dictionary, and protests that
he has very little money (only a small annuity which may be
withdrawn). He also alleges the clandestine nature of his
appointment, for he says he was never asked his consent until

[1] Westm. Archives, XXXVIII, 120.

after the Breve of appointment was issued. Till then he had heard nothing of it, and so was practically forced to consent. Even so, he had refused for two months until

> a certain person of distinction was desired to induce and bring me along with him to Mr. Fowler's[1] chamber where, after my plain refusal of accepting the office, he desired us to say the *Veni Creator Spiritus* with him, which being done, he laid his command upon me to accept the proposed office. This unexpected and despotick proceeding startled me, not a little, and I replyd that if I was obliged in conscience I would, not otherwise. Some time after His Lordship writ me a letter that certain Divines named therein had given it as their opinion that all circumstances considered I was obliged to submit; and amongst other things promise was made by His Lordship that if I continued under the same unwillingness and uneasiness after a year tryall, he would use his endeavors to get me freed and nominate some other in my place. This did not fully satisfy me, for I would have sent an appeal to His Holiness, if I could have persuaded a proper person to put it into Latin for me. But not succeeding in this, and being assured by my Director that notwithstanding the conviction of my unfitness, I should do better not to appeal, but to submit, I followed not my own, but his opinion, and therefore did consent to be consecrated. And now for this twelvemonths I have experienced the effects of my insufficiency and incapacity, have lost all tranquillity of mind, and that peace which surpasses all understanding; my inward repugnance to the enjoyned office has increased by the tryall I have made of it. . . . If you have any regard for me, or concern for the good of your country, I beg you will presse for my speedy discharge. . . .[2]

In reply Mayes sent a very long and wise letter of encouragement and counsel, refusing to submit the petition to the Pope. It is a model of what such a letter should be, despite the delicate position in which it placed Mayes, and as such is well worth reproducing here in part :

> Sir,
> I have now in my hands the favour of yours, Nov. 8, with the inclosed Petition. It would have been extremely accept-

---

[1] Bishop Giffard's.

[2] Ep. Var., VII, 373.

able had it been upon any other subject. I am the more concerned, because I am not able to procure you the satisfaction
you so earnestly desire. . . . It is a matter of the greatest
consequence to our concerns, and certainly not to be concluded
in haste. . . .

I observe that your complaints of incapacitie are not backed
with the opinions of others, not of Mr. Fowler especially, for
whom you justly have the greatest deference : much less am
I confident it is the opinion of others, that supposing a present
incapacity, it is an invincible one; yet nothing less than this in
my mind can excuse your present resolution. The said complaints proceed from the opinion you have of yours, which
certainly is the worst and most deceitful guide that can be :
the surest way upon earth in these cases is submission and
obedience to the judgment of others, especially Mr. Fowler.

After saying that Petre would have done ill if he had sought his
own promotion, and that since he did not seek it he has nothing
to answer for on that score, he added :

All kind of presumption is in favour of your continuance,
and stands good till there be evidence of your unfitness. This
so far does not appear; and if this were really the case it would
appear to others and you would be advised of it by friends,
and then would be time to sue for what you are seeking at
present, and we are all content to wait this time.

He has just cause for complaint as to the way in which he was
induced to accept the office, but

this does not argue that it was not the order of Providence.
If anything was wrong, surely the actors are responsible, not
the sufferer; but in the present case, all circumstances considered . . . neither [side] can be blamed.

There both have been, and are still, examples of persons so
employed whose education as well as engagements afterwards
have been far less suitable to the employment, than yours ever
were, and yet have and do acquit themselves very well. What
you observe of others there, and their antecedent qualifications,
make no more than a mere accidental difference between you
and them, as all know; and all know likewise that a good and
ingenious man may have spent his life among books, and yett
may be very unfitt for that employment [sc. episcopacy], may
want conduct, temper, prudence, experience, humility and
such like qualifications which are far more essential than titles

[sc. degrees], and the want of them far more dangerous than what you miss in yours, in regard of others who have gone before you : so that I am really surprised to see your fears of falling into doctrinal mistakes, which even ignorance, if I must needs suppose this, when accompanied with humility and diffidence in one's own judgment, seldom or never engage men in; but forwardness and presumption easily may and frequently do.

I think likewise you have very little reason to complain of your want of knowledge of antient rules, laws, etc., because it is very plain that your circumstances render the use and observation of them in a great measure impracticable; and you cannot but know something more or less, or may know something, as occasions offer, of the usual and common practices there, and the methods hitherto employed by others, in whose footsteps you may tread with great security; for, as I said before, exactness is impossible. . . .

As for help and consultations with friends there, I should not of myself have thought it a thing so very difficult and impracticable, as you seem to make it. But let this be as it will, when the case requires it you can write. Now, you say, you cannot write Latin letters; nor is this necessary in the least. For when you write to your Correspondent here in English, and he translates your letter either into Latin or the vulgar tongue of the country, and delivers the original together with the translated copy, tis of the same force and authority as if the original had been written in the purest Latin. . . . In case you do not approve this method and, wanting the assistance of another hand, chuse yourself to write in Latin, tis sufficient it be purely intelligible : grammatical faults are very pardonable in a person so much better employed. Let it be as it will, I am willing to suppose your Latin at the very lowest ebb; yet am I positively sure that you want no more of it than what you have.

He then assures the bishop that he was not chosen from a belief that he had large private means.[1]

It is certainly convenient for a person so employed to have something of his own, and in sending information about persons on such occasions, amongst other things it is usual to mention also something of this particular : but then it is not the motive of the choice; no more than it enters into the

---

[1] Actually, as we have seen, it was *one* of the reasons given for recommending him.

personal character, which, tis plain, it does not. After all, suppose your temporal circumstances were worse than they really are, methinks in these occasions there ought not to be forgotten the surer fund of Providence.

As to disquiet and trouble, and this on many occasions, as you mention, I am truely sensible of it for your sake, and I wish it less; or rather, give me leave to say, I wish you more courage, which in many respects would really make it less. I pray God it may be so. He is the best of Masters, whom you serve, and cannot forget your labours. You cannot expect that all things will go right, much less ought this to disquiet you; for that would be wrong on your side. All that you are, or can be obliged to do is to use an honest moral care, such as you would take in the discharge of any other employment, and let the success be what it will, nothing will be imputed to you, nor on your side any unwillful mistakes.

I now perceive that by endeavouring to excuse, what I do not own to be a fault, I am become guilty of a real one : that is, being desirous to give you reasons why I do not comply, at least so hastily with your desires and orders, I have taken too much liberty in setting forth my own opinions, and this unasked, and in a kind of instructive way, which I own to be unbecoming me on many accounts. But, as I said before, I could not forbear; and setting aside the manner, I am very confident that there is not one of our friends who would not subscribe to the import and substance of what I have said. And this makes your security, and lays all the blame, if any, at your friends' door; for which they are willing to be counted responsible. In fine, in my poor judgment, you yourself have nothing to fear so much, as so much yielding to your own fears. I beg a thousand times pardon for the great liberty I have taken, for the tediousness of this long letter, and to be believed with all imaginable respect, etc.[1]

This wise and soothing letter should surely have brought peace to Bishop Petre's troubled soul, but it does not appear to have had much effect, for he subsequently made several further efforts to be freed from his burden, all of them unavailing. In 1726, when his quinquennial faculties expired, he asked not for a renewal of them, but that he might resign; but, though Mayes presented the petition, he asked Propaganda to console and encourage and confirm the bishop in his office. That same year

[1] Westm. Archives, Rom. Coll., III, 163.

even Dr. Giffard's patience with him wore thin. Writing to Mayes he declared :

> Mr. Prusensis[1] who should be a comfort to me in my old age, is often a great trouble to me, by his uneasiness and complaints and continual threats of laying all down. I have borne the burden much longer, and in much more difficult and dangerous times; I allso was sufficiently sensible of the weight, yet would never think of casting it off, till I had provided for so important a concern. Should he lay down the office, as things now are at Rome, another Dominican[2] in all likelyhood will be put in his place,[3] especially when I drop off, which both age and infirmities sufficiently dispose me for.[4]

The next year, 1727, brought a further appeal from Petre to Rome, but both Giffard and Mayes wrote to Propaganda praising him. All this makes it the more surprising that when in 1728 a rumour spread that ' King James ' might soon have the nominating of an Englishman to be Cardinal, Robert Witham said that many thought that Bishop Petre was the best qualified for this honour in every way.[5] And in the following year the same Witham told Mayes :

> Though Bishop Petre makes great complaint of his heavy burden, and has writ strange letters of his own incapacity to the Nunce at Brussels and to Propaganda, yet at the same time [he] acts with a great deal of fervour and firm zeal; instructs every Sunday to the satisfaction of all that hear him; keeps good order in all the Embassadors Chapels; keeps under him the Irish Priests and the Regulars, who thereupon make all the complaints they can about him, tho without reason.

Indeed this bishop was a puzzling character. On the face of things his extreme diffidence and his hatred of public attention and of active occupation seem to mark him out as quite unsuitable for his position, especially in those stormy and difficult days. And in fact he appears to have been of little practical help to

---

[1] Dr. Petre. He was Bishop of Prusa (Epis. Prusensis).

[2] Fra Dominic Williams, O.P., had recently been made Vicar Apostolic of the Northern District.

[3] One cannot but feel that here is the real reason for the determination to prevent him from resigning, and for the praise so constantly accorded him.

[4] Ep. Var., IX, 5.

[5] *Id.*, IX, 180.

Bishop Giffard, and when he himself succeeded to the Vicariate he obtained a coadjutor (Dr. Challoner) as soon as he could and then promptly retired to his family estate in Essex for the rest of his life, leaving the active control of the London District to his coadjutor. And yet, as we have seen, he received encomiums from those who ought to know. Reluctantly one is almost forced to the conclusion that the above letter by Dr. Giffard lets the cat out of the bag; if not, then the Bishop of Prusa remains a complete enigma.

Chapter VI

CATHOLIC LIFE IN THE PENAL TIMES

THIS would seem a suitable point at which to break off the narrative in order to examine the conditions of life in England in the first half of the eighteenth century, so far as they affected Catholics. It is difficult for the modern reader to realize the conditions of life for Catholics during the long, weary penal times; but some knowledge of them is necessary for an appreciation of the difficulties and labours of the bishops and clergy.

And first of all, what of the daily life of the bishops? Inevitably that of the Vicar Apostolic of the London District, living as he did in cheap and obscure London lodgings and concerned mostly with the slum districts of the city, differed considerably from that of his three colleagues in the country. These last, like the vast majority of the clergy, lived in the country houses of the Catholic nobility and gentry, on whose hospitality they were to a great extent dependent, and whose generosity was the mainstay of the Catholic missions up and down the land. For there were no public chapels in those days in the towns, and hence the faithful tended to congregate in the neighbourhood of the large Catholic houses in which alone they could practise their religion. And thus to those old Catholic families in all parts of the country a very great debt is owed, the more so since they themselves were wellnigh crushed by penal taxation for the crime of being Catholics, were systematically ostracized by their Protestant neighbours and were excluded from all public service under the Crown, so that no career was possible for their children, while in addition they were persistently fined large sums for refusing to attend the Protestant churches. But in spite of all these disabilities and sufferings they for the most part (despite some lamentable apostasies due to the economic and social causes mentioned) endured for generation after generation with a loyalty and a courage and an ' otherworldliness ' that is beyond all praise. In their houses, then, the bishops found refuge, and from them they were able to govern their Districts and to make their constant tours of inspection. It is a strange and moving picture that they present to the modern eye, and one can but marvel that the Church, persecuted and in the catacombs, in such circumstances survived at all.

But the Bishop of the London District, even though his District stretched as far west as Dorset, always lived in London (save when in periods of special danger he had to flee to some refuge in the country); and the danger he ran of arrest and imprisonment was much greater than was the case with his provincial brethren. It has already been mentioned that Bishop Giffard was imprisoned many times, and narrowly escaped on several other occasions; and as he himself wrote :

> The continual fears and alarms we are under is something worse than Newgate. . . . In one prison I lay on the floor a considerable time; in Newgate almost two years; afterwards in Hertford jail; and now daily expect a fourth prison to end my life in.

And to another correspondent he wrote :

> Where to get a lodging in London, such as I may admit people to with security, and transact business, I cannot tell. I do all I can, and suffer a great deal : having no certain abode, but forced sometimes to change lodgings four times in a week, and once lodged at four different places in four dayes time. One poor garret is palace, cathedral, table of audience, diningroom, bedchamber and often kitchen too. I thank God; this is my glory, and my joy. I would not change my condition for that of the greatest cardinal.

One is vividly reminded of a similar passage in St. Paul's Epistles. Similarly Bishop Challoner used to preach in an unsavoury inn in Holborn, for he had no chapel; and the congregation sat around him at table, each member being supplied with a pipe and a mug of beer, in order to disguise what was really going on. Except in the chapels belonging to the foreign Embassies, Mass was said only with the greatest secrecy, generally at dead of night and in an obscure attic to which entrance was gained only after a secret password had been given. Small wonder, then, that Bishop Challoner, writing to a newly-appointed bishop (John

Hornyold of the Midland District) whose humility made him shrink from such an honour, remarked: ' After all, prelacy in our circumstances has nothing in it to be coveted but the benefit of more labour and trouble and the opportunity of serving a greater number '.[1]

This secrecy in carrying out the functions of the Church and the work of the clergy was essential throughout this century (as it had been for the previous one hundred and fifty years), owing to the ever-present need of not fanning into flame the smouldering hatred of the Old Religion which was liable to flare up at the slightest provocation. Naturally, it was essential for priests to conceal their real occupation and consequently to adopt the dress of laymen, and indeed it was not till after the restoration of the Hierarchy in 1850 that the wearing of clerical dress became general. One has but to recall the Gordon Riots which broke out as late as 1780 in furious protest against the measure of relief, meagre though it was, afforded to Catholics by the first Relief Act, to realize how deep-seated (and unreasoning) was the distrust and hatred of the Church amongst English Protestants, and the great need for caution on the part of Catholics.

One form which this caution took was the use of aliases by the clergy, very many of whom were known by two or even three names, and another was the ' code-writing' so common at the time, of which some examples are given elsewhere in this book. A few instances of the aliases may be mentioned here. The Pope was often referred to as ' Mr. Abraham ', or sometimes as ' the Old Gentleman ', Catholics in general were alluded to in letters (for some inscrutable reason) as ' Mrs. Yaxley's family ', Queen Anne was ' Mrs. Hobbs ', Bishop Giffard was ' Cousin Bona ', Bishop Dicconson was ' Mr. Eaton ', Bishop Williams ' Thomas Rogers ', and Bishop Challoner signed himself ' J. Fisher '. Bishop Smith of the Northern District had at least four aliases of which the most commonly used was ' Tarlton '. The Jesuits were sometimes called ' Birlies ' or ' Etiamites ', while Rome was nearly always ' Hilton ', and a District and its clergy were the bishop's ' wife and family '. Bishop Smith was always particularly guarded in his letters, so that some of them are by no means easy to understand even with a knowledge of the code-language. A typical example of his less obscure writing is this account he gives

[1] Ushaw Archives, The Hornyold Papers.

of a Visitation of his Vicariate and of confirmations carried out
which he wrote to Mr. Mayes[1] in 1709 :

> I have been three months from home in the visits of such
> friends[2] as are dispersed up and down in Westmoreland,
> Lancashire and Cheshire : taking the opportunity of a present
> favourable calm,[3] and doeing everything with as much caution
> and circumspection as was possible; goeing only with one
> companion and a servant; and performing everywhere by
> myselfe all parts of instruction and exhortation suitable to the
> occasion. These visits accompanied with such constant and
> almost daily performances,[4] as they were very laborious, soe
> they have been of great comfort in the good dispositions and
> effects with which, through the mercy of God, I have reason
> to hope they have been everywhere blessed. Not to disappoint
> poor friends comeing in great numbers[5] and to prevent the
> offence of unnecessary meetings, I seldom ended the burden
> and business of the day before 3 o'clock : a fault humbly sub-
> mitted, and I hope easily pardoned by Fathers[6] to us and our
> necessities.[7]

And on the subject of persecution in general, the following from
Dr. Betham (chaplain to the Queen Mother in France) to the
same Mayes in 1707 gives a further example :

> Mrs. Hobbs of her own nature is no enemy, but a chip in
> porridge, leaving Yaxley's family pretty quiet; but the laws
> are such that if any peevish person prosecutes, she dare not
> stop it. But none have suffered much [of late], but here and
> there one, among whom B. Giffard had the greatest share.
> No new laws have been made in her time; but the malitious
> ones made by her predecessor stand in force and might soon
> ruin all, if executed.[8]

The saying or hearing of Mass was, of course, a ' criminal
offence ' punishable by the severest penalties, and so for a very

---

[1] The clergy were, of course, always called ' Mr.'   Mayes was the Agent
in Rome of the English bishops.
[2] Catholics of his Vicariate.
[3] Cessation of persecution.
[4] Conferrings of Confirmation.
[5] For Confirmation.
[6] The authorities in Rome.
[7] Ep. Var., II, 271.
[8] Westm. Archives, Par. Sem. Col., I, 231.

long period it could only be done in the utmost secrecy. Here is a contemporary description of such a Mass which was written by a Mrs. Marlow about the year 1771 :[1]

We started from our lodgings about 5 in the morning, to be present for the first time at a Catholic religious service, or at prayers, as it was generally called, for the word Mass was scarcely ever used in conversation. We arrived at a public-house in some back street near the house in which Mr. Horne (the priest) resided. I felt rather frightened seeing some very rough looking people as we passed through the entrance, tho all were very quiet. . . . We hurried past them, but I could not help clinging to Marlow, having an undefined fear of what was going to happen. We mounted higher and higher. At the top the door of a garret was unlocked and we saw at the far end what seemed a high table, or long chest of drawers with the back turned towards us. A piece of carpet was spread before it by a young man, who pointed us to our seats. In a few minutes the door opened, and the Ven. Dr. Challoner, accompanied by Mr. Horne and another priest, entered the garret, the door of which was secured inside by an assistant, who then unlocked some drawers behind what, I found, was to be used as an altar, and take out the vestments and other things for the service.

. . . Soon after we heard the door-key turned and several rough footsteps entered the garret, some gentle taps and words were exchanged between a powerful-looking Irishman who kept his post close to it, and those outside, which were pass-words of admission. The key was again turned each time anyone entered, and just before the Bishop vested himself to say Mass bolts were drawn also, and no one else could pass into the garret. In the meantime the young man had pre-pared all that was needed for Mass, taken from behind what was used for an altar, which was covered with a white linen cloth. A crucifix and two lighted candles were placed on it and in the front was suspended a piece of satin damask, in the centre of which was a cross in gold lace. . . .

When all was over, I heard the door-key turn once more, and all the rough footsteps leaving the garret. The Bishop, having unvested, remained kneeling before us while the people departed. The two priests, assisted by the young man, replaced the vestments, candle-sticks, and all that was used

[1] This account was printed in Dr. Burton's pamphlet on Bishop Talbot (C.T.S. Tract, No. 49).

at Mass, behind the altar, locking all up carefully, and leaving the garret an ordinary one in appearance as before.

The same need for unobtrusiveness influenced the appearance of the Catholic chapels when, later on, a few were built. Until the passing of the Relief Acts towards the end of the century there were no public chapels (save those in the foreign Embassies), but when they were eventually built they were as concealed and obscure as possible, generally in back streets and with no external sign of their sacred character. And even inside their appearance would surprise a modern Catholic. There were no side-altars, largely because it was not usual to say Mass daily; and there were no confessionals, for confessions were heard in the priest's lodgings. Nor were there any statues, and processions were quite unknown, as also were votive candles and tablets. It is hardly necessary to add that the Stations of the Cross, as well as Benediction, were also never to be seen. Gradually all these things began to appear, chiefly as the result of the influence of the French émigré priests, after the French Revolution had broken out, but they were long regarded askance by English Catholics as being ' Continental abuses ', and it was not until those who had been brought up under the penal laws had died off that the newer generation learned to adopt such things whole-heartedly and eventually to take them for granted.[1]

It has already been pointed out that the Catholic centres were the homes of the Catholic landed gentry, and that the Faith had almost died out in the towns. This meant that the maintenance of the Faith in any given locality depended to a very great extent on these Catholic gentry, who alone could maintain a chapel and support a priest. And so, if for any reason such a family ceased to perform these functions the local congregation soon ceased to exist and many left the Church altogether. Unhappily this kind of thing frequently occurred, either because the local Catholic noble or squire moved away to another locality, or because the family died out, or even because they apostatized. Joseph Berington, writing in 1780, stated that ' In one district alone, eight out of thirteen [such families] are come to nothing : nor have any new ones risen to make up their loss. . . . I recollect the names of at least ten noble families that within these sixty

[1] See Ward, *The Dawn of the Catholic Revival*, II, 234.

years have either conformed [i.e. apostatized to Protestantism] or are extinct; besides many Commoners of distinction and fortune.'[1] He instances the apostasies of the Earl of Surrey (heir to the Duke of Norfolk), of Lord Teynham and of Sir Thomas Gascoigne; while Bishop Milner, some forty years later, enumerated those of Lords Gage, Fauconberg, Teynham, Montague, Nugent, Kingsland, Dunsanny, the Dukes of Gordon and of Norfolk; and the four baronets: Tancred, Gascoigne, Swinburn, and Blake.[2] These were grievous losses, and it was tragic that so many should have fallen just when relief at long last was beginning to come into sight. After many generations of fidelity under the most diffi·ult and exacting circumstances they collapsed just as the goal was in sight. When one of these great country houses passed into non-Catholic hands the priest perforce disappeared, the congregation melted away, and the mission ceased to exist. Occasionally the results were not quite so disastrous, since sometimes special arrangements were made for Catholics. This happened in the case of the apostasy of Lord Montague whose palatial home, Cowdray, had for many centuries been Catholic, and had been openly so even when Queen Elizabeth stayed there. The Blessed Sacrament was always reserved there and it was an unfailing shelter for hunted priests.[3] When he abandoned the Faith Lord Montague closed the chapel in his house, but he did at least build and endow a mission house in a neighbouring village to take its place. When at last he came to die he bitterly repented his apostasy and the great harm he had done. 'In his last illness he called up all his people, and told them that he had never been convinced of ye truth of ye Protestant religion, but he had changed [to] it out of pride, avarice and ambition. He received all the sacraments, and gave great signs of sorrow.'[4]

The Faith was dwindling steadily in those dreary days, but though many fell by the wayside under the tremendous economic and social temptations held out to them to conform to the Established Religion, yet very many more held fast, and they

[1] Berington, The State and Behaviour of English Catholics from the Reformation to 1780.

[2] Milner, Supplementary Memoirs of the English Catholics.

[3] Cf. Burton, The Life and Times of Bishop Challoner. The place was known as ' Little Rome '.

[4] Westm. Archives, William Gibson. Cf. Ward, The Dawn of the Catholic Revival in England, I, 51.

kept the flame alive until the coming of the ' new people ' whom
Bishop Challoner had foretold as about to arise : the people of
the cities, the industrial classes of a later age, together with the
products of the Oxford Movement and of the Irish immigration
of the nineteenth century. And so, though Dr. Burton in a
moving and haunting phrase could lament : ' Where are now the
Gages, Shelleys, Mordaunts, Teynhams, Ropers, Gascoignes?
Where the Giffards, Seftons, Swinburnes? Not without anguish
of travail did religion in this country bring forth its " new people "
nor without loss of the old ';[1] yet a shining example continued
to be set by many of the old families who continued to bear the
crushing burden of double taxation, of exclusion from society
and from honourable employment, combined with the fear of
crippling fines and actual imprisonment; and it was upon these
families that the plans and methods of the bishops perforce
continued to depend.[2]

Naturally the Vicars Apostolic were deeply concerned by those
apostasies that did occur, and a letter from Dr. Giffard to Mayes
in Rome, dated August 5, 1717, enables us to see how he reacted
to the matter :

Hond. dear Sir,
    I writ to you at the beginning of June and gave you an
account of all our little affairs. . . . The Parliament is up,
and without acting any new severity against us : on the
contrary it has shown some favour in granting a further time
for registering our Estates.[3] The Act made in the former
sessions appeared so dreadfull that it caused some[4] (very, very
few in respect of the great number) to prevent the ill consequences by taking all the Oaths, and signing of the Test, which
is directly opposite to our Religion.

[1] Burton, Op. cit.

[2] For instance, the Eystons of East Hendred, which they have held since the
reign of Henry VI, and still hold to-day. They kept their estates, despite
sequestrations, by compounding. More important, they have always kept the
Faith, and their chapel, dating back to the thirteenth century, has never ceased
to be Catholic. Wonderful has been the generous fidelity of this family (and
many others), generation after generation of which suffered imprisonment,
confiscations, and fines. So to the Carylls of West Grinstead, the Throck-
mortons of Buckland, the Darells of Scotney Castle, and the Vavasours of
Hazlewood, to name a few at random.

[3] Catholic Estates had to be registered for the working of the threatened law
confiscating two-thirds of the property.

[4] Robert Witham said ' about a dozen lords and gentlemen '.

G

As soon as I heard of this, and was rightly informed as to the few persons who had committed this great crime, I writ to some of them and spoke to others to make them sensible of their fault, and God was pleased to give a blessing to my words. I then considered what method was to be taken with them both for satisfying the justice of God, so highly injured, for repairing the great scandal given both to Catholics and Protestants, and also for preventing the lyke failing in others. After I had resolved on such a method as I thought proper and practical in our present circumstances, that we might proceed uniformly in this affair, I communicated my thoughts to all Superiors of Regular Bodies [Orders], some of their penitents having transgressed as well as others, who all approved of the method I prescribed and promised to act accordingly. I thank God this has had a good effect and brought those cowardly Christians back to a due sense of their Religion.

As to the few who, besides taking Oaths and signing the Test, are gone to the Protestant Church, I cannot give so good an account of them. Indeed I fear they are lost, and will ruin their succeeding generations. The love of the world, of greatness, of riches, has always prevailed to keep some from owning of Christ, and make others deny Him. But as the Prince of this world has gained some few proselytes, so the powerfull grace of Christ has triumphed in great numbers of the inferior, or middling sort of people, who have embraced the Faith. . . .

The frequent marks I see of God's mercy in [regard to the zeal of the clergy] gives me comfortable hopes of His religion continuing in this Kingdom. I must also do justice to the lay Roman Catholics, many of whom are great patterns of virtue, and all of them have given signal proofs of their great charity in relieving a vast number of prisoners, many whereof, from plentifull fortunes were reduced to the utmost necessity. Their charity has been so great both to Protestants as well as Catholics in this time of misery, that it has moved many of the former to embrace our Religion. This charity of Catholics is so much the more admired that they even exhausted themselves at a time when they were under dreadfull apprehensions of having two parts of three of their estate taken from them. . . .[1]

At this point it may be well to give a more detailed account of just what were the powerful inducements to the Catholic

[1] Ep. Var., VI, 141.

nobility and gentry to turn Protestant, in other words to outline some of the penal laws. Some of these have already been mentioned. From as far back as the reign of Elizabeth I it was high treason (with the punishment of hanging, drawing and quartering) ' for any man who is proved to be a priest to breathe in this kingdom' (Q. Eliz., 27, c.2), and a later, rather milder statute of William III condemned any priest convicted of exercising his priestly functions to perpetual imprisonment (King Wm., 11 and 12, c.4). It was also high treason to reconcile anyone to the Church. Under both William III and Queen Anne many of the most savage enactments were passed, and at the time we are considering (the reign of George I) Bishop Stonor reported to Rome that the chief hardships endured by Catholics were: (1) Exclusion from all places of trust and profit in the State, so that Catholic families have no way of repairing their losses nor others of acquiring fortunes. (2) The Act of 1700 allowing a Protestant next-of-kin to dispossess the Catholic heir of estates, and making Catholics unable to acquire landed property by gift or purchase. (3) The double land-tax, applied only to Catholics. (4) The confiscation of all property given for the support of priests or religious, with compulsion to reveal where such property is concealed. Thus the State ' contrives to starve those whom it ceases to persecute '. He added that there was reason to fear that the sequestration of two-thirds of all Catholic property, which had recently been threatened, might soon become the law. The Act 1 Geo. I, c. 50, appointed a Commission ' to enquire of the estates of certain traitors and popish recusants, and of estates given to superstitious uses, in order to raise money out of their security for the use of the public ', and by 9 Geo. I, c. 18, £100,000 was to be assessed on Catholics above 18 years of age, over and above the double assessment of the land tax. For the rest, the laity were cut off from public life and debarred from sitting or voting in either house of Parliament (30 Car. II, c. 2); while in private life, in addition to the disabilities mentioned by Stonor above, they were forbidden to keep arms (1 W. & M, st. 1, c. 15), they could be deprived of any horse worth more than £5 (*ibid.*), they could not hold any office in the army or navy (25 Car. II, c. 2), or practise as a barrister, doctor, or schoolmaster (7 & 8 Wm. III, c. 24), they could be fined if they sent a child to be educated abroad (which was the only way in which the child could have a Catholic education), and there were also heavy fines for non-attendance at the Protestant church. Thus, in effect they were forced to live the life of recluses, shut away on their estates, with no outlet for the activities and ambitions of the younger sons. In addition there were most severe penalties for performing or attending any Catholic religious service, for educating their children as Catholics *at home;* and Catholics had no vote at parliamentary elections. Well might Burke declare that the penal code 'was a complete system, full of coherence and consistency . . . and as well fitted for the oppression, impoverishment and degradation of a people and of the debasement in them of human nature itself, as ever proceeded from the perverted ingenuity of man'. The verdict of Charles Butler, the celebrated lawyer of a century ago, was that the penal laws ' depressed Catholics so much below their legitimate rank in Society that they hardly entered with the look or attitude of free men into the meetings of their Protestant neighbours. " Such was their situation ", to avail myself of Mr. Burke's strong but just expressions, " that they not only shrank from the frowns of a stern magistrate, but were obliged to fly from their very species; a kind of universal subserviency that made the very servant behind their chair the arbiter of their lives and fortunes." '

It is true that many of these laws were not enforced as time went on, but they were always liable to be put into force at any time, and so long as they remained on the Statute Book Catholics could have no ease of mind and no security. Even after the passing of the first Relief Act in 1778, the well-known priest Joseph Berington wrote :

> Shall I sit down satisfied because the good humour of a magistrate chooses to indulge me; whilst there are laws of which any miscreant has daily power to enforce the execution? My ease, my property, and my life are at the disposal of every villain, and I am to be pleased because he is not at this time disposed to deprive me of them. Tomorrow his humour may vary, and I shall then be obliged to hide my head in some dark corner or to fly from this land of boasted liberty. It is surely better *not to be* than to live in a state of such anxiety and dreadful uncertainty.[1]

[1] *The State and Behaviour of English Catholics,* viii.

And Catholics lived in this condition for three centuries. Is it any wonder that they became ' a people fleeing the light ', of whom little was known and of whom the wildest and most absurd of stories was believed? The reign of George II was the first since the Reformation in which no fresh laws were enacted against Catholics, yet in that reign there were plenty of prosecutions of Catholics for the practising of their religion, and the smouldering hatred and fanaticism found its outlet as late as the Gordon Riots of 1780. Even after the passing of the second Relief Act in 1791, which swept away most of the penal laws, all chapels had to be registered and the clergy had to take the oath of allegiance, no chapel might have bell or steeple, cassocks or habits might not be worn out of doors, and still no Catholic might sit in either House of Parliament or vote at elections, or be a judge or barrister, and the army and navy were still barred to them. Catholic marriages still had to be held in Protestant churches, and Catholic funerals were forbidden. Actually the first *repeal* of the penal laws did not take place till as late as 1844, for the Relief Acts had not repealed the laws but merely made exceptions to them, allowing further latitude. The laws still remained on the Statute Book, and anyone denying the spiritual supremacy of the king was still liable to forfeiture of all goods, and if the offence were repeated, to punishment by death for high treason.

It is small wonder if, after enduring all this for generation after generation, a few families fell away and conformed to the State Church; but the great majority held fast, and they were the ' hard core ' on which the bishops depended. And from this fact arises another peculiarity of seventeenth- and eighteenth-century life : the strange position of the clergy in relationship to the landed families. As has been explained, it was these families who formed the backbone of the system, for on them the clergy had to rely for financial support. Each Catholic country house would have its own resident priest, and this priest was chosen and appointed, not by the bishop of the District, but by the head of the family, and this because of the dependence of the mission upon the patron. Neither bishop nor priest could afford to offend such a patron, and so the squire or nobleman chose his own chaplain without reference to the bishop, so that the latter frequently did not even know where a given priest might be.   A further result of this was that the priest came to be looked upon merely as an employee, and in fact was very often employed in a purely secular position such as estate agent or secretary.   Much therefore depended on the personal character of the landowner, as regards the treatment received by a priest, and if the former were autocratic or harsh the priest's lot was apt to be extremely unenviable.   He could be dismissed by his employer without any reference being made to the bishop, and sometimes he even had to wait at the altar before starting Mass until his employer should say to him : ' Mr. —————, you may begin '.[1]

Of course this subservient position also served the very necessary purpose of helping to conceal the fact that any priest was living there, for the liberty and possibly even the life of both priest and employer depended on the authorities being unaware of the presence of a priest on the estate; and so, partly for reasons of security, and partly in order to gain a means of livelihood, many priests were forced to take up purely lay occupations.   In some cases none but the squire and a mere handful of the faithful would have any idea that an apparent layman whom they had known for twenty or thirty years was in reality a priest.   Then, too, many of these families had special ties with one or other Religious Order and so always chose their chaplains from those Orders.   This practice was on the one hand sometimes a cause of heart-burning amongst the secular clergy who were thus debarred from those positions, and on the other hand a source of difficulty for the bishop who, of course, had no control over the movements of the regulars.   And yet this custom and the general control exercised by lay patrons was never questioned either by clergy or by the Vicars Apostolic, all realizing the special rights possessed by the laity by reason of the great service they performed for the Church by making the missions possible at all.   In the curious circumstances it is remarkable that disputes and difficulties were not far more frequent than they actually were.   But it will be realized that the bishops had considerable difficulties in these matters, and had to exercise much patience and tact, and the more so since they themselves were generally dependent on such a lay patron for their own board and lodging.

The position was made worse for the clergy by their extreme

[1] Burton, *Op. cit.*, I, 142.

penury, for few were those who had private means. Yet as a rule a priest had to keep a horse and groom, since he usually had to say two or three Masses at places far apart on Sundays, and therefore had to undertake long rides fasting.[1] However generous the laity might be, the fact remained that even the great Catholic lords were themselves very hard hit by the penal taxation and fines, and in the eighteenth century their lot was made worse by the penalties inflicted on those who were in any way suspected of being concerned in the Jacobite risings of 1715 and 1745. In fact the extreme poverty of the English Mission continually prompted appeals to Rome for financial help, but not much was forthcoming. Even the bishops needed such help, although most of them had private means, even if they required this mostly in order to keep their priests out of the debtors' prisons for not being able to pay for board and lodging. In this matter the London clergy were in a much worse plight than their brethren in the country who mostly lived with the local land-owner. Thus in 1702 the English Agent in Rome was instructed to apply for a subsidy for the bishops, but this was not forth-coming owing to lack of resources in Rome itself and great expenses incurred through a recent earthquake. There were endless demands on the scanty resources of the bishops, both from indigent priests and even from the laity, and Dr. Giffard stated in 1722 that he always gave away three-quarters of his own patrimony and of gifts he received. By 1720 Bishop Witham, despite his ' very considerable annuity ', was sadly lamenting his extreme poverty which was such that he could not even pay his share of the salary due from the bishops to their Agent in Rome. Meanwhile this unhappy agent, Lawrence Mayes, was in great embarrassment from the non-payment of this salary. On protesting to Giffard he was told that Witham could not afford it, but that Stonor (of aristocratic birth and comparatively wealthy) should be able to, since he could keep many servants. As for himself, Giffard continued :

I thank God I have been taught to want [lack] many con-veniences of Secretary, coach, horses and servants (having but one, and that to serve others rather than myself); that I may help our poor indigent brethren. I shall therefore continue

[1] Much as many a poor priest, nowadays, must, by hook or by crook, have and maintain a car, and for the same reason !

my poor allowance to you, and shall be glad to procure you some pension from the Grand Duke.

Four months later he wrote to Mayes :

> . . . Just as I was writing this, came to me a gentlewoman of a very ancient and honorable Catholic family, who, with her two Sisters, are in a most miserable condition; so far, that with extraordinary acknowledgments and tears of joy, she accepted of half a crown for their relief. If some pity be not shown us, we shall shortly see many, both priests and lay gentry, goe begging about the streets.

But so far were the Government from showing pity to Catholics by remitting some of the cruel taxation levied on them for their religion, that that same year Giffard reported :

> . . . Now to complete our misery, a Bill is prepared to be brought into Parliament which will reduce all Catholics to the extremity of want; so that no further charity can be expected from them.[1]

But meanwhile the unfortunate Mr. Mayes in Rome was still unpaid, and in 1726 he complained that the President of Douay had said there was no hope of the bishops and clergy of England being able to pay for his (Mayes') maintenance. And so he wrote :

> . . . I have answered that I will retire, and leave the post to someone who either has a better purse than I have, or better friends. In case of death I hope my effects here may be sufficient to pay my debts. The truth is, Bp. Giffard has allowed me nothing since July 1723, and tis very certain that I must not let things run on thus, but must retire. I am very tender in giving Bp. Giffard the least molestation : but what can I do? I cannot maintain without some assistance. The Clergy seems unconcerned. . . . However, after what I have done to hold up so long, it cannot be taken ill that I provide for myself.[2]

Bishop Giffard came to hear of this, and sent him £10 with a promise of more to come, but added :

> . . . I have been twice stripped of all I had in the world [sc. by the Government]. No less than £600 taken from me

---

[1] Ep. Var., VII, 378.
[2] Par. Sem. Col., I, 553.

James Smith,

688   1711

Bp. of Callipolis.

George Witham,

1715   172.

Bp. of Marcopolis.

at the first time. At the second, all my fine ornaments and whatever belonged to my office, taken away. Besides which, how many, how long, and how expensive imprisonments have I suffered? Well; my treasure is in heaven, and I beseech God to keep my heart fixed there.

But in spite of his threats of resignation, Mayes continued to be Agent in Rome until his death twenty years later, after having performed for forty years in that office invaluable services to the English bishops.[1] These themselves were in desperate straits, and in 1722 Giffard appealed to Rome for money to relieve distress among his priests and laity. Six months previously even Stonor had received money from Rome, and in December of the same year Witham similarly appealed on behalf of the Northern District and received two hundred crowns in reply. And if it were so with the bishops and their officials, how much worse must have been the plight of the rank-and-file clergy?

And now, of what sort were these clergy? What of the men themselves? Of course generalizations are apt to be misleading, and the clergy were of many varying types, just as they are to-day; but on the whole in those days they inevitably suffered from the defects produced by their special mode of education, although at the same time they reaped many benefits from that same up-bringing. Necessarily all priests had to be educated overseas, since nothing in the nature of a seminary could possibly exist in England at that time. Even long after the more savage features of the penal laws had ceased to be inflicted, so that the chances of execution or even imprisonment had become slight, those laws were still on the Statute Book and might be enforced at any moment. It was therefore still illegal to bring up a child in the Catholic religion, or even to send him abroad for the purpose, let alone to train him for the actual priesthood. And so it followed that during their formative years the English clergy were inevitably completely out of touch with their compatriots. Most of them spent at least twelve or fourteen years in the English seminaries on the Continent (Douay, Lisbon, or Rome, for the most part), first as schoolboys and then as students for

[1] He was succeeded by Mgr. Christopher (' Kit ') Stonor, nephew of the bishop, who held the office for the next fifty years. Thus these two men between them held the post throughout the eighteenth century (1703–1795), and their correspondence is a rich mine of most interesting information.

the priesthood, and so when in due course they returned in secret as priests to this country they were cast in a very definite mould, while at the same time their long segregation from the ways of ordinary life inevitably meant that they were apt to lack that polish as well as that knowledge of contemporary affairs and familiarity with secular branches of learning which were to be found in most of their contemporaries.   What they lacked in this respect many of them made up for by their holiness and zeal (which were vastly more important), but at the same time these defects undoubtedly did to a considerable extent hamper them in their work by making an unfavourable impression on the laity.

In this connection a letter to be seen in the archives of Ushaw College throws much light on clerical customs in the eighteenth century.   The writer, one Simon Bordley, was a very old priest who was widely known as a ' character ', and he was certainly an ardent *laudator temporis acti*.   The letter, of which an extract follows, was written on the Feast of St. Joseph, 1789, and was addressed to Bishop Matthew Gibson of the Northern District.

. . . I am now an old man within half a year of fourscore, and I love the old ways and old customs better than new ones, and I think myself authorized to do so both by the Old and New Testament. . . . Our Saviour says ' No man drinking old wine calls for new, for the old is better.' And so think I; for the Catholics I found in Lancashire fifty years ago were incomparably better than what we have at present.

You must know my neighbour Mr. Caton sets up new customs unknown hitherto in these parts. 1st: He acquaints his people that he is not willing to hear confessions in a morning, but they must come overnight, and he will hear them from six in the evening till midnight. . . . Now this is directly contrary to our practice in these parts hitherto; and amounts nearly to a prohibition to many for coming to the Sacraments. For those of his people that have anything to take to market have at least twelve miles to Liverpool with as many back again, and cannot get home till late at night; and those that have nothing to sell are obliged to work all day at home to earn a poor living. And can these in this weary condition be expected to come overnight? We old missioners on the contrary encourage them all we can to come to the Sacraments; if women and children and such as can spare time come overnight we are glad of it, as we have more time for those that cannot spare time, the next day : we take care in the morning to be ready to hear them as soon as they are desirous to make their confessions. Question : which is the better way : the new or the old?

2ndly : He has told his people that he will not say Mass for less than half a crown, which is more I believe than any of his people can afford to give. This again is contrary to the practice of us old missioners. You must know the people of Formby are very religious in getting their parents etc. prayed for; they used to come to me with a shilling in their hand, saying, I desire you for God's sake to say a Mass for my father and accept of this. Which pleased me well, as they did not ask for a Mass for a shilling as the price of it, but for God's sake. And not only there, but all over the County, it is the custom to offer us a shilling to say a Mass, and to my knowledge all the best priests say a Mass for a shilling. It is a custom when a person dies to send shillings a-piece to three, four, five or six priests in the neighbourhood to say Masses for the deceased. The richer sort send us half-crowns or two shillings enclosed in letters, but whether they send shillings or half-crowns all our best missioners say or get a Mass said for them. If Mr. Caton will not say a Mass for a shilling he need not tell the people so, but say as I have always done : ' I will either say a Mass or get a Mass said for you.' Your priests in Yorkshire who do not get a shilling for a Mass in the course of a year would be very thankful for some of his Formby shillings.

3rdly : There is a pulpit in Mr. Caton's chapel. . . . He has now been a year and a half and never yet has set his foot in it. . . . This again is contrary to the present practice of us old Missioners; who think it our duty to preach to our people and not content ourselves with reading a bit out of a book. Any old woman can do that. The Monks and Exjesuits in these parts are excellent preachers, at least the people think them so; our priests [sc. the secular clergy] are backward in discharging themselves of this duty, tho some few of ours can preach well. . . . For any of ours not to preach at all is a disgrace to the order of the clergy; as it shows they either cannot do it, or are too lazy to do it. . . . If Mr. Caton knows not how to make a sermon, if he pleases to come to me, I will teach him, as Dr. Witham our worthy President[1] taught me, and I believe I can teach him in the very same words . . . but Mr. Caton may think it a disgrace to be taught by me;

[1] I.e. of Douay College.

though I am not ashamed to own myself taught by Dr. Witham. . .

4thly : Mr. Caton's way of travelling is on a full gallop generally, and even in the late hard frost when he and his horse were in danger of breaking their necks. This again is contrary to the practice of all old Missioners, and not only of them, but of all Protestant parsons and Quaker speakers, who would be ashamed to ride in that manner, as not becoming teachers of any profession. . . . And the Catholics groan to see it, at least it makes Protestants merry, who jestingly tell our Catholics : ' So your priest is gone to a Labour to-day on a full gallop,' because Men-Mid-Wives commonly go on that speed, when they go to lay women. Those and Rakes commonly go on that speed, but none use it that desire to be esteemed serious and grave men. . . .[1]

One wonders whether Mr. Caton received an embarrassing communication from Authority after the receipt of this letter at Bishop's House.

Complaints on the score of the lack of polish and secular knowledge on the part of the clergy (to which allusion has been made above) abound in the letters and manuscripts of the time, not merely from the laity but from the clergy themselves, and especially from the bishops. Bishop Giffard, Bishop Stonor, and Bishop Challoner (to name but a few) frequently lament the unsuitable type of man turned out by the ecclesiastical colleges, and methods of reform in the system of training, with suggestions that more suitable candidates should be chosen, were constantly put forward by the various Vicars Apostolic. For instance in an official document drawn up in 1737 by either Bishop Petre or his coadjutor Bishop Challoner, entitled *Praesens Status Missionis Anglicanae*, the language employed is very outspoken. After saying that the leakage caused by the apostasy of so many was largely the fault of the landed gentry (for reasons already seen), the document goes on to say that the clergy are even more greatly to blame, and that there could be many more conversions if there were suitable priests. Many have no zeal for souls, but seek their own ends; many are rough and ignorant, and give scandal. And the remedies suggested are greater care in the selection of candidates for the priesthood, reform in the

[1] Ushaw Archives, III, 279 C.

administration of the colleges abroad (especially Rome and
Valladolid), that these colleges should only have students who
have been sent by the Vicars Apostolic, and that the course of
studies should be better adapted to the English Mission. The
opinion of Joseph Berington, one of the most prominent priests
of the day, was similar :

> Our priests in their general character are upright and sin-
> cere; but narrowd by a bad education, they contract early
> prejudices which they very seldom afterwards deposit. . . .
> Moderately skilled in the Latin and Greek languages, they
> know nothing of their own, nor do they become sensible of
> their manifold deficiencies till it be too late to attempt improve-
> ment. . . . A priest is seldom seen in the company of
> Protestants. The Catholics he is told to herd with either are
> unable to improve him, or, if able, are seldom willing. Con-
> tracted in his circumstances, he has not the means of drawing
> information from books; and unfashioned in the forms of
> elegant life, his company is not asked for. Thus denied all
> occasion of improvement, if his native dispositions will allow
> him, he soon sits down sullenly contented and looks no further.
> If he ever had ambitions disuse will in a short time lay them
> asleep; and at 60 he will be found the same man as at 25. . . .
> It is the complaint of our gentry that priests are rough and
> unsociable : they would be less so, perhaps, if their patrons
> were less proud, less ignorant, and less imperious. On both
> sides are faults which should be corrected.[1]

Elsewhere the same writer sums up the Douay clergy thus :

> They are open, disinterested, religious and laborious; steady in
> the discharge of their duties; fond of their profession and
> emulous of supporting the character of primitive clergymen;
> but they are austere in their principles, confined in their ideas,
> ignorant of the world, and unpleasant in their manners.[2]

But all that does not amount to much in the way of condemnation : it boils down to little more than a lack of culture and a
freedom from worldliness, the latter of which, at any rate, is no
bad thing. We have to remember, too, their extreme poverty,
and the hunted, or, at the least, the obscure lives which they had
to lead. Nor should it be forgotten that these men had in many
cases sacrificed bright prospects of a worldly life in order to

[1] *Op. cit.*, p. 162.
[2] *Op. cit.*, p. 174.

become priests, and were therefore motivated solely by super-
natural zeal. The Catholic Church was at least spared the snare
spread for the Church of England, in that it provided no enticing
bait of a comfortable living for a younger son who never
professed to have a religious vocation. For the priest, his occupation was necessarily a spiritual vocation, for it offered no sort of
worldly career or prospects whatever. Still, the fact remains,
with which we started : that the Vicars Apostolic were for
generations much disturbed by the deficiencies in the training
given to aspirants to the priesthood, and made no bones about
roundly saying so on many occasions.

Moreover, the efforts of the Vicars Apostolic to spread the
Faith, or even to keep it alive, were constantly hampered by the
chronic shortage of priests : a shortage due not so much to a lack
of candidates as to a lack of funds wherewith to educate them,
and later to maintain them. This was a dominant factor at all
the colleges and is often referred to in the letters of the time. In
1734 the President of Douay wrote to Rome that

> Clergy-missioners[1] were never so much wanted and
> demanded in England as at this present time; in so much that
> Bp. Stonor (though much contrary to the judgment of the
> other Clergy Bishops, and his Predecessors) made some
> endeavours to get and introduce Irish Clergy-men, of whom
> he may have plenty, there being now at Paris alone about 400
> Irish priests, Clergy-men, and there are scarce above that
> number of priests, both seculars and regulars, put together in
> all England.
> In England they can hope for very few Clergy-Priests unless
> it be from this College only. Very few of late years have
> reached [England] except from Douay College, that is, very
> very few bred up under the Jesuits at Rome[2] or in Spain.
> Lisbon College is in a very low condition as to students. 36
> Clergy Priests are dead in England in less than three years
> time. It is true we are now 39 in our Ecclesiastical Quire, and
> the Pope's Pension to this College can only maintain about 20.
> In taking such a number we rely upon Providence, as we have
> done hitherto. . . .[3]

[1] Here, as elsewhere, the word ' clergy ' denotes ' secular ', as distinct
from ' regular '.
[2] The English College at Rome was conducted by the Jesuits.
[3] Ep. Var., X, 185.

This letter raises the interesting subject of the Irish element in Catholicism in England, or rather of its absence at that time. For this was, of course, long before the great Irish immigration of the 1840's which so changed the external aspect of Catholicism in this country. It must strike the most casual reader that none of the bishops or clergy mentioned in these pages have Irish names; the Church in fact was composed throughout this century of the dwindling remnant of the English Catholics. But it would have been thought that in their great need for priests the bishops would have turned to the great numbers of Irish clergy available on the Continent (Ireland itself was under an even more severe persecution than was England, so priests could not be got from there). Yet that source remained quite untapped, and the comparatively few Irish priests who did get into England were unwelcome to the bishops. In fact the above letter shows that here again we have another subject on which Bishop Stonor was at loggerheads with his colleagues and brethren. A quarter of a century earlier Bishop Giffard had ventilated his unwillingness to have Irish priests in his Vicariate, or at any rate Irish regulars. Thus, to Mayes on July 26, 1708 :

. . . I am much troubled with a number of Irish Regulars, who come hither in their way to Ireland, and cannot be got to move thither, pretending persecution and danger of imprisonment. But I think that ought not to stop them. Some of your friends here, and particularly Mr. Leveson, has been thrice in prison, and for almost two years. He's allso continually in danger of the lyke, and yet he quits not his post. I must write to Sacrapanti [of Propaganda] to put a stop to this, and am resolved not to give faculties to any. This placed is overstocked,[1] and all English Missionaries of all Bodys [sc. seculars and regulars] complain of the supernumerary Irish. Besides this consideration there is not one in ten that is proper for this place. . . .[2]

And six weeks later he returned to the subject :

I am resolved to admit no more [Irish regulars]. I have seen an order of the Propaganda forbidding their staying here, but tis twenty years since.

[1] This refers presumably to the actual city of London. There was certainly no overstocking in the rest of the country.
[2] Ep. Var., II, 103.

Nor was this a new attitude on the part of the English clergy, for if we go back a further generation we find Airoldi, the Papal representative visiting England in the reign of Charles II, reporting to Rome in 1670 that ' The presence in London of Irish priests is a great annoyance. Not a single Irish priest is a true friend to the English '.[1]

But that is a digression. We were considering the state and the paucity of English priests, and have seen that there were comparatively few students in the various colleges abroad.   It may here be stated that on leaving Douay for England the clergy could choose to which District they would go, but several times the Northern clergy complained when those who were born in the North did not go thither. They wanted Rome to decree that all priests must go to the District in which they were born. Actually many of the clergy moved about from one District to another, often at the invitation of some landowner who wanted a chaplain, though this practice was naturally distasteful to the bishops and inconvenienced them.   In consequence in January, 1725, there came a letter from Mgr. Spinelli in Rome to Bishop Stonor forbidding secular priests to wander from one District to another, and telling him not to give faculties to such without the consent of their own bishop. Dr. Stonor said that though he himself was glad of the order, he thought it had been caused by a complaint made by Bishop Prichard of the Western District. Others, however, were convinced that Stonor himself was the cause of it. Actually, Dr. Stonor replied to Rome with four proposals. These were : (1) None should give faculties to priests ' newly come over ', or from another District, without the written consent of their original bishop, which he may refuse or qualify. (2) A priest permanently leaving a District shall not retain the faculties he had in it, and if he wants to return to live there he must obtain new faculties.   (3) But anyone approved for one District shall be approved for all [Districts] for a period of six weeks, after which he would have to apply for ordinary faculties. (4) All coming from abroad must come straight to their own bishop, without staying anywhere except with permission of their bishop or of Propaganda.

But the chief problem was that of raising enough priests, and

[1] Brady, *The Episcopal Succession in England*, III, 126.

it was clear that Douay alone could not do this, for as a rule it sent over to England only four or five a year during the early eighteenth century. In the twenty-three years (1715-1738) for which he was President of Douay, Dr. Witham received 95 students and sent over 60 to the English Mission. Further light on this subject is thrown by a letter from the Vice-President of Douay, Edward Dicconson (later V.A. of the Northern District, 1740-1752) to his brother William, and dated July 14, 1735. It is, incidentally, a quaint example of the guarded code-writing of the period used in case the letter should fall into the hands of Government agents. For the reader's convenience the meaning of the code-words used is here inserted in brackets.

. . . It is necessary that you should know that of the Secular Clergy alone there have dyed since the year 1715 near, if not fully, 140 workmen [priests] : now in January 1737, when I copy this out, I find they exceed 160. In the mean time so few hands have been trained up to the business, that the Rulers of the Manufactory [the Superiors of Douay] cannot by a deal answer the calls upon it. Indeed Mr. Wyvill [Robert Witham, the President] has supplied as many as his circumstances could allow. But Hilton [Rome] and the other two places [presumably Seville and Valladolid], which were better able than Mr. Wyvill—being under the direction of men who have a separate Interest [i.e. not secular priests : they were Jesuits] have all that while sent out so few that it appears as if they designed by that method of proceeding to break the Company [the English Mission] instead of supporting it, to which last their undertaking that administration does not strictly oblige them. Hence in November last Mr. Nelson [Bishop Stonor] and his brother Petre [Bp. Petre of the London District] joyned in a long letter to the Directors [Propaganda] in which they fully set forth their reasons for complaint against the Padri [Jesuits] : 1. on account of their having from those places brought up and sent out so very few heads; and 2. on account that many of those [new priests] whom they had despatched hither were manifestly unfit for their business. From whence they proceeded to the reasons by which it is hoped the Directors may be prevailed upon to reduce those nurseries, particularly that at Hilton, to its primitive institution; and to give the management thereof to them whose property it was by its original foundation [the secular clergy].

A letter from the Jesuit Provincial to Bishop Stonor shows that

H

the English College in Rome sent on an average two a year from 1723 to 1725; and Dr. Dicconson said of this that judging by the finances of the College it should send out seven a year.

Turning now to some of the statistics which crop up from time to time in the documents of the period : it is shown by a list of priests living in London, apparently drawn up in 1685,[1] that there were then 65 in the city. That was, of course, during the brief period of liberty afforded by the reign of James II, and includes regulars as well as seculars. But it is surprising to find a letter to the Pope, dated 1704, stating that there were then one hundred thousand Catholics in England with nearly a thousand priests.[2] This is certainly a great exaggeration, as regards the priests; indeed Dr. Betham told Mayes two years later[3] that there were about ' four score thousand ' Catholics in England, adding ' they are rather increasing, than lapsed, since we had bishops ' (i.e. since 1688); and he estimates the number of priests to be only 400, made up of 250 secular priests, 70 Jesuits, 40 Benedictines, 30 Franciscans, 12 Dominicans, and a few Carmelites. Forty years later, Bishop Challoner reported to Rome that the London District numbered 25,000 with 60 priests, excluding regulars, and said there had been no perceptible change for the past 30 years. The same figure was given by his successor, Dr. Talbot, who, however, said they were diminishing, and that four-fifths of them were in London, with the remainder scattered over ten counties. The priests then numbered about 130, of whom half were seculars; and two-thirds of them were in London. Indeed under this bishop the number of missions, priests and laity steadily fell (not through any fault of his), and complete extinction before very long seemed inevitable. So low did the figures drop that Joseph Berington in 1780 estimated that there were only about 56,000 Catholics in all England and Wales, distributed as follows : the London District 25,000, the Midland District 8,500, the Western District 3,000 (with less than 50 priests), and the Northern 20,000 (with 167 priests). As the population at that time was about six millions these figures mean that Catholics numbered well under one per cent of the whole. Berington's analysis of the situation

---

[1] Westm. Archives, XXXIV, 271.
[2] Westm. Archives, XXXVIII, 271
[3] *Idem.*, Par. Sem. Col., I, 251.

is worth reproducing, even if he tends to paint the picture in rather too sombre colours :

> The few Catholics I have mentioned are also dispersed in the different counties. In many, particularly in the West, in South Wales, and in some of the Midland counties, there is scarcely a Catholic to be found. After London, by far the greatest number is in Lancashire. In Staffordshire are a good many, as also in the northern counties of York, Durham and Northumberland. Some of the manufacturing and trading towns, such as Norwich, Manchester, Liverpool, Wolverhampton and Newcastle-on-Tyne, have chapels which are rather crowded. . . . Excepting in the towns and out of Lancashire, the chief situation of Catholics is in the neighbourhood of the old families of that persuasion. They are the servants, or the children of servants who have married from those families. . . . The truth is, within the past century we have most rapidly decreased. Many congregations have entirely disappeared. . . . In the nature of things it could not possibly be otherwise. Where one cause can be discovered tending to their increase, there will be twenty found to work their diminution. Among the principle are the loss of families by death, or by conforming to the Established Church; the marrying with Protestants, and that general indifference about religion which gains so perceptibly among all ranks of Christians.

But Berington wrote just as the position of Catholics was at its worst. It was the nadir of Catholicism in England. From then on matters began slowly to improve with the passing of the Relief Acts, and the numbers began to climb. They have climbed ever since. The tide had begun to turn, and the inherent divine vitality within the Church was again beginning to tell, so much so, indeed, that although only scanty relief had then been given, yet when Bishop Douglass of the London District died in 1812 the Catholics in England were estimated to be 400,000.

Away in the West the story was worse : but that District had always lagged far behind the others. Although the West had fiercely resisted the Reformation and in the later sixteenth and early seventeenth centuries was noted for its Catholicity, the picture had gradually but radically changed, largely owing to the tragic shortage of priests which could not be remedied, so that the Faith almost died out in those parts, and they were later on captured by a militant nonconformity. In 1773 Bishop Walmesley, O.S.B., of the Western District, reported to Rome that there were only 750 Catholics and nine priests in all Wales, and only seven public chapels. In 1802 there were only two Catholics in Cardiff,[1] and the report by Bishop Collingridge (1809-1829) stated that in 1813 there were but two missions in Wales (Brecknock and Holywell).

In the North matters were very different. It had all along been the most Catholic part of the country, and in 1787 Bishop Matthew Gibson gave the total for his District as 33,685, with 141 priests, half of them seculars, half regulars. No less than 23,000 of them were in Lancashire. It is curious to discover that in Lancashire the average flock for each priest was 371, while in Yorkshire it was only 117. In the Midlands, which comprised fifteen counties, Catholics numbered less than 15,000 in Bishop Milner's time (1803-1826), and as he himself said: ' It is a long way from Ipswich to Oswestry '.

[1] See Donald Attwater's, *The Catholic Church in Modern Wales*.

CHAPTER VII

CATHOLICS AND JACOBITISM

DURING the first half of the eighteenth century one of the greatest problems for Catholics was that of deciding what their attitude was to be towards the rival Houses of Stuart and Hanover. Nor was this a merely theoretical matter; on the contrary it was intensely practical, for it seemed at one period that the whole future of Catholics and their religion was involved in it. There was no doubt where the loyalties and affections of the great majority of Catholics lay, but could they afford the luxury of sentiment or must they bow to the stern facts and thereby ensure their survival and the preservation of their worldly goods? It was a cruel dilemma, and it is not surprising that great passions were roused.

All the Vicars Apostolic of the period, save one, were ardent Jacobites, and so also were the great majority of the clergy and the laity. That this was so can occasion no surprise. Was not the last Stuart king himself an ardent Catholic? Had he not very greatly ameliorated the lot of the down-trodden Catholics of his kingdom, and in the end even forfeited his throne for his devotion and fidelity to the Catholic Church? And above all was he not the lawful, rightful, and divinely appointed king? How, then, could Catholics support the usurping Dutch William, or enthuse over the German Protestant George? Such were the thoughts of most Catholics, and their attitude was very natural. The one exception amongst the bishops was Dr. Stonor, and in this he was, as in so many other matters, hand in glove with his *alter ego,* Dr. Strickland.

Bishop Stonor took the coldly realistic view of the matter. Putting aside all question of sentiment and of romantic attachment to the Stuarts, he held, in a word, that the Stuarts were finished with, that they had no prospect whatever of regaining the throne of England, that Catholics had therefore nothing to hope from them, and that consequently it was madness for them to penalise themselves and probably ruin the prospects of the Church in England for the sake of mere sentiment. The matter was too serious for that, and if they wished to escape utter ruin the English Catholics *must* face facts and come to terms with the all-powerful Hanoverian Government. That was the gist of his argument. His case was a strong one, and to modern eyes eminently reasonable; but in the early years of the eighteenth century it appeared to his fellow-Catholics to be utterly scandalous and treasonable. To them the words 'the King' always meant the exiled James II, and, after his death, it meant his son 'the Chevalier', while 'Her Majesty' was Mary of Modena, wife and widow of James II, and mother of 'James III'. It was to the exiled Court at St. Germains that they looked for guidance, and in ecclesiastical affairs, as appears frequently in this book, the Queen Mother and the young Chevalier had powerful influence, and they expected to be frequently consulted by the Vicars Apostolic. Naturally this state of affairs made Catholics more suspect than ever in the eyes of the English Government, and the years which immediately followed the Revolution of 1688 were marked by the passing of some of the severest of the penal laws. Nor did the Rebellion of 1715 help matters. It was this state of affairs that forced Dr. Stonor to take action.

In view of the failure of the Rebellion, Stonor maintained that whereas in the past it had been best for Catholics to keep quiet under accusations so as not to add fuel to the fire, now the case was different owing to the political charges levelled against them by reason of 'the 1715', and because of the greater severity of the Government. Therefore he said: 'We should publicly apologise for the past, or rather swear for the future all that we can prudently think may give satisfaction to the Government, and conscience will allow'. So he thought that Catholics should express willingness to take a simple oath of submission and non-resistance, the oath of allegiance to George I, and the oath of abjuration (of the Stuarts). He rejected, of course, the Oath of Supremacy and the Test Act, neither of which any Catholic could take. It was the Oath of Abjuration that was the really bitter pill for most Catholics, but Stonor held it to be essential for them to take it.

But almost to a man the Catholic leaders, clerical and lay, totally disagreed with Stonor. Many of them thought the Oaths would only divide Catholics and would not appease the Government, and they agreed with Bishop Giffard that no good had ever yet come to Catholics by approaches to Parliament, and that in any case it would be no help to them to take these Oaths so long as they did not renounce and deny the power of the Pope to dispense the faithful from oaths they had taken, for nothing less than this denial would satisfy the Government, and this denial they could not make.   Here, indeed, was a very great crisis, for Catholics were threatened with complete ruin.   Stonor thought that the Government would not press the matter of the Pope's dispensing power if Rome allowed Catholics to take the Oath of Abjuration.   Rome therefore, he said, should give definite instructions as to what is or is not lawful, for the ruin of the great Catholic families must be averted.   The fetters of erroneous conscience in Catholics should be broken and punctilios (about loyalty to James) exploded.   Rome did in fact allow Catholics to take the Oath of Allegiance and of not acting against the Government, but it would not permit them to deny the Pope's power of dispensing from oaths.   But Stonor's proposals only aroused greater anger in his opponents, and while recognizing the good sense of the one, we can hardly do other than admire the determined loyalty and honour of the other.   After outlining his attitude as above, Dr. Stonor, in writing to his chief opponent, Robert Witham, declared :

And indeed, as far as my observation has led me, these are not ye sentiments of the cowardly and weak of faith, but on ye contrary of those who are most to be depended on no less for piety and courage than for prudence.   Whereas, generally speaking, I find that those who are most averse to ye offering any terms of submission are either hurryed on by extravagant hopes of all things being soon set right again, or cast down by a womanly despair of escaping utter ruin and destruction, or lulled asleep by a stupid, unaccountable, illboding indolency in the midst of such pressing dangers.   Since I came to France the Duke of Norfolk was pleased to write to me a pressing letter to use all my endeavours to get a speedy definition from Rome of this matter.   And I know that [some] of our most considerable Catholicks, both of the Church and laity, desire ardently the same.   I can not therefore blame Dr. Strickland for preparing memoirs upon that subject for the court of Rome.   I shall willingly join my labours to further on ye same end, and though I am apt to think that he is for allowing more than I yet or perhaps ever shall see to be allowable, I shall not take it at all ill that he bring the best reasons he can think of for his opinion, or anyone else for theirs, though it should be equally distant from mine. Farther, I make bold to desire of you, that you yourself would prepare on ye same subject some memoir which I would carry along with me to Brussels [sc. to the Nuncio there], viz. upon these three heads, a simple oath of submission and nonresistance, the oath of Allegiance, and the oath of Abjuration. As to ye oath of Supremacy and Test, there is no subject of dispute.[1]

Dr. Witham's reaction to this is shown by his letter of June 17, 1716, to Dr. Dicconson :

I think it will be necessary that you let your Bro. Dicconson know the rash and illegal methods that are now carried on by Bp. Stonor and his tool Dr. Strickland to ruine our King's interest, and to make divisions among all the Catholics in his dominions. They are upon a project of offering an oath of submission and nonresistance to George, also for allowing the oath of allegiance and abjuration, at least they are for proposing memoirs to Rome on these heads and would have me to joyn with them which I shall never think of. . . .

Your Brother will easily see that great caution must be used in this affair, yet no time to be lost to prevent their attempts. I had found out that Strickland had motioned these things to the Internunce Santini, and that Santini had proposed them to Bishop Stonor, but I had endeavoured to convince Mr. Stonor that such proceedings were never more illegal, improper, and less to the purpose than at present. Tis certain our King never had more friends in his dominions than at this time, notwithstanding the late miscarriages,[2] and they wait only for an opportunity to assist him to assert his right and venture their lives and fortunes to settle him on his throne.[3] And can his Catholic subjects now think of swearing allegiance to the present tyrant and usurper, and of abjuring their lawful sovereign, and even of swearing according to ye oath of abjuration that he never had or has any right? Some to save their estates may go in with such proposals whilst it may be hoped most of them will remain firm to their duty and be highly scandalized at the very proposals. Besides tis an

[1] Ushaw MSS., I, 44.
[2] The rebellion of 1715. Here the wish was clearly father to the thought. James's prospects had quite vanished.
[3] It is easy to realize what great harm this letter would have done to Catholics if it had fallen into the hands of the Government.

extravagant folly[1] to imagen that the present tyrannizing government will be content with oaths and methods of our proposing. They do not desire the Catholics should qualify themselves, but remain under the lash that they may profit by oppressing them.   When these foolish people have swallowed the oaths they propose they'l still be cheated as they deserve by ye oaths of supremacy and test.   This I have already signifyed to Bp. Stonor . . . but to no purpose, as I find by his answer. . . .

Pray desire your brother to keep what I think it necessary he be informed of as private as he can, and if he thinks it necessary to inform her majesty I hope he'l represent to her majesty that it may be proper to proceed with secrecy and caution, tho as tis my duty I am ready to incur anyone's displeasure or to suffer any inconvenience that may fall on me sooner than be wanting in my duty in what regards her majesty or our King. I'll write tomorrow to our agent Mayes that he may use his utmost endeavors to stop these pernicious consequences at Rome.   Bp. Giffard is altogether of my opinion, as he has expressed himself in a late letter to me. He will never consent to such unwarrantable proceedings.   But I suppose the Queen at St. Germains and ye King as soon as he can be acquainted will write to Card. Gualberi.   Strickland, you know, works all his mischief by Card. Fabroni. . . .[2]

But Stonor still thought that 'we ought to be ready to lay hold of any occasion of trying even a doubtful remedy' in view of the gravity of the occasion, and in view of the permission given by Rome to take the oath of allegiance and non-resistance, Bishop Giffard and Bishop Prichard (of the Western District) wrote to Propaganda regarding the scruples thus raised amongst Catholics.   They asked four questions : (1) Whether by swearing fidelity to George they did not deny that anyone else had a right to the throne? (2) Will it not give great scandal if Catholics swear fidelity to a Prince of a hostile religion, while Non-Juror Protestants refuse to do this and maintain their fidelity to a Catholic sovereign (James)? (3) If Catholics hear of Protestant plans to restore James (e.g. by the Non-Jurors), are they bound to reveal these to the Government?   This seems clearly to be demanded by the oath of allegiance.   (4) If James invaded

---

[1] Here he was on much firmer ground.
[2] Ushaw MSS., I, 109.

England, and George orders Catholics, by virtue of their oath, to join in the war against James and to kill or expel him, are Catholics bound to do this?   The oath seems to oblige it.

In February, 1717, Robert Witham expressed his annoyance that Mayes had written to the effect that he had nothing to say against Strickland.   Witham said he would change that opinion when he heard that, in addition to other Superiors, the three bishops were opposed to the oaths; meanwhile the bishops awaited the reply from Rome to the above *Dubia*.   When it came, it made no mention of the questions asked, but expressed the sympathy of Rome for the plight of the English Catholics, and said that Rome had urged foreign powers to order their envoys in London to do all that was possible to mitigate the persecution, and that it was sending a subsidy of five hundred scuti for the needs of Catholics.   In May, both Ingleton and Stonor reported a slight easing of the tension.   The danger of a new persecution by reason of the rebellion seemed to have passed, owing to assurances given by the Catholics to the Government, but they still have to register their estates (with a view to extra taxation being levied on them), and there is no real prospect of relief.

So matters remained until two years later, when Strickland suddenly took a sensational step.   In June, 1719, he tried to force the hand of Rome and of the English Catholics by drawing up for presentation to the Government a list of the conditions on which (he suggested) the Government should agree to have mercy on the Catholics, and he went so far as to propose to the Government that if Catholics (including the bishops) should not agree to these conditions they should be arrested.   This extraordinary episode appears to have been hitherto ignored in histories of the period, but the facts are in the Westminster Archives in papers copied from Secretary Craggs' MS. in the library of the Marquis of Buckingham at Stowe.[1]   This astonishing document issued by a would-be Catholic prelate, and headed ' Papers relating to a Scheme for inducing English Catholics in general to become by degrees truly and heartily well affected to his Majesty's Government ', declares that a delegation of influential Catholics must inform the Pope that if English Catholics are to be saved from utter ruin he must agree to four

---

[1] Westm. Archives, Kirk's MSS., III, 63.

conditions: His decree[1] allowing the Oath of Allegiance to be taken must be published and made known to all;[2] the office of Protector of England must be taken from Card. Gualterio, 'the Pretender's publick and declared Agent', and be given to some-one not obnoxious to the British Government; he must revoke the Indults given to the Pretender for the nomination of the Irish Bishops, and must promise 'to govern these missions' with-out any communication, direct or indirect, with the Pretender; and lastly, any cleric accused of any offence by the Government shall be recalled by his Superior. 'As the Emperor has engaged to bring the Pope to these terms, it will be necessary to send also a proper person to him with a letter to desire his Mediation in this affair.' It would suffice if these letters be subscribed by the Duke of Norfolk, Lord Stafford, Lord Montague, and Lord Walgrave for the Nobility, and by Sir John Webb, Mr. Charles Howard, Mr. Stonor, and Mr. Arundell for the Gentry. The document concludes:

> As any delays or tergiversations in coming into these Measures can never be coloured with any pretence of religion or conscience, so if any should be made by persons obstinately disaffected, ye Government would then have no means left . . . but in the real and full execution of the penal Laws, and more particularly the Act for transferring ye right of succession [to estates] to the next Protestant heir, upon the immediate heir not conforming at the age of 18; and of the late Register Act for taking away the two-thirds. . . .[3]

The whole plan was thus an effort to force Catholics to give up James under a threat of putting the penal laws into full execution. A letter from Secretary Craggs in Whitehall to Lord Stanhope, a member of the Government, dated June 30, 1719, says that Strickland called on him with this paper, and they both showed it to three leading Catholics: Norfolk, Waldegrave and Howard. But though the first two were inclined to agree with it, Howard persuaded them against it, and they refused to consult Mr. Stonor, 'the best intentioned of them all'.

---

[1] Rome had said, as regards loyalty to George I: ' *posse et debere, si requisiti fuerint, plenam fidem et obedientiam, etiam cum juramento, promittere* '.

[2] Hitherto it had been ' held dormant ' by the Nuncio at Brussels, Mgr. Santini.

[3] The dreaded law confiscating two-thirds of the property of every Catholic.

The Doctor [sc. Strickland] is so piqued [wrote Craggs] at this usage and so hearty in the business that in case the Gentlemen come to the resolution he apprehends, he would be for taking up [arresting] immediately Bishop Giffard, Mr. Gray (the true Earl of Shrewsbury, who enjoys the Estate, though another possess the title), and some other heads of that set of people, and by that glaring instance exert a power which may effectually and quickly terrify them into a compliance.

That a Catholic ecclesiastic should advise the Protestant Government to arrest Dr. Giffard is surely unpardonable. In the event, after a dramatic meeting at Strickland's house at which feelings and words ran high, the three noblemen refused to sign; and Craggs, reporting this to Stanhope on July 7, wrote :

. . . The matter being thus broke off, I have determined to put the thing in execution which I said in my former I intended in that case, by tendering the Oaths to Howard, and seizing Giffard and Gray. But because this proceeding is chiefly with a view to make them squeak, I would contrive to do it in such a manner as not to put them out of my own power by overacting it into that of the Law. For which end I have desired Delafraye to pick out a couple of discreet Justices of the Peace of his acquaintance that will, as of themselves, take up Howard and Giffard, and afterwards do just what Delafraye shall bid them, without carrying their Zeal too far. And as for Gray, I think some trusty and understanding messenger must be sent to manage him, for he is 17 miles off. Strickland persuades himself this method will have its effect, and make them ready to sign even stronger letters than those proposed to them.

We are irresistibly reminded of William Cecil or Walsingham in the reign of Elizabeth I. That same day Bishop Giffard wrote a letter giving an account of an attempt to arrest him that morning, and of his escape through the back door. And Bishop Stonor? What was he doing all this time? He was the ' proper person ' designated in the above plan for taking the proposals to the Emperor, his was the figure standing in the shadows behind Strickland; and for his part in this affair he was threatened by Rome with deposition from his Vicariate, but this made no difference to his attitude. He was convinced that he could win Parliamentary favour for the Catholics without prejudice to religion, and at the cost of merely taking the oath of allegiance.

After saying that Norfolk, Shrewsbury, his brother Stonor, and the Duke of Powis had signed, he gave his view by saying that he and Strickland had got nearer to success than had anyone since Elizabeth I's time; but the foolish attitude of many Catholics makes him think the relief cannot be gained this year, though he would try again later. He held that his duty to religion came before his duty of loyalty to the Stuarts; and indeed, if the two were in conflict he was, of course, certainly right. As it was, he felt sure that most Catholics would eventually take the oath, even Giffard, who :

> is now in an uneasy sort of situation, being afraid, and I believe with some reason, of being taken up [arrested]. But for any extraordinary danger he may thank his unaccountable behaviour.[1]

But there was nothing definite offered by the Government in return for capitulation by the Catholics. All the old disabilities would still remain, and it was very uncertain whether anything at all would be gained. But the Government were saying that they expected Catholics to take the oath of allegiance which their own bishops and priests had said they could take, and therefore if they refused to do so they deserved to be treated as obstinate rebels. It may well be imagined that most Catholics did not thank Stonor and Strickland for having raised up this storm. Yet Stonor wrote to Mayes at this time a strong and reasonable defence of the proposals, and it was proposed to go ahead with the plan of getting in touch with the Emperor in Vienna and with the Holy Father in Rome. However, when the eminent lawyer, Sir Edward Northey, heard of this he gave it as his opinion that to authorize anyone to go to Rome or Vienna for this purpose would be contrary to the Statute 5 Eliz. 1 (against maintaining the Pope's authority), and would also subject such persons to the penalty of high treason by the Statute 13 Eliz. 2. This opinion naturally much strengthened Giffard and the gentry in their opposition to Stonor, and Witham, after a long tirade against Stonor and his laxity as regards visiting his District, said the whole plan was ' due to the selfish politics of the two Abbots '.[2]

---

[1] Ep. Var., VII, 43.
[2] Stonor and Strickland. Both had been given Abbeys in France as a benefice.

Yet, as has already been said, Stonor's case was a really strong one, *if* the Government could actually be trusted,[1] and *if* (more doubtful) the Ministry could control Parliament. Giffard, for his part, did not believe that either of these conditions would be fulfilled. He was convinced that Parliament would never favour Catholics, even if the King or the Ministry did, but would only pass Acts more severe than ever before. He also pointed to the difficulty there would be of getting unanimity amongst Catholics on the wording of the Oaths, and that in any case the dispensing power of the Pope would be a fatal stumbling block. In fact, the situation was a curiously accurate foreshadowing of that which arose at the end of the century over the efforts of the 'Catholic Committee' to win emancipation for Catholics by appeasing the Government and taking Oaths, in which policy it was strenuously and successfully opposed by the great Bishop Milner. And just as now Giffard believed that no good had or ever could come to Catholics from approaching Parliament, so too did Bishop Walmesley believe in that similar crisis seventy years later. Meanwhile Stonor again argued his case with Mayes in Rome, and his letter contains so much shrewd insight that it should be quoted in part before this subject is closed :

> . . . Tis plain to anyone that will attend that the Catholic Religion is at present, particularly as to the Gentry and Nobility (its chief supports)[2] in a very declining way amongst us. Certain laws are in actual execution which are very uneasy and ruinous, viz. that of 1700 and the constant law of double taxes. And we are in continual danger of the execution of the other still severer laws, whether upon any indiscretion or misbehaviour of the Catholics themselves, or upon some emergency of State. I must add too, to our general confusion, that zeal and fervour are at a very low ebb, both with Priests and people. So that upon an increase of persecution or even upon the continuance of our present uneasy circumstances, the little remains of religion amongst us seem to be in a most imminent danger.
>
> Now these greater severities cannot possibly be staved off, much less an Act of Parliament be obtained to mend our

---

[1] It is interesting that Stonor said four years later (1723) that there would be no persecution but for Jacobitism, ' so wonderfully is the nation now changed, and so averse is it become to anything that looks like persecution for religion '.

[2] A curious contrast with the position in modern times.

circumstances, without obtaining the favour of the ministry, and good will of the King. And these being obtained there was and is very good grounds to hope for both. Here an occasion happens that on our submission and compliance we are promised this favour and good will.[1] Tell me, supposing it to be lawful to comply, is it not more prudent to doe so, than to cast our [hopes] upon the uncertainty of a new Revolution? And even after that uncertainty there is another still remaining, whether our circumstances would be much bettered by it.

But there is still something stronger in the case. There is all manner of reason to believe that tis a fixed and settled resolution with our Masters that they will not leave us in the condition we are now in : too much aggrieved to love them, and yet too powerful to be neglected; but so that we either behave to them like other subjects or else expect shortly to be ruined. Now put into the balance this extraordinary danger of one side, and on the other the two above-mentioned uncertainties of relief, and tell me which you think overweighs and deserves most to be regarded. For my part I am so much persuaded of the greater weightyness of the former that I cannot think even those who are most concerned for, hope, and wish it most, can take it amiss if we postpone the consideration of it. So that our case, if the measures be followed which I have been for, is reduced to this dilemma. If the present Government stands, we shall be better; if it falls, we shall not be worse.[2]

Catholics were indeed in a difficult position and were faced with a most unpleasant choice. But fortunately for them at this critical juncture public attention was suddenly distracted from them by the excitement of the South Sea Bubble and its eventual disastrous collapse, so that they were not for the present further molested. The crisis passed, and no more was there any talk of embarrassing oaths—until the question of Relief and Emancipation arose many years later, and by that time Jacobitism was long since dead and buried, so far as practical Catholic politics were concerned.

Of course the second Rising, that of 1745, inevitably brought fresh anxiety to Catholics, all the more so since the attempt

[1] Here again the situation is a striking anticipation of that of 1791 and the Relief Act.
[2] Ep. Var., VII, 57.

came so near to success. Once again they were faced with the painful dilemma and many a Catholic family was divided on the subject. But by then two generations had passed since the Revolution of 1688, and many of the younger people did not feel the same obligation towards the Stuart cause. Moreover in London the powerful influence of Bishop Challoner was exerted to restrain Catholics from joining Prince Charles, for he was very sceptical of the chances of success and he dreaded the inevitable severe reprisals which would fall on Catholics in the event of failure. Douay College was still extremely Jacobite, and soon after the Battle of Prestonpans its President (Dr. Thornburgh) wrote to Mayes, who was now very old but was still in charge of the Agency in Rome :

> Our news from Scotland has hitherto been very good, and we are in great hopes, and pray daily that heaven may prosper the just army of our glorious Prince, whose praises are in everybody's mouth. Besides our daily prayers for his success we sing a solemn High Mass at least once every week for the same intention.[1]

When the Highlanders reached Derby in December all Catholics were ordered to leave London, and something approaching panic seized London and the Court; and this very fact made the anger and suspicion against Catholics all the more intense when the danger had begun to recede. After the failure of Charles was manifest, persecution flared up, the prisons were full of Catholics, houses were searched over a wide area, and schools and chapels (even the Embassy chapels) were closed, while many people were tried for their lives and some executed. Catholics feared the worst, and they appealed for the intercession of foreign Powers. Challoner himself tried to inform the Pope by a roundabout means, through a letter to a merchant in Antwerp, asking him to forward it to a M. de la Vacquerie, which was presumably a code name for somebody at Douay, as the letter was sent thither, and from there to Mayes in Rome. Dated 12 September, 1746, it ran :

Sir,
    This is to let you know that your friends here are very much alarmed with the apprehension of a storm, that they are told

---

[1] Ep. Var., XII, 75.

by knowing people is gathering, and will break and fall upon
them at the next meeting of Parliament. They are the more
surprised at this, because they did not expect it, having given
no just occasion for it; but on the contrary, having behaved
remarkably well in the late troubles. This comes therefore to
desire two things of you; the one that by your prayers and
those of other servants of God, you would endeavour to prevail
with the King of Kings to deliver us; and to change the hearts
of our enemies : the other, that you would with all convenient
speed (for there is no time to be lost) acquaint Mr. Abraham[1]
by the means of Mr. Laurence [Mayes], or otherwise, with the
danger that threatens us; that he may make without delay the
best interest he can at Vienna, Turin, etc., to divert by their
mediation here the blow we apprehend.[2]

Next day Alban Butler wrote a similar letter to Mayes to the
same effect, but pointing out that it was necessary to distinguish
between joining the Prince and being Catholics ' otherwise the
Queen of Hungary will not stir '. But slowly the storm died
down, no new penal legislation was passed, and Catholics
gradually settled down again. It was the last occasion on which
a serious persecution of Catholics in England seemed really
imminent.

[1] The Pope.
[2] Ep. Var., XII, 87.

I

Chapter VIII

BISHOP WILLIAMS AND THE NORTH

Meantime (to resume chronological sequence) Bishop George Witham in the Northern District had been growing old, and he was extremely infirm. Already in 1715, a year before his transfer from the Midland District to the North, he had asked to be allowed to resign, but Bishop Giffard (to whom he had sent it for forwarding to Rome) refused to pass it on, for he feared the resulting vacancy might be filled by a regular. ' Many things ', wrote Bishop Witham to Mayes, ' there are which in these parts give me great trouble and vexation; and I heartily wish that . . . I might be allowed to lay down this too heavy burden, and to transfer it to someone more able and more courageous.' But Giffard added a note saying he did not think this ' proper at this present time ' and that he was keeping back the application till a more reasonable juncture. ' In a short time I hope we may both be discharged, some younger and abler coming to take up our places.'[1] His brother, Robert Witham of Douay, also refused to help in this matter and for the same reason, and because he feared that Dr. Strickland might be appointed to the vacancy. As he was thus unable to resign, Dr. Witham then asked for a coadjutor, and this he continued to do almost every year until his death, though without success. Two years later (March 28, 1718) he wrote a truly heart-rending appeal to the Cardinal-Protector imploring to be allowed to resign because of his lack of ability and his physical infirmities which included what he called ' trembling paralysis ' and incipient dropsy. He said that the thought of the grave was constantly with him and that he wished to prepare for approaching death and judgment.[2] His brother at Douay, who had previously stopped two such applications, let this one go through, as there

[1] Giffard then had 18 more years as a bishop in front of him, and Witham in the following year was transferred to the Northern District, where he ruled for another nine years.
[2] The whole letter will be found in Appendix III.

was now less danger in asking for a successor or coadjutor, since
Strickland was by now largely discredited. But he lamented the
lack of unity amongst the Vicars Apostolic[1] which would prevent
them from uniting in presenting one candidate. ' There's room
enough to doubt, not only of Bp. Prichard, but even more perhaps
of Bp. Stonor, being of the same mind with Bps. Fowler and
Markham.'[2] Three months later Bishop Witham wrote to
Mayes :

> If His Holiness and their Eminences will have the charity
> and goodness to let a poor old weak man, now near the end
> of his grand climacteric year, and maybe too fearful (which
> he knows not well how to remedy), lay down, as I trust in
> God they will, his too heavy burden that he may better prepare
> himself to dye, and that the burden itself may be better born
> and the dutys better discharged by some good and able Brother
> of ours,[3] of more courage and strength and better abilitys
> both of mind and body : and if they please to demand whom
> I recommend that may succeed me, I shall and do recommend
> to them three of this District.

The three he mentioned were Edward Parkinson, James Barker,
and Lawrence Rigby, and he added that his own brother, the
President of Douay (Robert Witham) is the fittest of all, but
would decline the offer. So also Lawrence Mayes. This was in
June, 1718, and next month he told Giffard that all those he
had recommended had declined the burden. His brother told
him that neither Parkinson nor Rigby would be approved in the
North, that Barker would not do because he was an enemy of
Stonor, that Mayes would be best, and that Dicconson would do,
if he could preach.[4] He ended with the sombre remark : ' I think
we have reason enough to apprehend a Regular.' It was curious
that he should have foreseen that so early, for seven years were
to elapse before an appointment was made, and then it *was* a

---

[1] These were Giffard, Stonor, Witham, and Prichard. Obviously there
could be no accord between the first two after Stonor's behaviour towards
Giffard as detailed in an earlier chapter; and Prichard, as a regular, was as
good as ' beyond the Pale ', though actually he generally was on good terms
with the seculars.

[2] These were the aliases of Bps. Giffard and Witham.

[3] I.e. of the secular clergy.

[4] He was afflicted with a bad stammer.

regular who was chosen.   It is also curious that the secular clergy in those days so often had difficulty in producing a really strong candidate, as for instance in the two lengthy vacancies in the West and the North already described above.   Such was also to be the case now.

Two years later we find the bishop begging Mayes to come home from Rome and be his coadjutor, but two years after that (1722) he was still without one, and his brother Robert said there was no prospect of getting one, as everyone refused it.   He also wanted Mayes to take it on.   Just before Christmas that year Bishop Witham made another attempt, telling Mayes to petition for a coadjutor for him and naming five, who were the above-named three, with the addition of Edward Dicconson at their head, and Thomas Towneley at the end; but this letter was criticized by his brother on four counts.   (1) He did not know why it was written to the Prefect of Propaganda (Cardinal Sacriponti).   A bishop wanting a coadjutor should write direct to the Pope.   (2) The Canons allow him to name only one person, whereas he has named five.   (3) He should also write to ' the King ' (i.e. James).   And (4) He should also write to the Cardinal-Protector of England.   So that application was scrapped and its place taken by one in which only one name was mentioned, that of Dicconson.   That cleric was time and again proposed for vacant bishoprics, but was constantly rejected by Rome, because he had (quite unjustly) been accused of Jansenism.   This was the best way of smirching anyone in those days, and thus stopping their promotion.   In March Propaganda said they would consider the matter, but in September Witham was still fretting with impatience, thinking he might die without a coadjutor, as had happened to Bishop Leyburn.   In December, 1723, Robert Witham said he had heard a report that a Benedictine might be chosen, and he raised the usual objections; Dicconson had by this time become Vicar General to Bp. Stonor.   In February Ingleton repeated the rumour of a regular being appointed : ' which would occasion great confusion ', etc., etc.   That month (February, 1724) saw yet another petition from the unhappy but persistent Witham, naming the last four of the previous five, i.e. without Dicconson, and begging Rome not to choose a regular.   He added, somewhat naïvely, that he still prefers Dicconson.   But the whole of that year wore away and no word came from Rome.

It would seem that the real cause of the delay was the failure of the clergy through all that time to produce anyone really acceptable. On January 1, 1725, the disconsolate Ingleton wrote to Mayes :

> The delay goes beyond all bounds, and looks almost desperate. Yet Bp. Witham is in so decrepit a state of health as ought to make that business very pressing. He desires you will still insist on Mr. Edward Dicconson, who is certainly the fittest and most desired. The others he named, except Mr. Towneley, are either very old, or infirm, or poor.

In April came one last appeal from the bishop, this time to the Cardinal-Protector (Gualterio), and naming no one. It simply asked that a regular be not appointed. Six days later the bishop was dead. The end of the stricken old bishop was reported by his friend, Bryan Tunstall of Wycliffe Hall, in a letter to Rome dated April 4 (O.S.), 1725 :

> What I said of Mr. George Witham's failing condition has proved too true. For though on this day sevennight Mr. Rigby and Mr. Addison had been with him about business most of the afternoon, and he even walked over his floor to show them how active he was, yet, when they were gone home, he having desired his man to pull his chair to his study and lay him his book before him to say his Vespers, and come up again to him in a quarter of an hour, and accordingly his man coming up again to him, found him leaning upon his book dead; and was buried last Sunday.
>
> I hope you [sc. Mayes] will immediately let Mr. Abraham [the Pope] know it, who I confide will break through those malignant objections and delays made in Mr. Eaton's [Dicconson] business, and give us him for Mr. George's successor. I do not know anyone more fit for it, or wished for by us, unless you'll come to us.[1]

But Mayes had long since made up his mind that he did not wish to be a bishop, and a month after Witham's death Bishop Giffard submitted the names of Dicconson, Parkinson and Rigby to Rome, while Ingleton at St. Germains was using all his influence with the Chevalier, with the bishops, and at Rome. Robert Witham wrote to Propaganda in July giving reasons why

[1] Ep. Var., VIII, 247.

the new bishop should not be a regular, and there was a petition to the same effect from the clergy of the North.   The question of ' loyalty ', i.e. to ' King James ', constantly crops up.   Bishops Stonor and Prichard were both annoyed that their opinions had not been asked.   There were already rumours of a Dominican getting the post, and on this Ingleton ingenuously commented : ' If we must have a Regular, I should rather wish for one of their Order [sc. the Dominican] than any other.   The post will here- after (in that event) more easily return to the Clergy.'[1]   Stonor's view was expressed in a letter to Mayes of August 3 :

. . . My present situation,[2] and more the temper of our Antient [sc. Bp. Giffard], makes me less acquainted than formerly of such business as passes through your hands, and less capable of being serviceable by intermeddling in it. Indeed I was very seasonably in London when the news came of Mr. Marcom's [Bp. Witham's] death; and I was very desirous that Mr. Petre[3] and I should have acted joyntly with him to procure a successor.   But this he [Giffard] declined, and even to let us know what he himself would doe.   So that . . . I was forced to sit still.   Tis true he has since excused his reserve and directly asked my pardon.   But this is a poor amends for the past, and I doubt no better security for the future.   Things, I believe, must now be so far forward that it would be in vain for me to make any representa- tion. . . . I believe it will be very disagreeable to the State, as well as to the generality of the Catholic Gentry, and par- ticularly prejudicial to the Secular Clergy, if at one time there be more than one of the Vicars Apostolic taken from among the Regulars. . . . Besides that, nothing is more difficult than for any one, who has long been member of a particular Body, to put on a spirit truly Episcopal, and make his chief interests those of his Flock.[4]

The Benedictines were reported to be confident that the new bishop would be one of themselves, and probably a Fr. Southcott,

[1] Ep. Var., VIII, 287.
[2] He was now no longer in London, but was forced to live in the country, i.e. in his District.
[3] Coadjutor in the London District.
[4] Ep. Var., VIII, 295.   The answer to this is, of course, supplied by the illustrious names of Bishops Walmesley, Baines, Brown, and Ullathorne, amongst a host of others.

but by October most of the clergy expected a Dominican. And this was perhaps the more probable by reason of the fact that the Pope of that time, Benedict XIII, was himself a Dominican. Into this atmosphere of speculation, dreads and hopes, there suddenly came from Robert Witham the news (it might almost be termed ' comic relief ') that Strickland had been made Bishop of Namur through the influence of the Emperor. The story, according to Witham (and it seems an unlikely one), was that Strickland had some time previously been promised a Cardinalate through Polish influence, and that he had now concluded a bargain with a Polish nobleman, Count Zizendorf, for the latter's nephew to have the Cardinalate, Strickland in return to have the first vacant bishopric in Flanders.

Hardly had this tale been digested in England when news came of the appointment to the Northern District. The actual appointment came not, as was usual, from the Congregation of Propaganda, but from the Pope himself. He chose Fra Dominic Williams, a Welsh Dominican, who was Prior of Bornhem in Flanders. Born in 1661, Bishop Williams was thus 64 at the time of his elevation, and he had the distinction of being not only the sole Dominican English Vicar Apostolic, but also the only regular to govern a Vicariate other than the Western until the coming of Ullathorne more than a century later. Like his fellow-regular, Bishop Prichard of the Western District, he was a native of Monmouthshire and also, like him, he had been professor of Theology in the College of his Order (in his case that of St. Thomas Aquinas at Louvain), where he had four terms of office as rector, while in addition he had also twice been prior of the monastery at Bornhem, and twice Provincial of the English Province of Dominicans, which position he occupied at the time of his elevation to the episcopate.

News of the appointment became public about the middle of December, 1725, and on hearing it Ingleton wrote to Mayes :

> Just now I received yours of the 12th with the afflicting news of a Dominican Bishop. The Pope's resolution, if unalterable, will cause great confusion, as well as chagrin in a District which makes the most considerable part of the English Mission. There is but one poor Dominican in the whole District, and in all England only seven.[1]

[1] Ep. Var., VIII, 339.

And six weeks later he wrote :

> Both the Clergy and Gentry of the North received the news with the greatest surprise and trouble; and this the more because they are persuaded this choice was not made by His Holiness *ex proprio motu*, and without the advice and suggestion of others. . . .[1] Tis certain the choyce of Bishop Williams will be attended with very ill consequences, and not less mortifying to him than to others. A friend of mine lately come from the North and well acquainted with the Catholic Families, assures me that not one Gentleman will give [the bishop] a residence in that District. He is a stranger, a beggar. . . . I have taken liberty to acquaint the King how much the Northern Clergy are offended at this choyce, and that they will not believe it made by the Pope alone *ex motu proprio*.

But Ingleton was always a diehard and an extremist, and in fact the Northern clergy, at least after they had come to know their new bishop, were not nearly so cold as one might gather from the above, and eventually they conceived a warm regard for him. Nor did any of the ' ill consequences ' actually materialize. There had been a long delay in the issue of the Briefs of appointment, as representations had been made to Propaganda of how unwelcome such an appointment would be, and for a time it seemed that some other vacancy would be found for Dr. Williams,[2] especially as Giffard and Stonor wrote a letter of expostulation to Rome. But the Pope remained firm in his determination to send the bishop to England, and on July 11, 1726, he himself, as a mark of special favour, consecrated him bishop in Rome. A certain amount of the displeasure felt at this appointment by the heads of the English clergy was vented upon the unfortunate Lawrence Mayes in Rome for not doing enough to prevent it. Robert Witham was especially angered, and in addition was extremely annoyed because Mayes had declined to deliver to Bishop Williams two letters sent by Witham. There is extant a very long letter from Mayes to Witham in which

---

[1] In this he was quite wrong. The Pope himself made the choice, without consulting Propaganda, as Mayes declared in a letter to Witham.

[2] Witham wished that Dr. Williams could be put over the Western District in succession to Dr. Prichard who was asking for a coadjutor, and leave the North to a secular.

the former defends himself in this matter.[1]   Before the appointment had been irrevocably made, Robert Witham (of all people) had written a congratulatory letter to Williams, because he hoped that the latter would be able to help him in a plan which he had in mind for Douay.   But Mayes realized that to deliver this letter might do great harm to the prospects of even yet getting a secular priest made bishop for the North, as it might just turn the scale.   He therefore held up the letter, and when a second one came he returned it to the writer.   He received a severe reprimand from Dr. Witham, but was consoled by Ingleton who wrote :

> As to Mr. President's proceeding in reference to you and his letter to Bishop Williams, tis certainly scandalous, and shows his dispositions towards you.   But you need not fear him, for he has lost all credit with the clergy, and both the bishops and others have an esteem and concern for you.

He also added that he had been told by the new bishop himself that his comfort was that he had not sought the bishopric himself, but that it had been decided by the Pope himself *ex proprio motu;* and that he (the bishop) had promised Ingleton he would be impartial in his dealings with the clergy and regulars and would take advice from the secular clergy.   To which Ingleton's characteristic comment was : ' I wish the latter part of these promises may be more sincere than the first.'

The opposition to the appointment, coupled with the fact that the new bishop was penniless, and that, as a regular, he could not profit by the endowment of the Northern bishopric left by the late Bishop Smith for the use of secular bishops, made it impossible for Dr. Williams to leave Rome for a considerable time, but at length he set out and reached Paris in October, 1726, bringing letters from the Pope to the King of France and to the King of Spain, asking them to grant him benefices that would afford him sufficient to live on.   But after six months stay there he had to leave without having received anything from either. It appears that he then spent some weeks at his old monastery of Bornhem, and from there went on to Douay which he reached in July, 1727.   From there Dr. Witham reported to Mayes on July 18 :

---

[1] The letter will be found *in extenso* in Appendix IV.

. . . Bishop Williams passed by [Douay] last week and lodged with the Benedictines,[1] which I told him looked odd and unkind to us, since he must know very well that we stood the most need of a Bishop, being the Regulars have always their Provincials and proper Superiors, and besides half of the Priests in the Northern District are of the Secular Clergy. He had also taken one with him from Paris, a monk, whom the monks here call the Bishop's Secretary; and as such he assisted him at giving Confirmation here at the English Monks. I expostulated a little with him on that account and told him none of the Bishops in England pretended to keep a Secretary. He answered me he did not design to keep him. He left him at Douay, and went for Brussels and those parts without him, where he is yet. By the discourse I had with him I perceive the reasons you had not to deliver my letter to him, nor any that gave him the title of Vicar Apostolic,[2] for he told me the use he made of a letter of compliment from Dr. Ingleton, and that it turned the Cardinals of the Congregation in his favour. He also told me the Cardinals of Propaganda offered him a maintenance of 800 crowns a year if he would stay at Rome and not go to the North of England. At the same time the English Dominicans set about that it was you who, in the name of the Clergy of the North, offered him this pension of 800 crowns; but I let them know this was a groundless story and what I was persuaded they neither would nor could do.[3]

At first it seemed that the bishop would have to spend the winter in Flanders owing to the difficulty of getting across to England and also owing to his poverty, but eventually he managed to avoid this further delay, and two and a half years after the death of Bishop Witham his successor took ship from the Low Countries and landed on the Northumbrian coast. It was not an inviting prospect that lay before him, and one cannot but feel great sympathy for Dr. Williams. A stranger to his District, unasked for and unwanted, knowing no one and not even knowing where to obtain shelter, with his pockets practically empty and not even a travelling companion, the new Vicar Apostolic may well have felt forlorn. None the less he at once made a favourable impression on his critical flock. Bryan

---

[1] At St. Gregory's, the community that is now at Downside.

[2] Dr. Witham had addressed the letter to ' the Vicar Apostolic of the North', though the appointment had not yet been actually made.

[3] Ep. Var., IX, 125.

Tunstall (the same who had sheltered Bishop Witham and had reported his death) gave the news of his coming to Mayes on December 26, 1727 :

> Mr. Williams is at last come to us, and of a Regular, I always thought we could not have a properer.   He landed at Shields and our Mr. Gibson [the priest] at Newcastle conducted him to Durham, where he remained about three weeks in an inn. Our Brethren and others eat with him mostly there, and took care to make the reckoning easy to him.   But he seemed a little balked not to have a private lodging found him; but I know not anyone there qualifyed for that purpose.   Dr. Rigby from Wycliffe went to pay him respects, and made him Cousin D. Tunstall's compliments to him, with an invitation to pass the Holydays [sc. the Christmas season] at his house.   I have great hopes he will be easie with us : and we with him.   He does not seem to be desirous of meddling with our private affairs; and in a dispute about some little matters given in to him as his due, referred the matter immediately to Dr. Rigby's decision. . . . He [Williams], upon his arrival as he had done before from Paris, confirmed all Cousin George Witham's Grand Vicars.

Thus from the start the new bishop displayed tact and consideration.   Dicconson (who was his eventual successor in the bishopric), writing twenty years later, told Mayes that Dr. Williams had himself told him that he landed in England

> so well supplyed with the *unum necessarium* for this world that being landed he had not sufficient to pay off all he owed for his passage oversea, nor did he know (as he said to me) where to go and find reception, till my good patron at Wycliffe,[1] hearing how it was, sent one over to him with an invitation to come and reside with him till he could otherwise be provided.   Where being well entertained for five months, he had time to think of gathering subscriptions etc. from the Padri[2] and the Benedictines.   Afterwards he lived in the house of a very worthy gentleman, Sir Edward Gascoigne, gratis.[3]

[1] Mr. Tunstall. This family had already sheltered Bishop Witham for some years, and Bishop Smith before him. As Dr. Dicconson calls him his own patron, it would therefore seem that four successive bishops of the North were indebted to this family for hospitality.

[2] The Jesuits.

[3] Ep. Var., XII, 148.

This Sir Edward Gascoigne had two houses in Yorkshire, one of which was Huddlestone Hall, six miles from Pontefract, and the other Parlington Hall, where Bishop Williams consecrated the chapel in 1733, dedicating it to the Transfiguration of Christ and to St. Benedict.[1] The bishop at once set about visiting his District and was especially assiduous in confirming the people. In his first year he confirmed 1,379 persons. Now there was the unusual situation that two of the four Vicars Apostolic were regulars (Williams in the North and his Franciscan colleague, Prichard, in the West); while in the other two Vicariates Giffard of London was now 84 and his coadjutor, Bishop Petre, was constantly seeking permission to resign. That left only Bishop Stonor, and he was by no means *persona grata* with most of the clergy at this time. Altogether the episcopal ' bench ' had rather an unsatisfactory appearance, from the secular clergy's point of view, though the only serious aspect of this was the lack of unity between the bishops. In this connection one has to realize how very seldom it was that any of the bishops met each other. The distances involved, the slowness and discomfort of transport in those days, and the poverty of the bishops, all told against such meetings; and indeed throughout the whole of the penal times there is no record of any organized or regular gatherings of the Vicars Apostolic. The vast majority of them must never have seen any of their colleagues, and this naturally handicapped efforts towards unity of outlook or policy.

It will be of interest at this point to look somewhat closer at the financial problem, as instanced by the case of Bishop Williams, and there are fortunately a few letters which vividly illustrate his difficulties and also cast a light on the conditions of the times. Being debarred, as a regular, from the enjoyment of the legacy left by Bishop Smith, Dr. Williams was always in great straits and had to devise various means to ensure his subsistence. How difficult was his situation three years after his coming to England is shown by a letter to him from his Vicar General, Dr. Rigby, dated March 25, 1730.

---

[1] The Gascoignes had strong Benedictine connections. One had been Superior of St. Edmund's, Paris (the modern ' Douai ') and Abbot of Lambspring, as well as President of the English Benedictines, and an Abbess of Cambrai (Stanbrook) was a member of the family.

Most Honoured Sir,

. . . Though in my opinion your Lordship might table at a cheaper rate, yet I cannot but very much approve of your Lordship's project of setling and keeping house in the manner you represent, and for the good reasons you give for it in your letter if Providence but enables your Lordship to go on with it. Methinks the good Benedictines, having the example before them of the Jesuits and Clergy, might be prevailed on to allow your Lordship £20 a year towards such an expense, and your Lordship I hope will have £20 a year more after the death of Mr. Rivers which, in all appearance cannot be far off. . . . At least all my best endeavours shall not be wanting to effect it.

What has ? done as to Contributions from the Clergy? Though all are not willing to contribute, some at least I hope will not refuse, and if your Lordship could but have in all £100 a year certain coming in, [with] other little perquisites merely casual, it might with good management possibly doe at least in a tolerable manner. I heartily wish your Lordship a good journey to London whenever you goe, and a safe return to us, and if your Lordship want money for that journey I will endeavour to prevail with Perkinson and others concerned, though the year is not yet expired, to procure for you the £20 from the Clergy, and Mr. Tunstall five guineas. In all £25-5-0.

When you see your Brethren, good Bp. Giffard and Bp. Petre, you'l be pleased to give my most humble respects to them both. I am surely sorry for the death of our Holy Father, and shall earnestly pray we may be made happy in a successor of the same good spirit.[1]

Nine months later a letter from Mr. Royden, the bishop's ' Grand Vicar ' for Lancashire and the western counties of the District, shows the difficulties continuing :

. . . Mr. Williams now a housekeeper at Hudleston Hall . . . has writ to Mr. Parkinson and to Mr. Rigby; and desired this latter to communicate the matter of his letter to Dr. Carnaby and myselfe. The heads of Mr. Williams' letter are to this effect :

That he could not find anybody willing to entertain him in their houses gratis; or as a Boarder or tabler. This forced him to a resolution of living entirely to himself in winter quarters.

[1] Ushaw MSS., II, 31.

That he had layd out almost all his ready money upon the furniture of his Chappell, lodging roomes, kitchin, stable, garden, etc.   That the income he can reckon upon will not answer his necessary expenses.   That he cannot live with[out] a Priest to say prayers to him when indisposed . . . , two servants at least, and three horses.   This obliges him to have recourse to his Vicars to consult what proper means may be taken to supply his necessities.   He proposes finally an alternative : either a contribution from the Laity to subsist him this winter.   Or if that fail a collection from the seculars and Regulars *per modum subsidii charitativi*.   Which a Bishop (says he) by the Canons may demand upon urgent occasions.

This to the Yorkshire Brethren seems a Nice Article. Especially after presents to the value of 32 guineas; and £20 yearly for two years, and promised to continue if the low ebbe of their Funds and ill payments will allow it, after many great losses by the Bank of Paris.

I have writ to all the Reverend Deans on this important Case, that we may act with deliberation, Prudence, and Concert, as such a weighty affair requires.

The main points are; whether we shall address the Laity for a Contribution : Or, if that be disliked, whether we shall make a collection.   Lastly, if a collection is agreed upon, what summe is to be raised by the Secular Clergy. . . .[1]

It appears from a footnote in the handwriting of Dr. Dicconson that as a result a meeting of the clergy was held at Preston at which a collection was taken, and thereupon a priest ' rid over into Yorkshire, and carryed the Bishop between £20 and £30 to satisfy this request of his '.   Some six weeks later (January 20, 1731) this same Mr. Royden wrote to the bishop a report on this Preston meeting, in the course of which he said :

. . . We are all concerned, my Lord, to hear of your Necessitys, and most are willing to contribute some Reliefe, as far as our narrow and unhappy Circumstances will permit. But in Good Truth our Funds at best were smaller than in other parts; and by the late Misfortune of the Times some are entirely lost, many are reduced, because the Estates whereon they were settled have been forfeited,[2] and the Owners indebted and impoverished by their late purchases, and former Incumbrances.

---

[1] *Id.*, II, 29.

[2] This refers presumably to the consequences of the Jacobite Rising of 1715.

The consideration of their great Hardships amongst the Gentry, who have been generally sufferers, cheifly on the North of Ribble, and whose losses are very well known to us, and the world, have discouraged us from all Application to them, whilst they are much straightened in paying their debts, and too many allso more pinched by the necessary Subsistence of their Growing Familys.

Notwithstanding these Difficulties, your Lordship, will receive some Assistance from the Laity.

The Necessitys of some Brethren [sc. Clergy] can scarcely be imagined. These poor, but zealous Labourers live on a mite, and have not a mite to spare. They lament the Misfortune common to their Prelate and to themselves; and are truly mortifyed that their Bishop is in Want : that they cannot relieve him, nor be relieved by him : which was one Comfort and Resource they had from and under your Predecessours.

The small number of those who are not absolutely able, but comparatively more able than the Indigent, have at this our Meeting Resolved a Collection, and sent it by the bearer . . . who is deputed to bring our little offering, and to report and explain the Case of our Clergy, and the Condition of our Circumstances in this District, where most of the Familys are possessed by the Regulars, cheifly by the Society [of Jesus].

Tis hoped their more plentifull Contributions and Gatherings will be a full supply to your Lordship's Necessitys.

Our mite is hastened to you for your more ready Ease and Present Relief, though the method to raise it is not yet put in execution.

Thus you have the result of our Meeting, and we hope your Lordship's Goodness will please to observe that we have exerted our Poor Ability towards your Lordship's Assistance *at this Dead Lift,* as you were pleased to call it.

There is onely one thing more in our Power, viz. a Representation and Petition to the Propaganda for a yearly Pension to supply your Necessitys; to support your character; and to ease our poor Mission. This will be cordially subscribed to by all our Brethren. . . .[1]

It must have been a hard struggle to make ends meet in such circumstances, and of course the same applied to his episcopal colleagues, especially Bishop Prichard whose District, the Western, was very much poorer than the comparatively wealthy North.

[1] Ushaw MSS., II, 30.

Presumably Bishop Stonor was an exception to this, for he was of high birth, with plenty of wealthy relations, and a patrimony of his own. It is worth noting that in matters in which the bishops were in disagreement with the regulars (and these were not a few) Bishop Williams always supported his episcopal brethren,[1] thereby differing markedly from the other regular bishop, Dr. Prichard.

[1] So also had the Benedictine Bishop Ellis.

CHAPTER IX

BISHOP PRICHARD GOES TO ROME

With the consideration of Bishop Williams' difficulties this narrative has now entered the fourth decade of the century, and it finds the aged Bishop Giffard still at his post in London together with his coadjutor, Bishop Petre. In the North is the Dominican Bishop Williams, and in the West the Franciscan Bishop Prichard, while the Midland District is occupied by Bishop Stonor. But the old warrior in London was nearing the end of his long journey. Already in 1729 Robert Witham had written: 'Bishop Giffard is grown so old that his memory seems to fail him very much, and as old men are apt to be jealous he is not pleased that most of the Gentry and Priests apply themselves to Bishop Petre.' Another four years passed by, and the indomitable old bishop had at last to take to his bed. He retired to the Convent of the Institute of Mary at Hammersmith (belonging to the Order founded by Mary Ward), to which community he had long been greatly devoted. There was only one other convent[1] then in England (all religious houses being illegal), and it is truly extraordinary that the Hammersmith convent was able to exist at all in those days of persecution, even though, of course, the real nature of the house was a close secret and the nuns never wore religious dress. They greatly venerated the aged bishop and rejoiced to be able to look after him in his last days. Early in 1733 he (being then 90) became very feeble, and he said his last Mass in the convent chapel on the Feast of Corpus Christi. In August Dr. Ingleton at St. Germains reported to Mayes in Rome:

> Bishop Giffard is in a very weak condition by several painful distempers, which leave little or no hopes of recovery. He is retired to Hammersmith, where he waits for his dissolution with wonderful patience. My correspondent tells me he is wholly rapt in God and continual prayer. I believe him one of the greatest examples which the Mission in England has produced; and his loss will be irreparable.[2]

[1] The Bar Convent, York.
[2] Ep. Var., X, 113.

Fifteen years earlier, Giffard himself had written :

> I have been full forty years in the practice of pastoral duties.
> Many failings must have happened. A dreadfull account
> approaches, the thought whereof very often makes me tremble;
> and yet as I entered not into my present charge, but by the
> pressing advice of persons the most pious, zealous and learned,
> so I dare not lay it down, but with the lyke advice.

Now he lay peacefully in the chaplain's house at Hammersmith,
and continued there for nine months more. His 91st birthday
came and went, and still he lingered. How his mind must have
travelled back in those days of quiet waiting! Back, perhaps, to
his boyhood at Douay in the days of Oliver Cromwell, to his first
chaplaincy in the house of Sir John Arundel at Lanherne in
Cornwall, to that strange interlude when he was President of
Magdalen College, Oxford, and then on to the wonderful scene
of his consecration as bishop in the Banquetting Hall in Whitehall
in those brief spacious days of James II, and after that the long,
weary, dangerous years, forty-five of them, of his hunted and
hidden episcopate under William III, Queen Anne, George I,
and George II. It was during these last months that, on
September 26, 1733, he made his will.[1] That done, he had the
happiness of being able to devote himself entirely to his spiritual
affairs, to commune with God, and to prepare for the end that
was now close at hand. It came at last on March 12, 1734, and
was reported to Rome by his coadjutor and successor, Bishop
Petre, in these words :

> Our Excellent Prelate, Bonaventure Giffard, worn out with
> his Apostolic labours and a far advanced age, having cele-
> brated Mass on last Corpus Christi Day, has almost ever
> since been confined to his chamber, where he wasted away by
> degrees under the torture of the stranguary, till being reduced
> to skin and bones he was constrained to keep his bed on the
> 1st inst. From that day he laboured under a continual strong
> fever, which often made him delirious; but even then it
> appeared that his heart had taken a strong bent towards God
> and his flock, by the expressions he let fall in those raving fits.
> His Lordship during the ten last months frequently desired and
> received the Sacraments with extraordinary fervour, humility

---

[1] It will be found in Appendix VI.

and confidence : and on last Tuesday, the Feast of St. Gregory, the great Apostle of England, half an hour after eleven at night, amidst the tears of his spiritual daughters in their Community at Hammersmith, just as their priest, his confessor, was concluding for the second time the Recommendation of the soul, he gave up his pious spirit into the hands of God, in the 92nd year[1] of his age, and 46th of his Episcopate.[2]

In accordance with his own special request, his heart was extracted and taken to Douay, where it was buried in the choir of the College with impressive ceremonial.

In the year following Bishop Giffard's death the secular clergy made an effort to put an end to the Jesuit control of the English College in Rome. Allusion to this has already been made in the letter written by Edward Dicconson in July, 1735,[3] just after Bishops Stonor and Petre had decided to take up the matter. But Mayes, who was on the spot, thought it would be impossible to dislodge the Jesuits because of their great power in Rome, as it would be impolitic for the Pope to offend those who had such great influence at foreign Courts, and he continued to maintain this defeatist attitude throughout the proceedings, much to the irritation of Stonor, who decided none the less to send in a petition on the subject. At this time, as at many others, Mayes was in a very delicate position, because as Agent in Rome he had to serve five masters : the four Vicars Apostolic and the President of Douay (Robert Witham), while they, for their part, held conflicting views and were often torn by dissensions. Bishops Prichard and Stonor had long been at loggerheads for a variety of reasons, partly personal, partly political, and partly ecclesiastical; and Stonor and Witham were also old opponents. Nor did Stonor have a high opinion of Bishop Petre. This state of affairs was by no means new. As long before as 1723 Bishop Stonor himself had lamented these dissensions when trying to get a decree from Rome against the regulars. For this purpose he wanted a

---

[1] Oliver (*Collections Illustrating the History of the Catholic Religion*) says he was 99, others give his age as 89, but the above appears to be correct, for it agrees with a statement made by Giffard himself some years earlier.

[2] Characteristically Bp. Petre ended his letter by requesting that he himself might now be allowed to resign and not have to succeed Bishop Giffard, and two months later he tried again. But Witham, Ingleton and others all wrote opposing this, and for the same reason: the danger of a regular getting the post.

[3] See above, p. 101.

petition signed by all the Vicars Apostolic, but this was a dream, as he himself confessed to Mayes :

> Who is it that will make us so unanimous as to join in such a request?   Madauris will not act; Prusensis dare not; Marcopol is afraid of every shadow; and my good brother, Myrenensis, is very waspish and intractable.   God mend us all, and those we have to do with.[1]

And so the unfortunate Mayes had no easy task in trying to please everyone, and to obey conflicting instructions.   And at this time, while Edward Dicconson (the future Vicar Apostolic of the North) was writing in friendly terms to Mayes, he was secretly denouncing him to Stonor and saying that he ought to be humbled.   Into this maelstrom Bishop Prichard then quite unwittingly blundered, for it became known that he was about to go to Rome.   At once all were asking the reason for this unusual step.[2]   What was the sinister motive behind it?   Stonor was quite certain that he knew what was afoot, for he declared that Prichard was known to be the tool of the Jesuits and therefore he was obviously going to Rome to help them to retain control of the English College.   It is rather curious, incidentally, that Stonor should have launched this charge, because undue friendship with the ' Padri ' was precisely the accusation that had constantly been made against himself in his younger days, and was for long one of the main reasons for the distrust felt for him by the clergy.   Curiously enough, too, Prichard's regular colleague, Bishop Williams, also thought that Prichard was going as an agent of the Jesuits, but Bishop Petre and Dr. Witham thought the contrary.   And Witham took occasion to point out that whereas Stonor was taking the lead in this matter of the English College, it was he who had refused (as a friend of the Jesuits) to sign the Remonstrance of 1728 on this very subject, although Bishops Giffard, Petre and Prichard had all signed it.

This was the situation when Bishop Stonor in 1736 proposed that Dicconson should go out to Rome to further the scheme, to urge Mayes into greater activity, and to keep an eye on the

---

[1] Ep. Var., VIII, 119.   This habit of referring to the bishops by their titular sees was quite a common one.   ' Madauris ' was Giffard; ' Prusensis ' was Petre; ' Marcopol ' was George Witham; and ' Myrenensis ' was Prichard.

[2] It was in fact unprecedented.   No ruling Vicar Apostolic had ever gone to Rome, and none did again until Milner, nearly a century later.

movements of Bishop Prichard. Bishop Petre agreed with this plan, but Dicconson himself demurred. He said that he had been looking forward to a quiet retirement in his old age (he was then 66) and had been laying by savings for that purpose, and that this business would spoil both prospects; though he added that he would agree to go from a sense of duty, especially as Dr. Stonor offered to raise funds for his journey. This attitude on Dicconson's part is of interest, because it shows that he, who had been time and time again proposed to Rome for a bishopric, had now abandoned hopes of one; yet in fact he was to succeed Williams as Bishop in the North within four years of this date. Point is added to this by a letter which he wrote to Stonor (agreeing to go to Rome), dated October 13, 1736, which added under great secrecy that he had had the 'good news' that Bishop Williams now wanted a coadjutor, and had fixed on Dr. Carnaby (a prominent secular priest). After saying: 'I wish he be not diverted from so good a design' (i.e. of restoring the Northern Episcopate to the seculars), he says that the clergy should at once get a written instrument executed by Bishop Williams in which he *petitions* Rome for Dr. Carnaby, for Bishop Witham had spoiled his applications for a coadjutor by *nominating* whom he wanted. It is clear he little thought that he himself was to have the succession. In fact he wrote to Mr. Royden (from whom he had had the news):

> The account you had from Yorkshire is most agreeable tidings. Dr. Carnaby would gladly have put me in that place. As he did that out of zeal for the public good and love of me, so from the same motives and also of gratitude to him for that good will of his, I shall think myself happy if I can contribute to sett the mitre on his head.

And he added that Stonor would help in this, and he would get Mayes to work for it.[1]

In the autumn of 1736 Dr. Prichard set out on his journey, and he passed through Douay and Paris on his way to Rome, protesting at both places that he was no agent of the Jesuits, and Dr. Witham added that he knew that Prichard had rejected the *offers* of the Jesuits with scorn. Dining at St. Gregory's College in Paris, the bishop declared that the sole object of his journey

---

[1] Bp. Dicconson's Papers, I, 126 (Ushaw).

was to obtain a subsidy from Rome to relieve the terrible poverty of his Vicariate, or else that he might be allowed to retire to his monastery. In November Dr. Stonor wrote to Mayes in most friendly terms, with no hint of reproof, and told him that Dicconson was coming out to help him. The instructions which Dicconson received from the bishops were that he should work for the restoration of the English College to the secular clergy and to obtain financial help for its upkeep; but there were also secret instructions from Bishop Stonor : ' You will get an account of what yearly income is annexed to the Agency, and endeavour to find out what are Mr. Mayes' sentiments as to the keeping of it, or having a successor; of all which you will give us an account, together with judgment on the matter.'[1]

In the new year Mayes was as despondent on the matter as ever, and his conversations with Bishop Prichard did not seem to make him more optimistic. In February the bishop wrote from Rome to Witham at Douay to say that he found the whole business held up by the illness of the Cardinal Protector, and so he himself had had no opportunity of giving any help regarding it, though he was ready to do so, as he had promised to Bishop Petre and Dr. Challoner[2] before leaving England. He also said that the Jesuits were confident of their ability to retain control of the College, and that Mayes thought nothing could be done. But Dicconson, who was now on his leisurely way to Rome, wrote to Mayes from Paris, saying that instead of desponding he should have induced Prichard ' to make a proper declaration in writing to be given to one of the Visitors to the College. This, if obtained, must have been of great service. If not, it would have let you see further into him ', and added that if Prichard were sincere he should surely have offered something of the sort of his own accord; and he hints that Mayes was remiss in his duty. Plainly Dicconson was still full of suspicion of Prichard's motives and intentions.[3] Only four days later (March 14), Prichard reached Paris on his way home, and there he had a long interview with Dicconson, who had not yet left for Rome, and who reported the substance of it to Bishop Stonor. In this letter of March 20

[1] *Idem.*, III, 351, 355.
[2] Challoner became Petre's coadjutor in 1740, but at this time he was working in London as a priest and had considerable influence with Bishop Petre.
[3] Ep. Var., XI, 15.

he said that Prichard ' seems mightily satisfied with the success he met with at Rome. He over and over again declared that he did not only wish me success, but that he would readily concur on his part to procure it ', and had agreed to write a letter that could be shown to Propaganda. ' In short he is either sincere, or has acted it to the life. He told me my going was necessary, because Mr. Mayes was quite cowed.' He then added that he had told Prichard how much harm had been done by the long coldness between Prichard and Stonor :

> This did not relish quite so well with him as the other topic; but before we quitted that head, I found him very much softened. . . . The which I set down here, [so] that if you think it proper you may perhaps have the opportunity of meeting [him] at London, and from thence forward be upon better terms. Which, if you do, I now really believe, by your address, he may be prevailed upon to do very considerable services in this affair. . . . I find him very much nettled at the Padri's [sc. Jesuits] proceedings in his regard.

He not only allowed his companion (Fra Chapman) to criticize the Jesuit management of the College, ' but often chimes in with him and approves it in all our hearing '. And he concluded by saying that what Prichard had told him about Roman affairs had been confirmed by others, which makes him believe that Prichard is sincere.[1]

But Bishop Stonor's long reply to this made no mention of the proposed reconciliation with the Franciscan bishop. Two months later Dicconson at last reached Rome, on May 13, and reported that he had been warmly welcomed by Mayes who was in bad health. Dicconson also took occasion to write of the ' lamentable ' condition of the English Mission, which, he said, had never had less than 300 secular priests and sometimes 400, but now had only 156, of which the great majority were educated at poverty-stricken Douay—far more than those produced by the Jesuits at richly endowed colleges. Soon after Dicconson's arrival Stonor rebuked Mayes for his pessimism in this matter of the College and ordered him to carry on with the task according to the instructions of the bishops. If he did not like this, let him come home and take Stonor's place, and the latter will

[1] Bp. Dicconson's Papers, I, 127 (Ushaw).

resign. It is pleasing to find, however, that in January, 1738, seven months after his arrival, Dicconson said that he now regretted the things he had said about Mayes before leaving England, and that he now finds him a truly good Christian. Although Mayes had been deeply jealous of him when he first came, that had now been obliterated by tactful patience. It was during this winter that there arrived in Rome a young student who was to play a prominent part in English Catholic affairs for very many years to come. This was ' Kit ' Stonor, the bishop's nephew, who came to Rome in December, 1737, to study Canon Law, and in the very next month Dicconson suggested to the bishop that his nephew might be trained to take Mayes' place eventually. He was then at the Academia, and ten years later he became Mayes' assistant, and on his death soon afterwards he succeeded him as Agent in Rome of the English bishops, holding the post for nearly fifty years.

But the affair of the control of the College languished, and Mayes in despair suggested a compromise, by which Italian Jesuits should be substituted for the English Jesuits then in charge. But this solution made no appeal to Bishop Stonor, nor to Dicconson, and in the end the whole matter petered out, and Dicconson returned home, after parting from Mayes with coldness on both sides. This was apparently in 1740, because Dicconson said several years later that the coldness had been partly caused by a belief on Mayes' part that Dicconson did not support Mayes' proposal of Francis Petre to succeed to the Northern Vicariate vacant by the death of Bishop Williams, which occurred in 1740. Mayes thought that Dicconson wanted the appointment himself. The position is rather piquant, because actually it was Dicconson who did get it.[1] But Dicconson declared in the letter alluded to above that he never desired or sought it, and was convinced he was unfit for it, and that in fact he had not even heard of Petre's candidature. He takes the opportunity of stating that when Bishop Witham of the Northern District urged him in 1722 to be his coadjutor he refused for two years until Bishop Giffard

as our Patriarch, layed his hands upon my head and *commands* me to submit, which then I did; promising to comply with his

[1] Twelve years later (1752) he was succeeded in the Vicariate by this Francis Petre.

Brother Witham's desires. But how these failed, and what followed after, I need not repeat to you.[1]

What did follow, of course, was the appointment of Bishop Williams to succeed to Witham; but now after fourteen years in charge of the Northern District the bishop was a very old man. The end came for him at 4 a.m. on Holy Thursday morning, April 16 (N.S.), 1740, at the house of his patron Sir Edward Gascoigne, Huddlestone Hall, six miles from Pontefract. Thence the body was taken some four miles to the historic chapel of Sir Walter Vavasour at Hazlewood (half-way between Leeds and York), where his tomb may still be seen.[2]

And now at last the man whose name had so often figured on the *terna* of candidates was to be promoted to the episcopate. It is extraordinary that almost thirty years earlier (five years before the consecration of Bishop Stonor who was now about to celebrate his silver jubilee as a bishop) Dr. Dicconson had been suggested by Bishop Giffard for the Northern District then vacant by the death of Bishop Smith; and since then his name had frequently reappeared on such lists. For all these years he had been considered eminently fitted for the episcopate, and it was unfortunate that he had had to wait so long, for by the time he was appointed he was 71 years old, and his activity was therefore naturally much restricted.

Edward Dicconson was the fourth son of Hugh Dicconson of Wrightington Hall, Lancashire, and was born in 1670. Entering Douay as a boy, he was a Professor there from 1708 to 1720, and for the last six years of that period was Vice-President to Dr. Witham, and then went to the English Mission where he was chaplain at Chillington, Bishop Giffard's old home in Staffordshire. A man of great ability, he always stood very high in the estimation of the clergy, but unfortunately he was afflicted with a stammer which prevented him from preaching. At this time he also became Vicar General to Bishop Stonor, and his administrative experience was doubtless enlarged by his four years in Rome on the affair of the English College, which afforded him

[1] Ep. Var., XII, 148.
[2] The present writer recalls the surprise with which some years ago, when wandering in the chapel and churchyard at Hazlewood, he came upon an ornate tomb which proved to be that of Bp. Williams (of whom he had then never heard); and a few minutes later a second which was that of Bp. Briggs, a later V.A. of the North.

an insight into Roman methods and procedure. On the conclusion of this he received the appointment to the Northern Vicariate and was consecrated at Ghent by the Bishop of that city on March 19, 1741, after which he departed for England. Hitherto the Vicars Apostolic of the Northern District had lived in Northumberland and Yorkshire, but Dicconson was a Lancashire man and he transferred his headquarters to that county, settling at his family home at Wrightington.

Chapter X

TWO NEW BISHOPS

THE coming of the seventeen-forties brought two new bishops on the scene, both of them as coadjutors, the one to the Western District and the other to the London District. In the West Bishop Prichard had been twenty-five years in charge, and it had been known for some time past that he wanted help. It was generally expected that he would secure another Franciscan as his coadjutor, but in fact the Holy See turned again to the Benedictine Order and selected the Prior (i.e. Superior) of St. Gregory's monastery in Douay,[1] Dom Laurence York. The new bishop-elect was a Londoner by birth, having been born there in 1687, during the brief reign of James II. As a boy he had gone to St. Gregory's for his schooling, and there he became a professed monk in 1705, and a priest in 1711. Ten years later he became Prior of St. Edmund's Priory in Paris[2] for the usual term of four years, and then was chosen to fill the same office in his own monastery at Douay for the next four years (1725-1729), after which he came over to the English Mission and was given charge of the mission at Bath. It was eleven years later that he was appointed coadjutor to Bishop Prichard, and he was consecrated as Bishop of Nisibi on August 10, 1741, at Douay. As coadjutor he continued to reside at Bath (his chief, Bishop Prichard, always lived in Monmouthshire), and he was there when the Jacobite Rebellion of 1745 broke out. This event had an unpleasant consequence for himself, for a certain anti-Catholic bigot saw an opportunity for making trouble for the bishop. He forged a letter which purported to be from Prince Charles to Bishop York, and which conveyed the Prince's thanks for help and encouragement given to the rebels, and a promise of the bishopric of Carlisle in return for the services he had rendered. This letter was taken to the Mayor of Bath, and although that official realized that the letter was a forgery, he suggested that it would be prudent for the bishop to retire from

---

[1] This is the Community which is now at Downside.
[2] Now Douai Abbey, Woolhampton.

143

Bath for a time.   This Dr. York did, but was soon able to return from his exile.

Five years more passed, and then the aged Bishop Prichard fell ill at Perthyre, the estate of the Powell family with whom he had so long lived.   He had been 37 years a bishop and had reached the age of 81[1] when at length he died at Perthyre on May 22, 1750, and there he was buried.   His tombstone may still be seen there under the 'Communion table' of the local Protestant parish church : perhaps the most peculiar place of burial that fell to any of the Vicars Apostolic.   In connection with that there is a story told by a modern parish priest of Monmouth.   After saying that the bishop's tombstone forms the predella under the Communion table or altar in Rockfield Parish Church, he continues :

> The late incumbent was a bigoted parson.   In doing some repairs to the church he had this [tombstone] and two other Catholic tombstones removed, and offered for sale as waste materials!   This I heard from some of the Protestant parishioners; so I walked over, and saw the stones reared against the boundary wall.   The Vicar happened to call upon me, with his wife, a few days after on some business; so I asked him why he had removed the Bishop's tombstone.   He said he did not think it right to have a 'Romish' bishop's tombstone there.   I said, 'Are you not going to replace it?' He replied, 'No, certainly not.'   Then I said, 'I will write to my friend the Rev. Dr. Oliver of Exeter, who has published the history of Bp. Prichard with a full description of his Lordship's burial there and the inscription on the stone, and I will get him to put a footnote in the next edition to the effect that, through the bigotry of the Rev. — this monument was removed in such a year.'   He then said he would have it replaced immediately.   I said, 'If you don't, I will hand down your name to posterity like Pontius Pilate's in the Creed.'   It has been replaced, and his successor, I am told, still repeats the anecdote to visitors.[2]

The death of Bishop Prichard made Dr. York automatically

---

[1] The longevity of these early Vicars Apostolic is surprising.   An examination of their ages reveals the fact that of the 14 bishops who figure in these pages, no fewer than eight lived to be over 80 (one of them over 90), and of the remaining six, five lived to be over 70.

[2] Letter from Fr. Abbott to Alfred Williams, quoted in Catholic Record Society, IX, 165.

Vicar Apostolic of the Western District, but the other bishops did not like the idea of the District remaining in the hands of the regulars, and so when in 1756 he wanted to have a coadjutor and put forward the name of a fellow-monk, Charles Walmesley, they demurred. Rome had, in fact, instructed the bishops to name two seculars and two regulars for the vacancy, but Dr. Stonor suggested to the others that they should refuse to name any regular, and this idea had the approval of both Bishop Petre and his coadjutor, Challoner. The latter wrote to Stonor, October 7, 1755 :

> Mr. White[1] is entirely of your mind as to the declining the recommending of any of the regulars for the reason you alledge. And as to seculars, he likes the persons you speak of; only he is more inclined to name Alban Butler (whom he thinks the gentry of that part of the world will be more taken with) than Mr. Walton.[2] . . . If the choice should fall on your nephew,[3] I know not what we should do for one to succeed him in his present state, in which he does us signal service.

Yet in the event it was Walmesley who was appointed.[4] The attitude of the bishops in this matter may well have been influenced by the recent issue of Pope Benedict XIV's famous Bull *Apostolicum Ministerium* of May 30, 1753, which at last put an end to the very long-standing dispute between the bishops and the regulars over the question of faculties and the rights of the regulars, and which reinforced the Decree of 1745 on the same subject. For Bishop Prichard had sided with his fellow-regulars in this dispute, and had refused to sign the bishops' promulgation of the decree; and moreover both he and his coadjutor, Bishop York, had protested to Rome against it, as having been surreptitiously obtained.

The same year, 1741, that saw the consecration of Bishop York to the Western District, brought about that of Dr. Challoner as coadjutor in the London District. With him we meet probably

[1] Bishop Petre.

[2] V.A. Northern District, 1775–1780.

[3] Mgr. ' Kit ' Stonor, the Clergy Agent in Rome. Like his predecessor in that office, Mgr. Mayes, he was frequently suggested for various episcopal vacancies.

[4] The names put on the *terna* by the bishops were Charles Howard, James Talbot (later V.A. of the London District), and Christopher Stonor.

the best-known to-day of all the Vicars Apostolic, and certainly one of the greatest; but most of his episcopate lies outside the period covered by this book. He was born at Lewes of Protestant parents on September 29, 1691, but while he was yet a young child his widowed mother became a Catholic and the boy was received into the Church by the celebrated Dr. Gother, and by him sent to be educated at Douay, where he remained from 1705 to 1730, and where he had a brilliant career. Ordained priest in 1717, he was Vice-President of the College three years later and won his Doctorate in 1727. He left for England in 1730 and the rest of his laborious life (save for a brief exile at Douay in 1737-38 owing to persecution in England) was spent in London, where at the time of his arrival Bishop Giffard's long episcopate was drawing to a close, and where Challoner himself fifty years later would still be Vicar Apostolic.

But in 1738 there arose a crisis in his life, for in May of that year, while Challoner was at Douay during his above-mentioned exile, Dr. Witham, President of Douay, died, and Challoner was chosen to succeed him. But before he could take up the position Bishop Petre intervened, declaring that he must have Challoner as his coadjutor in the London District. A long struggle then took place for the services of Dr. Challoner. What had happened was that when dying Dr. Witham had nominated him as his successor, and the Nuncio at Brussels appointed him as President and wrote to Bishop Stonor to that effect. Thereupon the bishop wrote to Dr. Hornyold (his future coadjutor and successor, and a close friend of Challoner) on May 14, 1738 :

> The disputes about the Presidency of Douay College are in a fair way of ending well, though in a manner much feared by my brother Peters [sc. Bp. Petre], for which reason he engaged strongly on Mr. Kendal's side.[1] The Nuncio has at last declared in a letter to me, that having Mr. Witham's choice of Dr. Challoner, signed under his hand, he actually deputed the said Dr. Challoner for the Presidency of that College; to which end a letter to the said Doctor was enclosed in mine to be sent to him by me, and I was desired to manage things in ye best manner I could with ye Bishop and ye Doctor, that ye latter might be dismissed immediately and repair to ye

---

[1] Kendal was one of the professors at Douay, and Bp. Petre wished him to be appointed President.

College.[1] In pursuance of these orders, I have sent ye letter to ye Doctor and writ to ye Bishop.

To this Bishop Petre reacted vigorously, and wrote a strong protest to Mgr. Mayes on May 15 :[2]

> I am told by a letter from Bishop Stonor that Mr. Witham has been prevailed upon, by what means or by whom I cannot absolutely determine, to sign a paper wherein he prefers and nominates the Doctor. To this nomination I earnestly desire that you make all the opposition that is possible, not only on my account, but for the good of my whole district, and I may truly say, of all in this mission [sc. England] : for he is frequently consulted by persons of all denominations in all Districts. I cannot satisfy my duties without his help and counsel; nor will presume to do it. If he be forced from me by Superior Powers, for I will never give my consent to his leaving this metropolis whilst I continue in my post, in that case be pleased to send me the usual form of resignation of my duty. Not only in that case, but at all times and hours, I will most heartily and joyfully resign my office to him, because I am certain it will conduce more to the general good and satisfaction of the people of England, than his going to Douay, for the government of which there are many sufficiently qualified. . . . I writ by last post to Mr. Tempi to desire his opposition to the election of Dr. Challoner, and amongst other reasons I mentioned the danger and risk of losing many hundreds lately converted, if he were to be removed from hence. I concluded my letter with these words ' Ille si mihi ablatus fuerit, ego muneri renuntiabo.'

In November Dr. Day (Dean of the Chapter), writing to Stonor of the plan to keep Challoner in London, mentions :

> the *fatal* settlement upon the Vicars, that when the Vicar Apos. of this [London] district dies, he is to be succeeded at once by the eldest [in Vicarship] of the others. You know also that if Bp. Petre and Bp. Prichard should die before you (as they probably may, they being older than you) then you of course are to succeed in this District.

This is a mysterious statement, to which no other reference can be found. If such an arrangement did in fact exist, clearly it

---

[1] He had by then returned from Douay to London.
[2] Ep. Var., XI, 45.

was set aside when Petre applied for Challoner as his coadjutor with right of succession. Be that as it may, Bishop Petre had made up his mind about Challoner and nothing would make him give way. It says much for his delineation of character that he picked out Challoner with an unerring eye as being outstandingly fitted to be his helper and his successor. At first it seemed out of the question that he should obtain Challoner, for Douay had already chosen him and obtained approval from Rome, where the Cardinals of Propaganda wished him to accept the post. But for once Petre proved immovable and undismayed. So vehemently did he write to Rome time and time again imploring the services of Challoner, and even threatening flatly to resign forthwith unless Challoner came to him, that eventually he got his way, so that instead of spending the rest of his life in the academic peace and dignity of Douay, Richard Challoner had before him forty years in the slums of London. The glowing encomiums which Petre wrote about him at this time remind the reader forcibly of Bishop Giffard's similarly enthusiastic praise of Henry Howard when applying for him as coadjutor. Thus, in his letter to the Pope, dated April 10, 1739, two years before the appointment was actually made, Dr. Petre wrote in these words:

Most Holy Father,
   Urged by advancing years I most humbly desire that the Rev. Richard Challoner may be granted to me as my Co-adjutor. For I am now in my 68th year, when, besides the weakness of body, which I feel to be growing on me daily, I recognise that I am in a measure breaking down and am thus incapacitated from the labour and care necessary in tending so large a flock, whose spiritual government calls for a Pastor of vigorous age, who can bring to the task all his strength and powers.[1] He has scarcely reached his 49th year, but by his many remarkable gifts of mind, his great humility and gentleness, by his assiduous fidelity in reclaiming sinners to the way of life taught by the Gospel and to the truth of our religion, by his marvellous power in preaching, in instructing the ignorant and in writing books both spiritual and con-troversial, he has won not only the esteem but the veneration of all who have heard him preach or who have read his books. And so, I seem to myself justified in my conviction that out of all whom we have on our mission I could not choose

[1] In point of fact he lived for a further 19 years.

anyone as my Coadjutor more welcome or more acceptable to my flock and to all Catholics. And I am persuaded that he, who in zeal for souls and in learning will prove himself equal to, and perhaps greater than, all that have gone before him, will be regarded as a shining and burning Light in the Church, a Leader beyond all cavil, and an Example to all labouring in our vineyard. By this estimate and expectation of Richard Challoner, Doctor in Theology of the University of Douay, which I have long had implanted in my mind, I am led to the hope that this, my humble suppliant petition, may be favourably received. And I confess that to have it granted would be to me a consolation and help past all belief.

And now I humbly beg the Apostolic Benediction for myself and the flock committed to me. Being the most humble and dutiful servant of your Holiness,

Benjamin, Bp. of Prusa and Vicar Apostolic.[1]

These were truly prophetic words. And in the end Dr. Petre got his way, and he himself consecrated Challoner at the convent at Hammersmith (where Giffard had died), on January 29, 1741.

And so began Challoner's long period of episcopal activity in London, for although it was not till 1758 that the death of Bishop Petre made Challoner Vicar Apostolic, yet in reality he governed the London District for all intents and purposes from the day of his consecration in 1741, for Dr. Petre left practically everything to him and himself retired to the depths of the country for the remainder of his days. Challoner's effective rule of the District thus lasted forty years, and they were years which contained not a wasted day nor an idle hour. A typical day in his life of prayer and labour has been described by one of his early biographers :

Summer and winter he rose at 6, and spent an hour in meditation, after which he offered the Holy Sacrifice at 8. At 9 he breakfasted, and then, having said the Little Hours of his Office, he attended to business till 1. When tired with writing he would take a few turns backward and forward in his apartment, then take some pious book to read, say some prayers, or, sitting in his chair, contemplate on some pious subject, and then return again to his writing. At 1 he used to say the evening part of the Divine Office, which finished, he used either to say some vocal prayers or else employ himself in meditation until 2, when, with his chaplains, he sat

[1] As translated in Burton, *Op. cit.*, I, 112.

K

down to dinner, at which time he unbent a little his mind from that close application, and was always very cheerful and agreeable, discoursing with them on different subjects. Dinner being over, he remained in conversation for half an hour, and then walked out to pay visits, or to take such exercise as he required. Between 5 and 6 he returned to resume his business or writing. Later in the evening he said his Office, and shortly after supper he retired.[1]

One of his chief characteristics was his great devotion to the poor, and, indeed, Bishop Milner declared of him :

> He considered himself as particularly commissioned to preach to the poor, whose cellars, garrets, hospitals, workhouses, and prisons were much more agreeable, as well as familiar, to him, than the splendid habitations of the great and opulent.

Those are words which are reminiscent of what was said of Henry Howard, the beloved assistant of Bishop Giffard. And Dr. Milner's formidable opponent, Charles Butler, was equally enthusiastic in his praise of Challoner :

> He carried piety and recollection with him wherever he went, and diffused them among all that were present. He was very cheerful, and the cause of cheerfulness in others, but he stopped very short of mirth. He was always serene, affable, unaffected, prudent and charitable, and never said anything which tended even remotely to his own advantage. He always listened with modest attention, and interrupted no one unless the glory of his God, or the defence of his neighbour made it necessary.

Yet all the while he was a hunted man (perhaps even more so than Dr. Giffard had been, although, unlike him, he did not actually go to prison), for his zeal and his controversial skill had raised many enemies against him, and this persecution lasted to the very end of his days. All his life he lived in poor lodgings, rather than in a house of his own, for the purpose of having thus more to give away to the destitute. His long life spanned the most desolate period of the penal times, when the numbers of Catholics sank to the lowest point they ever reached in England,

[1] Dr. Barnard, quoted by Burton, *Op. cit.*

when hope was well-nigh dead amongst them, and when courage
and faith were very necessary qualities in a Vicar Apostolic. Yet
through it all faith and hope burned brightly in his soul, and his
confidence in the future of the Church in England never wavered.

And while Challoner was thus beginning his laborious ministry
in London, far away in Rome another great labourer was
drawing near the end of his days. Mgr. Lawrence Mayes had
become Agent in Rome of the English bishops as long ago as
1706, as a young man of 33 (having been born at Yarm in
Yorkshire in 1673). He had been educated at Douay from the
age of 14, and continuing there as a student for the priesthood,
had in due course been ordained, and later became Professor of
Divinity until he took up his post in Rome which he was to fill till
the end of his life. His success in that capacity was marked by
his appointment as a Protonotary Apostolic in 1721, and it is of
interest that in 1727 he was Preceptor to the Young Pretender,
Prince Charles. Now, at the period of which we have been
writing above, he was an old man. He had had a vast experience
of Roman ways, and routine, and etiquette, had known many
Popes and a multitude of Roman prelates, and through his hands
had passed all the most important and most secret business of the
English bishops. In 1748, at the age of 75, he was ready to hand
over his charge into younger hands and to give another the benefit
of his ripe experience. Fortunately such a one was at hand and
ready to take over.

Christopher ('Kit') Stonor was an ideal successor to Mgr.
Mayes and had been carefully trained with a view to succeeding
to the post since his first arrival in Rome as a student twelve years
earlier. Nephew of Bishop Stonor and grandson of Lord
Teynham, he had entered St. Gregory's College, Paris, in 1739,[1]
after concluding his studies in Rome, and it was in 1748 that, at
the age of about 36, he returned to Rome as assistant to Mayes,
from whom he took over before the end of the year. He, in his
turn, was to hold that post till his death 47 years later, and to
acquire a wealth of experience and a reputation equal to that
of his predecessor. Meanwhile, at the threshold of his career
in Rome as Agent, he wrote from Paris to Mgr. Mayes on
'April ye 15', 1748, a letter that is attractive in its modesty and
in its deference to the old priest :

[1] Kirk, *Biographies*.

Sir,

The enclosed for you I had from my unkle[1] at parting, with orders to forward it to you as soon as possible. I hope you will excuse the liberty I take of accompanying it with a few lines of my own. The forwardness with which you accepted of the proposal made you by our Bishops in my regard, and the obligeing manner in which you was so good as to mention me to my Unkle, deserve to be always gratefully acknowledged. I propose doing it soon by word of mouth in a more ample manner, and hope by my future behaviour to merit the continuation of the same sentiments from you, and by following your example, profiting of your instructions, and punctually obeying your orders will use my best endeavors to render myself not altogether unworthy of the good opinion, which you and the Bishops in England seem to have conceived of me. I arrived here last Wednesday from Calais, having taken Douay in my way, and got here just time enough to have a sight of poor Dr. Thornburgh,[2] who set out the next day back to Douay, but in such an ill state of health that I think it impossible for him to hold out much longer.[3] As to his successor, my Unkle is entirely for Dr. Green, and I found the gentlemen at Douay unanimous in the same opinion. . . . I propose, God willing, to be with you towards the middle of June. In the mean time believe me always

Dear Sir

Your most obedient Humble Servant

Christopher Stonor.[4]

In due course he arrived in Rome and took over the Agency, and at first had the benefit of the help of Mgr. Mayes, but the latter died in Rome just over a year later, on August 23, 1749. For some time Stonor lived in the household of the Cardinal of York with, we are told, £60 a year. Before very long he was made a Papal Chamberlain, and as such had apartments in the papal palace. He is described as being ' an exemplary Prelate '.

In Rome one of his first tasks was to help Bishop Dicconson of the Northern District to obtain a coadjutor. The bishop was at this time (1748) 78 years old, and he wanted to have as his

---

[1] Bishop Stonor.

[2] President of Douay.

[3] Four days later Thornburgh reported to Mayes that he had reached Douay ' in a very weak condition, though better than when I left Paris '.

[4] Ep. Var., XII, 132.

helper and successor the same Francis Petre who had been
himself proposed for the vacancy that had occurred in 1740 on
the death of Bishop Williams. On that occasion Dr. Dicconson
had been given the vacant bishopric, but he had always thought
Petre the right man for it. He therefore wrote to the Agent in
Rome asking for information as to the right way of making
application for a coadjutor, and on December 4 Christopher
Stonor replied :

Hond. Dear Sir,
. . . You have on the other side a sketch of a postulation
for a Coadjutor. Mr. Lawrence [sc. Mayes] indeed could
not find any old formulae for that purpose; but as you seemed
desirous of one, I have by his advice put this together from
the different hints mentioned in your letter. The character
of Mr. Petre may seem too much particularised for one who
is not personally acquainted with him; but I have so often had
occasion of hearing him spoken of, and always in the same
manner, that I thought I might venture to say of him what
I knew to be the general voice and opinion. As to the number
of persons to be named in the petition, Mr. Lawrence is
of opinion that you ought to mention two or three besides him,
though always with a special commendation in his favour. . . .
I need say nothing more, that what I mentioned in my last,
of the vanity of the Frati's[1] boastings in regard of M. Englefield. I am still persuaded that if the Congregation grant you
a helper it will at least be one of those mentioned in your
petition. But if contrary to all expectation and common
practice on those occasions, they should cast their eyes upon a
Regular, the Franciscans[2] would be the last thought of : their
more strict profession of Poverty making a stronger objection
against them than others. And I question much whether his
brother, Sir Harry, would be willing or even able to supply
out of his own pocket what would be wanting for his
maintenance. . . .[3]

This petition for Francis Petre,[4] if it actually was sent in at that
time, was not immediately effective, for it was not until two and
a half years later that Dr. Dicconson was given a coadjutor. But
in the end he obtained the man he wanted, and on July 27, 1751,

---

[1] I.e. the regulars.
[2] The Order to which Fra Englefield belonged.
[3] Ushaw Collection, II, 69.
[4] He was a nephew of Bishop Petre of the London District.

Petre was consecrated at Douay as coadjutor for the Northern District. Ten months later he became its Vicar Apostolic.

And so the middle of the eighteenth century is reached, and it finds the Catholic strength in England at its lowest point. As yet there was no glimmer of the coming Dawn, nor did there seem to be any hope or prospect of such a phenomenon. It is true that for over sixty years no Catholic in England had been called upon actually to shed his blood for the Faith, but on the other hand there was no sign whatever of a lessening of hostility on the part of the State, and gradual but steady ' leakage ' and apostasy still marked the passage of the years. Well might Dr. Burton say of the Church at this time : ' Her present lot was persecution without martyrdom, her future was without prospect of relief '.[1] All the more credit, then, to those steadfast and faithful leaders whose heart-breaking task it was to nurse the flickering flame, to preserve as they might the feeble remnants of the Faith in this land, and, where no grounds for hope seemed to exist, to refuse to abandon hope. This task was staunchly and unwaveringly fulfilled by the Vicars Apostolic, and we may fittingly conclude these pages by echoing the proud declaration of Bishop Milner :

The writer is bold to say that no Christian Kingdom could during the same period (1588-1788) boast a list of prelates more worthy to succeed to the chairs of the Apostles than Bishops Smith, Bishop, Giffard, Petre, and Challoner.

[1] Burton : C.T.S. Tract on Challoner.

DOCUMENTS CONCERNING THE OLD CHAPTER

A

An eighteenth-century half-sheet of notepaper in the Ushaw Archives (Ch. 1) states the following on the foundation of the Chapter:

> R.R. William Bishop, Chosen Bishop, consecrated at Paris in 1622,[1] deputed seven Vicars and erected a Chapter called of the Church of England, consisting of 24 canons, gave them a seal with the image of St. Thomas of Canterbury, created Archdeacons dividing the counties of the kingdom amongst them, to whom he substituted Rural Deans, with many other good regulations concerning good spiritual government and ecclesiastical discipline and ministered to very many the Sacrament of Confirmation. He died in 1624.

B

Many doubts were expressed from time to time as to the legality of the Chapter's position and authority in the absence of explicit confirmation by Rome, and there would seem to have been much correspondence over a lengthy period on this subject, some of which documents have survived. The following, dated August 2, 1656, is a letter from Mr. Leyburn (the future Vicar Apostolic) to the Chapter on the subject of the recognition at Rome of the Chapter's authority (Ushaw Archives, Ch. 5).

> Mr. Plantin's transactions att Rome contayned in this letter, which I heard from his owne mouth my selfe.
> Hond. Sir,
> Nothing occurring of late in order to oure maine business, and many of our Brethren desiring to know upon what grounds Mr. Plantin writ from Rome that our Chapter was sufficiently confirmed to proceed with it: I thought good to make it my taske at this time to give you satisfaction in that concerning point. I expressed the said desire in Consult, where our Agent being present, rendered his reasons after this tenor:
> that first, whereas he stood upon it to the Cardinals on all occasions, that our Chapter had sufficient Authoritie, they never

---

[1] Mazière Brady (*The Episcopal Succession in England, Scotland, and Ireland, 1400–1875*) gives the date as June 4, 1623.

contradicted him therein, nor never denied, or soe much as questioned the said Autoritie as dubious.

Secondly, that whereas he expressed to His Holiness that we desired not a confirmation of it, as tho it were not sufficiently autorized alriddy, but out of our particular Addiction to the Apostolick See, and our desire to depend on it in all waies which might express our more submissive obedience, His Holiness never questioned nor gainsaid the sufficiency of its autoritie avouched by our Agent in his presensce to himselfe, nor showed the least dislike to that pretence.

Thirdly, that after His Holiness had desired us to expect seven months for a Bishop, comming to speak of how wee should be governed in the meane time, himselfe voluntarily asked the question, numquid habetis capitulum, Decanum et subdecanum, nor did he the least word afterwards expressing or intimating the insufficiency of the said autoritie, or his disallowing it as such, but was far from it, as shall bee seene. Now what those words could signifie in those circumstances but that if wee had a Chapter and were actually governed by it, acknowledging noe other immediate authoritie over us, and alledging reasons why noe other form of government was comformable with our safetie, save that onely till wee should have a Bishop, His Holiness seemed very well satisfied with those reasons against other (?) autoritie, nor opposed in the least the said government by the Chapter, upon which he ? avouched our present and future procedure upon it : nay more, since it was mentioned by him selfe in these circumstances and upon that occasion, that he thought and adjudged it the fitest.

Fifthly (sic) : In all his expressions and carrage att the same time, as our Agent attests, he plainly signified his agreement of the Chapter, which in our circumstances did soe fully please him that such were the . . . .[1] to all our friends in Rome, that His Holiness had granted us a Bishop after seven months, and till wee had a Bishop approved of our Chapter, which argues that the Pope's expressions were satisfactory in that point to a prudent man. Nor need wee wonder that nothing was given publickly in writing, it being the best policy to countenance us on this fashion (?), whereas a publication of thus favouring us would have occasioned clamours and opposition from the adverse partie.

Sixthly : The Pope, by receiving Mr. Plantin as sent from our Chapter, and by wishing the Chapter to send the names of those persons they nominate to succeed the former Bishop,[2] doth plainly acknowledge the Chapter as the boddy upon which the Clergy is to depend untill we have a Bishop.

Lastly : our Agent being to take his leave of Cardinal Barberini, one who cannot be thought to bee ignorant what the Pope's

---

[1] At this point, owing to a crease in the paper, a whole line in the MS. is indecipherable.

[2] Bishop Richard Smith, Vicar Apostolic, 1624–1631.

intentions in this point are, as being both our Protectour and the cheife of those deputed by him to treat the business, and telling him that His Holiness had granted us a Bishop after seven months, and in the meane time confirmed our Chapter : he never signified his own doubt, or our Agent's mistake, but on the contrary replied : ' You see then you have not lost your labour ', which insinuates his assent that the thinge was soe.   Wee need not add the delaying a future Superior or appointing no other, nor one in the interim teacheth us that they have either left our ? an Anarchy in the meane time, which cannot bee Imagined by prudent governours, or else that they like well and approve of the government of the Chapter intimated by the Pope's words to bee ? in the interim.   And on the other side, nothing is more evident then this, that they not onely knew that we intended to proceed with it, but that actually we doe soe,[1] they seeing it, and yet neither in the dew opportunitie which was stood upon by our Agent as sufficient, nor afterwards, in the leastwise contradicting it, which is a most ample and undeniable testimony of a tacit confirmation of it, though wee should take all the stronge presumptions arising from the other favorable expressions.   This 'tis I was desired to communicate.

C

The following letter (Ushaw Archives, Ch. 7) concerning the Chapter's authority and rule is undated, but the writing is clearly of the seventeenth-century style :

Hond. Sir,

   Beeing solicitous on all occasions to contribute to ye conservation of that peace and amity amongst ye Brethren which Christ lefte unto his church, and which becomes people of our vocation, and haveing been lately surprized a little at ye contents of some of ye letters, wee conceived it our obligation with candidnesse and civility to represent unto you ye griefe wherewith we are touched to find yt when our Deare Brethren in all other parts of ye Nation so unanimously conspire in a perfect harmony without ye least sign of dissatisfaction in our government[2] establisht so many year ago by our first venerable Bishop[3] of happy memory by ye advice of most grave and learned persons of diverse nations, and in like manner so vigorously confirmed by our second [Bishop], you or ye neighbours should seem yet dissatisfied, and invent objections never alleadged by our Adversaryes conduceing to no other end yt we can imagine, only our disquiet, you praying in one line for peace, and in another prophecying faction and dis-

---

[1] I.e. that the Chapter continues to exercise authority in England.
[2] I.e. in the rule of the Chapter.
[3] Dr. William Bishop, 1623–1624.

turbances, this we cannot but resent and with brotherly affection intimate unto you hopeing you will also acquaint ye Neighbours.

And first passing by as you desire that strange comparison of our government (which is according to ye most Antient modells in God's Church) to the long Parliament or Cromwell which were ye most extravagant in civill matters, we neither leading nor driveing, as you object, but onely demeaning ourselves in a peaceable way according to the orders and rules prescribed us; and to come to ye difficulties :

The first, which you father on the Council of Trent in generall terms reaches us not at all, first because yt Council was never received in our Countrey except in dogmaticall things, wherefore in points of reformation it obliges not ours no more then divers other Countreys; secondly because were yt sacred Councell's decrees of force here, yet they concern not such Chapters as ours, but onely such as have benefices annexed unto them, as you may easily see in ye Councill itself, Sess. 21, Cap. 16, where it sayth : Capitulo sede vacante ubi fructuum percipiendum ei munus incumbit oeconomum unum vel plures, etc. descernat item officialem seu vicarium infra octo dies constituendum etc. si secus factus fuerint ad Metropolitanum deputatis hujusmodi devoluatur, vel ad antiquiorem Episcopum, vel propinquiorem in casu negligentiae, and not His Holiness as you urge. Thirdly, our Bishops constitutive letters give us power to chuse officers, even our Deane, and whereas the Councill supposes a Chapter dayly and hourly together tis often a long time ere wee can either heare of their death or meet, and Canonists generally agree that if ye neighbouring Bishop do not stepp in and appoint officers, the Chapter looses no right but may do it at their convenience.

As for ye second difficulty, concerning Archdeacons, which you looked uppon as so strictly belonging to ye persons of a Bishop that ye Church hath no power to choose or constitute them, wee desired you to looke uppon ye gloss on ye first part of ye Decrees in Disc. 6, where you may see ye like objection urged of ye collation of an Archdeaconshippe as belonging to ye Bishop and ye same glosse answering in these words : sed contra 93 di : legimus de extra de Electione ad in cunctis ubi dicitur quod ad Canonicos spectat, and this supposes ye Bishop liveing, a fortiori ergo sede vacante.

Now for ye third difficulty of granting faculties which you saye deserving consideration for ye good of poore soules, wee finde no Canons that hinder either Bishop or Chapter ye communicating such a power either to vicars, Archdeacons, Arch-Priests, Praefects or private Priests. And for your saying yt you like our Bishops advise not to goe before our head ye Pope in censuring even a private person, if you meane accordingly, wee hope you will upon reflection much more forbeare censuring our Bishops themselves and ye generality of ye Clergy in and since their time, being no

Pope hath done it as yet.   But on ye contrary they and their
Ministers treated us as a Chapter and his present Holiness made
a clear acknowledgment of it in a publicke Bull, accounting ye
being a Canon of our Chapter a qualification befitting a man for
a Bishopricke.   Neither can wee doubt but ye Pope and our Protectour Card. Barberine have as great care of soules as you or ye
neighbours; and so well do they know what passes here in all our
affaires that they have desired us to let them have ye changeing of
our Deane hereafter, and some officers, unto which wee modestly
replied yt it was contrary to our consitution, as also that then
we might through misinformation of our adversary (?) come to
want officers, as long as we have done a Bishop.   Thus you see
we have complied with your desire in as calme a manner as we
could reasonably expresse ourselves, referring you in other occur-
rences to your Superiours, our Vicar Generall, and the Arch-
Deacon of your District, hopeing hereafter to have as Brotherly a
complyance and correspondence from yours as from ye other
respective parts, whereby peace and unity may be preserved
amongst us till it please God to send us a Bishop, which is ye
dayly prayer of (Unsigned)

D

A certain amount of light on the circumstances of the times and
of the interests and actions of the Chapter is afforded by the next
document which is a contemporary report on the Meeting of the
General Assembly of the Chapter in May, 1667, and sets out the
reasons for the calling of that Assembly (Ushaw Archives, Ch. 6).
It is headed : ' The Occasion of the Assembly '.

It was ordered in ye Assembly of 1657 yt there should be held
every three yeare a generall meeting of ye Chapter.   But noe
extraordinary business occurring at that presise tyme which could
make ye Venerable Deane and his brethren of Consult judge it
convenient just then to give our Brethren the trouble of comeing
so farr, it was waved that season till some occasion worthy of soe
great cost and paynes should occurr, which wee had some reason
to hope would happen in a short tyme.   After this succeeded
yt dismall plague yeare, which overpast, the desire of seeing our
Brethren, and the care of not permitting ecclesiastical discipline,
as is apt to slide back into forgettfullness of our respective
duetyes, but rather if it might be to knitt our body into a firmer
union, made them in September 1666 againe determine of a
generall meeting.   But our care not to disgust our Governours,[1]
obliged us againe to retract those resolutions apprehending that
ye zealous humor of the tymes might administer occasion of

---

[1] I.e. not to annoy the State.

offence to some who misunderstood our honest, loyal, and every way inoffensive intentions and actions.

At length, those disturbances being to a great degree composed, ye Consult in London could noe longer sustaine to be debarred from ye comfort of seeing there Brethren and fellow members with whome it may with perfect truth be said that they have Cor unum et animam unam. Nor indeed the publick any longer bear ye want of there assistance, for at this tyme Dr. Leyburne, President of Doway, not onely by his courteous and brotherly letters, but alsoe by efficacious endeavoureing to secure yt Colledge to our body, did so in the estimation of all his brethren give us both hopes and eaven an earnest of a freindly corresponding with us for the future, nay more, had already initiated that most desired commerce by professeing in his answere to our sumons sent by Mr. Courtis his hand, that he would have come in person could he have discovered in what might advantage our body, and in his absence appoynting Mr. John Leyburne,[1] a person most welcome to the whole Assembly, to be his Deputy.

Alsoe our Venerable Brethren in France were with ye assistance of ye Lady Abbess aboute ye settling of a new house for the perfecter seasoning of our missionaryes, the nature and circumstances of which it was needfull our Brethren should thorowly understand in regard their concurrence to it was required. Againe, the right Honble Abbott Montague, Lord great Almoner to her Majesty the Queen Mother,[2] had sent a Letter to the venerable Deane proposeing the sending an Agent to Rome to obtaine for us a Bishop in which business wee could not act without the advice and consent of our Brethren. And lastly, a favourable peacefullness and harmony of mindes in our whole body disposeing it to a straiter union seemed to make it now apt to beare a more perfect regularity and a stricter obligatoriness of the mutuall duetyes of one member towards another, and consequently our government capeable of receiving further advances. These reasons and some others made the Venerable Deane and his Brethren for the Consult of London resolve absolutely to order the convening our Brethren, which was accordingly performed and ye Assembly began to sitt May ye 6th, 1667.

The document then gives the roll of Chapter-Men and the resolutions which were passed at the five sessions on the following five days, together with the rules for Archdeacons. The whole is signed ' Humphrey Ellice, Dean '. These periodical ' Assemblies ' performed most useful service in maintaining discipline and fervour amongst the clergy, indeed the regulations promulgated at the meetings were sometimes surprisingly detailed. As illustrating this,

---

[1] His nephew, the future Vicar Apostolic.
[2] Henrietta Maria, widow of Charles I.

and also for its own intrinsic interest, the following document is here printed. It dates from nine years later than the above (Ushaw Archives, Ch. 9).

E

An Extract of several Orders tending to the Government of the Clergie of England made in the Generall Assemblies held in the several years of our Lord God 1653 : 1657 : 1667 : and 1672. All which were confirmed in the Generall Assembly held this present year of our Lord 1676, and ordered to be communicated to our Brethren by the Superiours of each respective District, who are not to give copies thereof to any.

1. Vicars-General and Arch-Deacons are to advise young priests how to comport themselves at their first coming over sc. from the Colleges overseas. They are likewise to endeavour by all means to prevent and compose all differences that may arise betwixt the Priests and their District.

2. The Vicar-General or Arch-Deacon is to tender the Oath to such as have not taken it, before they present them to any employment or residence.

3. No priest is to enter into a Residence, nor to sleight a Residence recommended unto him, if indifferently convenient, nor to desert it without first acquainting his Superiour : and if any General-Superiour displace any Priest, let the Particular Superiour of that District be first advised.

4. The Superiours of Particular Districts are to convene every year the Priests under their charge, to see that all Orders of Generall Meetings are complyed withal, and that the Poor are sufficiently supplyed with Instruction and Sacraments.

5. The Superiours, and other Priests under them ought mutually to vindicate and stand for the credit of each other.

6. Priests ought to be wary and discreet that they stand not litigiously in defence of one Partie against another without sufficient cognizance of the Cause, and hearing both Parties speak : that they be not forward in resolving doubtful Cases, especially when other Mens Interests are concerned. That they venture not upon practises that may sound ill, but take advice from the Superiours, or some others.

7. There ought to be such Correspondence among those of every District as may keep the Superiour sufficiently informed of the employments of their subjects, as what places they frequent, what places provided, what unprovided, or likely to be so; what notable alterations have happened, or likely to happen, that if there be any evil towards, it may be prevented.

8. There ought to be such Correspondence betwixt the Superiour in London and those in the Countrey, that each of them may have a competent understanding of all things in London, Countrey, and abroad as far as they may concern the Clergy.

9. A true cordial Correspondence ought to be betwixt the Superiour at London and both the Presidents of Doway and Lisbo, in order to which it is the request of the Chapter to the Presidents : ffirst, that unlesse extream necessitie force the contrary, no Missioners be sent over before they have finished their Courses, or drawn well towards an end.[1] 2ly : That before they be sent, the Superiour of London may have notice of the time, and their abilities. 3ly : That they may be recommended, first to the Superiour at London, and thence to the Superiours of the Particular Districts. 4ly : That if any one of those who are sent over for the end of the House, or otherwise, shew themselves after convenient Tryal incapable of progresse, the said President sc. of Douay or Lisbon, or some by his appointment give timely notice of it to those that sent them.

10. Fraternal advice is to be given to all Priests, rather to address themselves to our own Brethren then to Regulars, not only in matters of ordinary advice and communication, but especially in matters of the sacraments.

11. All priests at their first coming into the Countrey are to present themselves to the Superiour of that District where they intend to reside, and the Superiour (after such Priests have taken the Oath) is to provide out of the Common Stock (if there be any) for them till places be found.

12. All priests are to consult their Vicars or Arch-Deacons when any occasion of practise occurs concerning Marriage of Catholics with Protestants.

13. Such of our Brethren that suffer great want either in Prison, or elsewhere, ought to be relieved by Collections amongst ourselves, so to prevent scandal of Laity, and give them good example.

14. Priests ought to be wary in their disputes concerning Controversies, or Cases of Conscience before Lay-People.

15. The Pope's Breve concerning Holy-Dayes is to be observed : to wit, that the Dayes defeasted by that Breve are not to be esteemed obligatorie to be kept; and the new Feasts more and more are to be brought into Custome, though not esteemed of strict obligation at the first : by that means an Uniformitie will be brought in every where by little and little.

[1] The large number of unsuitable and only partly trained priests sent over from the Colleges abroad was a constant cause of complaint, especially on the part of the Vicars Apostolic in the next century. Bishops Giffard, Stonor, and Challoner, amongst others, often alluded to it.

16. The Frydayes, and three dayes in Rogation Week betwixt Easter and Ascension are not to be fasted, but observed as Dayes of Abstinence.

17. All Clergy-Men[1] are to leave something to their Body[2] at their Deaths according to their several abilities.

18. Every Clergy-Priest is to say a Masse for every Clergy-Priest that dyeth, as soon as his Death is signifyed unto him.

19. The Monasteries of Louaine and Paris are recommended to all Clergy-Men, as worthy of their Protection whereunto they may recommend Gentlewomen, either for Nuns, or to be bred.

20. The Superiours of every District are to endeavour to raise Founds towards the maintenance of indigent priests in their Districts.

21. Priests are forbidden to censure, or intermeddle with any Actions of his Majestie, or any of his Officers of State, but humbly to obey, and to expect God's, and their pleasure.

22. The Superiours of every District are to acquaint those in London at every Generall Assembly with the several Founds in their respective Jurisdictions to be registered, and kept by the Superiour of the Clergy; as also who are Sureties, and in whose hands the Securities are lodged. This to be understood without Alienation of any Fund from the District where it was given.

23. The Arch-Deacons are to send to Mr. Dean a Catalogue of all our Brethren under their Charge, and where they live.

24. None of our Brethren is to maintain any Opinion, Practical or Speculative against the Common Doctrine, and Practise of the Church, nor to practise any extravagant Cases.

25. St. George, Patron of England, and St. David Patron of Wales are to be observed respectively as duplex majus following the Antient Custome.

26. No youths are hereafter to be sent to either of our Colledges, Doway or Lisbo, out of the Countrey who are intended for Missioners, according to the end of the said Colledges, without the approbation of the Arch-Deacon, or Vicar General of the District whence the Youths come.

27. No Ex-Jesuit hereafter is to be received into the Body of the Clergy, nor have Faculties given him without the unanimous consent of the Consult, in London.

28. All Chapter-Men at their death are to give some part of their debtlesse goods to the Fund at London.

29. Agreed in the Assembly: that all Chapter-Men present should say three Masses apiece for Mr. John Hammond for an old debt to be struck out of the Treasurer's book.

---

[1] The word ' Clergy ' was always used to designate a secular priest
[2] I.e. to the fund for secular priests.

30. No Clergy-Man is to print any thing except it be first approved by the Consult in London.
31. All Chapter-Men are obliged by their own unanimous agreement in the Generall Assembly of 1676 to say three Masses apiece for every Capitular Brother that dyes.

F

THE RELATIONS OF THE CHAPTER WITH THE VICARS APOSTOLIC

It will be convenient here to illustrate further the fortunes and the aims of the Chapter, even though this necessitates anticipating to some extent. With the coming of a Vicar Apostolic in 1685 its position had, of course, been radically altered, and for some years there was considerable uncertainty as to what its powers might now be (if any) and as to how it stood in relation to the bishop. It has already been shown that the Holy See had tacitly recognized its authority in England so long as there was no bishop in the land, but nothing to this effect had been given in writing, though Leyburn had wanted the position and the jurisdiction of the Chapter ratified by a Brief from Rome, and had blamed the Chapter for being satisfied with merely oral approval. When, in 1688, the number of Vicars Apostolic in England was increased from one to four the position became yet more difficult, and in addition there then arose a desire on the part of many (including the bishops themselves) that there should be not merely one Chapter for the whole of England, but a separate Chapter for each of the four Districts. This proposal was constantly put forward.[1] It was, for instance, urged by the Chapter itself in the subjoined Address to the bishops, and Bishop James Smith of the Northern District instructed the English Agent in Rome (Dr. Witham) in 1700 to ask for this to be sanctioned. Similarly in 1707 both Bishop Giffard of the London District and Witham himself (now Vicar Apostolic of the Midland District) instructed the new Agent, Lawrence Mayes, to secure it. None the less this change was never brought about.

But the chief anxiety of the Chapter was concerned with what might happen when a bishop died if there were no Chapter to govern *sede vacante,* and above all to present a *terna* for a new bishop. The underlying fear, of course, was that in that event a Regular might well be ' intruded ' into the Vicariate, and this, above

[1] In 1703 Dr. George Witham, the Agent in Rome, drew up a petition for an extension of the faculties of the Vicars Apostolic, which included a plan for a chapter to be formed in each District (Westm. Archives, XXXVIII, 21).

all things, must be prevented. Both these matters will be found reflected in the remaining two documents, of which the first, dated November 16, 1693, is ' An Address to the three Lords Bishops ',[1] and is to be found in the Westminster Archives, XXXVI, 39 :

To each thus :

My Lord,

We, the Dean and Capitulars of the Consult at London, as representatives of the whole clergy, and having full power to act herein, having seriously reflected on the past attempts of our Adversarys,[2] and of the great interest formerly made against us; and now foreseeing that whenever Allmighty God shall take your Lordship to himself we shall most probably have those sett over us whom our Adversarys shall recommend, as having the power of both Courts[3] to favour them; we see in this a Gate opened, whereby all that mischief will easily, and of course, be brought in, which for a long time has been designed against us. And then we must either by submitting consent to our own ruine, or else by standing uppon the defensive run hazard of great disorders, if not of schism. Both these are evils so great, that we are confident your Lordship's zeal for our,[4] and the public Good, will oblige you to use all possible means for their prevention. And for this end we make it the subject of ye present Address humbly to beseech your Lordship to take it into ye serious consideration, and with your most Reverend Colleagues to conclude upon some effectuall means for the securing both us, and the Public, against these Evils, which we so justly apprehend.

We do not pretend to prescribe, but with due submission lay before your Lordship what in justice and duty we are strictly bound to desire, i.e. that since the present Chapter was first erected by William Lord Bp. Bishop, *with the advice and judgment of divers Bishops and learned Doctors beyond the seas,* as appears by the words of the Breve of its Erection dated September 10, 1623, and after confirmed by Richard Lord Bp. Smith with this clause that it should endure *donec pluribus in Anglia Episcopis Catholicis constitutis, plura in regno erigantur Capitula,* we cannot but hence joyn our hearty wishes that by this method of erecting in each respective Diocese, Chapters, which may succeed with Ordinary jurisdiction, an end might be putt to all these fears, and so the clergy being maintained in its rights, and many disorders prevented, it may likewise be secured against all attempts of ill-wishers.

[1] The fourth, Dr. Michael Ellis of the Western District, was in Rome, having been exiled from his Vicariate by the government.

[2] Apparently meaning the regulars.

[3] The Court in exile of James II at St. Germains, which always sought to exercise influence in ecclesiastical matters, and especially in appointments to vacant bishoprics; and the Papal Court in Rome.

[4] I.e. for the secular clergy.

L

But if this cannot be, we then humbly request your Lordship to conclude together with your Reverend Colleagues on some means of securing us in our rights and privileges of Ordinary Jurisdiction, and of *nominations and due share in* the election of ye successive Bishops etc., sede vacante, as bequeathed us by your most worthy Predecessors. For thus it was left us, as absolutely necessary for the preservation and wellbeing of our Body, and this we cannot lay down, without forfeiting that trust reposed in us, and being false to our Body, and the Oath we have taken for its support, and also injurious to the memory and whole proceedings of ye H. Bishop and ye predecessors.

This affair, and we think it of very great concern, we in all humility and spirit of peace recommend to your Lordship whose charity we hope will not rest till by some expedient you have settled us in peace, and put us out of danger of being made a prey to any other interest whatever.

One year later the Dean and Chapter set out for Dr. James Smith, Vicar Apostolic of the Northern District, the arguments for maintaining the Chapter in existence. This document (Ushaw Collections, I, 33) is dated December 3, 1694, and is as follows:

Reasons given to the Bishop of Calliopoli by the Dean and Chapter of the London Consult for Capitular government and Episcopal Jurisdiction in England.

My Lord,

In pursuance to your Lordship's desires, in your answer to our last address, made by the General Assembly, of having such reasons offered, as might show the necessity of a Capitular government, and standing Ordinary Episcopal jurisdiction in our nation, above others, where the state is not Catholic: These following are humbly presented by the Dean and Capitulars of the Consult of London, in the names and autority of the whole Chapter of the Secular English Catholic Clergy.

1. Because a Dean and Chapter Governing and exercising Ordinary Episcopal Jurisdiction, sede vacante, is the ancient ecclesiastical government in Catholic times of this our country; established by the sanctions of the Church and the laws of the Realm. It is that, the possesion of which we have been cast out by the Protestant English Church; and to which primitive way of government we have more hopes, in progress of time, to be restored, than any other Catholic clergy living in a nation separated from See Apostolic. And therefore we may groundedly confide His Holiness as the Common Father of the Catholic Church will not deny ours, which hath the honour to be styled Primogenita Ecclesiae, to proceed in this ancient and established way of government.

2. Because the government of Dean and Chapter is grown by long continuances, as it were, natural to this kingdom, easy and suitable by its genius; which is evident allso, because the Protestant Church, here established by law, follows and embraces the same Hierarchicall way of government, by Bishops, Deans, and Chapters; altho many foreign Protestants dislike thereof; so that any other sort of Church government amongst Catholics here in England cannot promise itself any favourable Reception as being contrary to the sanctions and lawes aforesayd, nor any peaceable continuance, if receavd; because intrinsically apt to create fears and jealousies in the Protestant clergy and laity, as if the Holy See had some new design upon England by pretending to methods of ecclesiastical government different, not only from those the Protestants here allow, but also from what our Catholic Ancestors were so long accustomed to; and the present Chapter hath so many years practised quietly, without any disturbance from the State, even in the most troublesome of Times. Now what manifold Mischiefs the Protestant fears and jealousys, fomented by our Adversarys, may produce is not hard to conceave; but will proove greivous for both our clergy and laity to be exposed unto.

3. Because this sort of government is not only ancient, establisht, suitable to the genius of the nation, obviating Protestant fears and jealousys, because known in all its parts and boundaries, but it moreover appears soe necessary for the dignity and support of the English Catholic secular Clergy, that it will prove the most Despicable and Contemptible of all Ecclesiastical Bodys in England, should it be without it : since all Regulars here, not only pretend, as missioners, to be of the clergy and have Pastorall jurisdiction, but have allso their Bodys Corporate, confirmed by the See Apostolic, for their greater strength, encouragement and emolument; whilst the Secular Clergy, should the present Chapter be ever thought or supposed to expire, and no new ones, in your Lordship's times, be erected, would not be capable of being properly styled a Body, but a contemptible Number multorum Capitum sine Capite, and not only sine Capite, but sine Capitulo, the Heir Apparent in the vacancy of Ordinary Episcopal Jurisdiction.

4. Because the Body of the Catholic Secular Clergy in England, as to its Qualifications and number, is far more considerable than any Body, or perhaps Bodys of English Regulars in the sayd kingdome : and what hath maintained it in its dignity and credit hath bin the government of Dean and Chapter, now in above seventy years Possession, from its first institution and exercise of Ordinary Episcopal Jurisdiction, in the most weighty concerns appertaining thereunto : during the intervalls of the two last Bishops, untill the Arrival of my Lord Bishop of Adramite.[1] And this being so, what a shipwreck of credit and

---

[1] Bishop Leyburn. The period alluded to is 1631–1685.

dignity would the secular clergy make, should it (being so considerable a Body) be left *Acephalus,* without Capitular authority and jurisdiction, so requisite for its right order and support.

5. Because if, before other Chapters be erected, the present General Chapter of the English Catholic Secular Clergy should be supposed to cease; all Contracts, Donations and Funds made and valifyed by authentic Deeds, under the seal of the present Chapter, for the education of students, provision of Pastors, Relief of superannuated or otherwise necessitous Priests, and other good uses would run great hazard in small time of being lost, having not any corporate Body or Bodys to look after them. And altho this were a great misfortune yet would it be accompanied with a greater. For we might bid adieu to all hopes of suchlike future charitable donations from the piety of the Nobility, Gentry, Ecclesiastics or other devout persons; since no prudent person can be thought willing (how piously soever inclined) to make any such donation or establishment, where there is no authorised Ecclesiastical Body able to give security for future performance of incumbent duties.

6. Because, altho it may seem that the government of Vicars Apostolic without Chapters might doe as well in England as in some other lands, yet here is this disparity, that such countries so governed either never had Chapters or not so long continued and universally receaved by the Catholics of these parts, as here in England; or at least the Clergy's Dignitys and Rights are there otherwise so well fenced that there is no fear of their being prejudiced, or Church government embroyled, of which we here have had so scandalous experience, that it is of the highest importance for peace and verity that a Capitular government should be continued.

7. Because again, in supposition of there being no Capitular government here, sede vacante, there will follow an inundation of evils. Who shall then inflict necessary Censures? Who shall provide Pastors with Flocks and Flocks with Pastors? Who shall govern both Clergy and Laity in a canonical way? Who shall give faculties to forreign Priests (flocking hither in greater numbers and more ? this country than any other) if they are found fitt? Or deny them if they be found otherwise? Who shall examine Extraordinary Facullties, of which there are here frequent abuses? Who shall approuve Preachers and Confessors? And who give leave to a forreign Bishop when requisite, to administer the Sacrament of Confirmation? And, in a word, who shall, or can supply all the other numerous comforts and advantages which Ordinary Episcopal Jurisdiction brings with it? All which has bin most laudably performed by our Chapter hitherto.

These reasons alledged, we humbly conceave, may sufficiently evidence to your Lordship, without further pressing the matter from other topics, relating to further mischeifs, that there is a necessity of a standing Capitular Government in this our nation, above others, where the State is not Catholic.

We further humbly pray your Lordship that for the more effectuall moving His Holiness the manifold Favours and Graces which his Holy Predecessors of happy memory have viva voce expressed towards the present Chapter may be represented to him. His Holiness Pope Innocent X professed to Mr. Fitton, our Agent at Rome, that *he would not disapprove our Chapter; but let us alone with our Government.* His Holiness Pope Alexander VII, having promised us a Bishop after seven months, or as soon as it should be convenient, expressly ordered Mr. Plantin, our Agent, that *we should govern in the mean time by our Dean and Chapter.* His Holiness Pope Innocent XI, being moved in something relating to the present Chapter by Mr. John Caryll, whom the King sent as Envoy to the See Apostolic for obtaining a Bishop, declared in these express words, that *the Chapter was of ancient institution, and he would not have the power of it lessened.*

From these so illustrious examples, we cannot but steadfastly confide that His present Holiness who, ever since his advance to the Apostolic Chair, hath so much studied and endeavored the peace of the Church and of all Christendome, will according to his great wisdome and goodness for the extirpation of all the least seeds of division and faction, which may arise at the respective deceases of your Lordships, about a remaining Ordinary Episcopal Jurisdiction, allready shewn so necessary for our circumstances, will, we say, either graciously declare, as His holy Predecessors have done, for the quiet continuance of the present Chapter, or else authorise your Lordships to erect new ones in your respective dioceses; upon which ours fairly ceases to be, according to our constitutive Breve, which hath established this present Chapter, *Donec pluribus in Anglia constitutis Episcopis, plura in Regno erigantur Capitula.*

Having thus offered your Lordships these reasons at present, for the necessity of a Capitular Government in our Nation, above others, where the State is not Catholic, as also what may the more effectually move His Holiness to support and comfort the English Catholic Church, by the same or like methods of Ecclesiastical Discipline, from the examples of His holy Predecessors. We, to conclude, most humbly beseech your Lordships favourably to receave, and with Fatherly regard to consider, what we have offered; that so, as to your wisdome may seem best, these or any other more pregnant reasons, which shall occur to your Lordships, may be represented to His Holiness, in the behalf of the whole Catholic Clergy of England and Laity with them; and that from time to time, we wayting on your Lordships may receave the Favour and Comfort of knowing what Progress is made in this so important Affair.

The Chapter, as already indicated, continued to exist, but the oft reiterated desire for a separate Chapter in each of the four Districts was never granted. An attempt made by a few malcontents in 1717 to have the Chapter broken up altogether came to nothing,[1] and Mgr. Santini, the Papal representative in Brussels, told the President of Douay College that nothing would be done against it so long as its authority did not clash with that of the Vicars Apostolic. In 1738 it was warmly defended by its Dean, Dr. Day, who, writing to Bishop Stonor, describes the great benefit the Clergy received through it, and declared that it was the best means for procuring a Bishop in Ordinary. He added that if the Chapter should be dissolved ' can we hope for any help to prevent the four Districts from being filled with Regular (Bishops) '; pointing out that two of them were already so filled.[2] Meanwhile many, and notably Dr. Day, wanted the Chapter to have the power of presenting names of suitable candidates when Vicariates fell vacant, and moreover a considerable number of the Chapter, including the Dean, wanted their bishops to be ' Ordinaries ' and as such to take their titles from ancient English sees (Dorchester was several times mentioned as an example) instead of bearing Asiatic titles. On this latter subject, which he had very much at heart, Dr. Day frequently wrote to Lawrence Mayes, the clergy Agent in Rome, but quite without effect.

[1] This attempt was made by Saltmarsh and Strickland in the course of their intrigues against Bp. Giffard, on which see above, pp. 51 sq. Seven years later Bp. Stonor was reported to be trying to get the Chapter annulled and to get control of its funds for himself.

[2] These were Bp. Prichard of the Western District (Franciscan) and the Dominican Bp. Williams of the Northern District.

THE 'BRIEF OF INSPECTION' GIVING BISHOP STONOR
POWER TO ADMINISTER THE LONDON DISTRICT IN
THE EVENT OF THE ABSENCE OR INCAPACITY OF
BISHOP GIFFARD

Clemens Papa XI

Venerabilis Frater salutem et Apostolicam Benedictionem.
Fraternitatis tuae in nos et Apostolicam Sedem fidei et devotionis
merita, cum eximia doctrina, integritate, et Catholicae fidei zelo
conjuncta nos adducunt, ut opera tua in iis quae nobis cordi sunt
libenter utamur firma spe atque fiducia in Domino freti, te
expectationi et desiderio de te nostris cumulate responsurum. Alias
siquidem nos te in Comitatibus Cestriae, Lancastriae, Eboracensi,
Northumbriae, Cumbriae, Westmoniae, in Episcopatu Dunelmensi,
et in insula Monae in Anglia, aliisque locis ibi assignatis Vicarium
Apostolicum cum solitis facultatibus ad nostrum et Sedis Apostolicae
Beneplacitum constituimus et deputavimus,[1] et alias prout in nostris
desuper in simili forma Brevis die Septembris anni proxime
praeteriti expeditis Literis, quarum tenorem praesentibus pro plene
ac sufficienter expresso et inserto haberi volumus, uberius continetur.
Nunc autem spiritualibus Christi fidelium in aliis locis moderno
Episcopo Madaurensi Vicario Apostolico in Anglia subjectis
degentium necessitatibus quantum nobis ex alto conceditur con-
sulere cupientes, de nonnullorum ex Venerabilibus fratribus S.R.E.
Cardinalibus negotiis Propagandae Fidei praepositis super rebus
Angliae a nobis specialiter deputatorum consilio, Tibi jurisdictionem,
ac omnes et singulas facultates per praesentes literas tibi a nobis
quomodolibet concessas ad omnia et singula loca jurisdictioni
ejusdem Episcopi Madaurensis subjecta in casu tamen defectus,
absentiae, et impedimenti ipsius Episcopi Madaurensis, ac
hujusmodi defectu et absentia seu impedimento tantum durante, et
non alias, ad nostrum et dictae Sedis beneplacitum eadem
Autoritatae tenore praesentium extendimus et ampliamus. Non
obstantibus . . . etc.
Datum Romae apud S. Mariam Majorem sub annulo Piscatoris
die xxa Martii 1716 Pontificatus Nostri anno xvi . . .

[1] The Northern counties are here mentioned because Dr. Stonor was at
first intended for the Northern District.

Concordat cum copia authentica. Ita testamur die 18 Aug.,
1716. Rob. Witham, S.Th.Licent.. Coll.Ang.Dua.Praeses.

E. Dicconson, S.Th.Prof., et ejusdem Coll.Vicepraeses.

Richardus Kendall, S.Th.Professor.

The document is superscribed on the outside : Venerabili Fratri
Joanni Episcopo Thespien. Vicario Aplco. in Anglia.—Concordat
cum originali, quod asservatur in Archivo hujus S. Nunciaturae.
In fidem etc. Th. de Nottolis Proths. Aplcus. ac Illmi. et Revmi
Internuncii Secrets., Bruxelles. 30 Aprilis, 1716.

PETITION FROM BISHOP WITHAM TO THE CARDINAL PROTECTOR FOR PERMISSION TO RESIGN

Emme. et Rme. Dne.,

. . . Quare scire dignetur Emma. Vra., quod cum ab initio fere currentis saeculi, satis intellexissem, SSmi. Dni. Nri. mentem esse, uti mihi misero nimisque indigno, formidandum Angelicis humeris onus imponeret, adiisse me Sua SStem., et coram Pedibus ejus provolutum, declarasse me tali tantoque munere nimis indignum, ineptumque fore, tum propter peccata mea, tum quia prorsus ignorarem, qua ratione fieri possit, ut apud Nostrates Ecclesiastica disciplina possit in multis observari. Consolabatur me pro Sua Paterna Summaque benignitate SSmus. Dnus., Suaque Benedictione, et liberalissimo Viatico donatum ditatumque dimisit. Sed o quantum me, quotiesque paenituit, quod adeo facilem assensum praebuerim : Non enim me SSmus. Apostolicis minis perterruit, sed affatu suavissimo delinuit, non satis, ut opinor, memorem illius dicti, quod hoc onus cum imponitur, *dignus* saltem inuitus, *indignus* autem (qualem me fuisse et esse sentio) *nullatenus* accipiat : et si nunc coram Apostolico throno prostratus adessem, arbitror equidem me non offensurum illius Summam bonitatem, si modeste dicerem : Vae mihi, Pater Se., quia elevans allisisti me. Nam a multis jam annis sub hoc onere terribili gemens et anhelans, multo profecto plures, multoque majores difficultates, curas et anxietates expertus sum, quam ab initio praeviderim, quasque si praevidissem, eo quo nunc animo sum affectus, nunquam, ut arbitror, adduci potuissem, ut hoc onus omnino debilibus meis humeris impar, in me susciperem.

Circumstant me undique curae multiplices, difficultates, anxietates, perplexitates rodunt me atque consumunt, et anni mei jam declinantes ad ultimum occasum, transeunt in gemitibus : jam senesco, jam canesco totus, jam prae debilitate nervorum (quam Paralysim non perfectam et mortiferam, sed *trementem* audivi vocari) subinde valde tremiscunt mihi manus, in tantum ut aliquando vix unam Litterulam, nisi valde deformem, exarare valeam : caligant oculi, doloribus podagricis saepe vexatus fui, quos et redituros experto : ex tumore pedis et tibiae, signisque compressionis ex tactu manentibus, medicus Hydropem, ut puto, inchoatam conjecturavit, quam et fatalem mihi futuram praedixit. Gravitas et infirmitas corporis mei Senilis ad movendum huc illucque, et ad visitandum (sicuti deberem) Provincias, vel minus idoneum, vel

omnino non idoneum me reddunt. Jam mihi Sepulchrum quotidie
velut ante oculos observatur, et corpus meum aetate atque
humoribus grave plenumque festinat ad pulverem, pastumque
vermium : quodque me terret magis, brevi Supremo Judici de
salentis mihi commissis, et de villicatione mea mihi ratio reddenda
est, et quid dicam ignoro, nisi hoc unum, miserere mei Deus per
Sanguinem Xti tui Domini mei.

Quapropter ut ad appropinquantem mortem atque Judicium me
melius tutiusque praeparem, humiliter et instanter obsecro, uti cum
bona venia SSmi. Dni. Sanctaeque Sedis Apostolicae mihi tandem
liceat ab hoc onere Vicariatus Apostolici libero feriari in Domino,
vacare mihi, et videre quam suavis est Dominus, simulque culpas
et omissiones meas plurimas (nam ut timeo multiplicatae sunt super
capillos capitis mei) non interrupta curis innumeris cordis mei
intentione, deflere atque purgare : atque ut ad hanc favorem pro
me obtinendum (quem summi beneficii loco semper aestimabo)
Emma. Vra. pro me veluti mediator et Advocatus existat, humiliter
supplex, rogo atque obtestor. Meticulosum me nimis, vel certe
Scrupulosum fortassis aliqui censebunt : nec ego facile Judiciis
eorum contradicam : sed qua me pungunt, melius egomet experior :
et si Scrupulositas est iste timor meus, eo minus huic officio
difficilimo sum idoneus, maxime cum velut in naturam abiit haec
mea qualiscumque timiditas, multorum (ut arbitror) jam annorum
consuetudine roborata, et fortassis invincibilis.

Nemo mihi hoc otium (si quod ardenter opto, diuque optavi,
tandem impetravero) nemo mihi hanc quietem, pacemque invideat :
hoc enim otium meum erit negotium, illudque maximum, scilicet
accuratior ad mortem praeparatio. Nec ero deses aut ignavus, sed
dum vita superest, pro meo modulo, et prout Dei gratia me
adjuverit, inserviam huic Missioni ut simplex Sacerdos, sine Juris-
dictione Episcopale, et sine Vic. Apostolici authoritate, si Sua SStas.
ita fieri concesserit, aliumque de Clero Nostro[1] me fortiorem,
saniorem, sanctiorem, uno verbo corpore et animo robustiorem,
deputare dignabitur : Cui has in Provincias misso, omnem meam
authoritatem, imo et Pensionem huic officio de fundatione piae
mem : Jacobi Episcopi Caliponensis, ut arbitror, annexam,
libentissime resignabo : atque interim dum hoc fiat, quod ut fiat
quantocius ardenter desidero, feram hoc onus ut potero, timens ac
tremens tum corporae tum animo. Confirmant me quidem in hoc
voto meo multorum Praesulum exempla, qui saltem in Senectute,
levamen ab hoc onere, secessionemque ab his gravibus curis
petierunt atque impetrarunt : Non desunt plures, ut arbitror, e

---

[1] I.e. one of the secular clergy.

Clero Nostro, qui omnibus consideratis melius hujus officii partes implere poterint, quam Ego jam Senex, et in votis emeritus miles : et multum spero meam cum SSmi. Dni. Nri. venia cessionem, ad majorem Dei gloriam vere cessuram : hoc est quod instanter et Supplex obsecro.

Emniae Vrae
humilimus Servus
Georgius Marcopol. V.Ap.   Die 28 Martii, 1718.

LETTER FROM MGR. MAYES TO DR. ROBERT WITHAM ON THE APPOINTMENT OF BISHOP WILLIAMS

Undated, but presumably 1726.

Although it may be what I write will be of no great credit, yet nothing shall be wanting on my side to justify a proceeding which I apprehend will have offended you.[1] It signifyes nothing to ye present purpose to enquire into ye wayes and means whereby Fra Williams came to be made a Bishop : of which I am not able to give a very good account, and might be guilty of setting down my own suspicions for truths. It is very certain he was made contrary to ye usual custome of Bishops desighnd for Missions, i.e. without ye consultation of Propaganda. Ye next stepp was to assign to him ye Northern District. Here ye Propaganda enterd, and made such a remonstrance to His Holiness of ye ill consequences, yt ye Pope orderd ye Secretary of Propaganda to speak to him to desist from that pretention. Bishop Williams acquiesced, and severall projects were sett on foot to provide for him otherwise than by ye Northern District. In ye mean time came congratulations which I did not wonder att, as from Regulars; for though some of these might be mortifyed to see an inferior body,[2] with respect to their number in England, preferrd before them, yet I conceivd it was an universal jubily of all to see ye Northern District wrested out of ye Clergy's hands. Att last came a letter of congratulations and compliments from a certain Clergyman.[3] Bishop Williams gave a copy of this letter to His Holiness who was made to believe, as I have been informed, yt what had been represented of ye displeasure and inconveniencys on ye Clergy side was a false supposition. Tis matter of fact ye Pope sent this very letter to ye Congregation, with orders pro expeditione Brevis, in his own handwriting. Ye Congregation was surprized, and I plainly understood yt we ourselves had ruined our own cause. Here I lost all hopes a second time, for whereas things were in such a fair way before yt I could not wish better : I saw now a most sudden change as appeared to me without redress. I excusd ye letter as well as I could, by saying it was

[1] He had purposely failed to deliver two letters from Witham to Bishop Williams.
[2] The Dominican Order.
[3] I.e. secular priest. It was Dr. Ingleton.

meant onely for a compliment, and written at a time when it was supposed Bishop Williams was at ye same time destined for ye North, that he was consecrated Bishop, and that I had no hand in ye said letter, whereas it had been written, sent and deliverd without my knowledge. Here then I supposed all was at an end, and sett myself down with all that melancholy you may imagine. I enquired from time to time if ye Breve had been given to ye Bishop and after I had observed an unusual delay, I gott some light, yt ye Congregation though in readiness to obey His Holiness's orders, yet had made another remonstrance which was, and I suppose is, ye cause of ye present delay and demurr about ye Breve.

In this state of things, I receivd your Letter for Bishop Williams and writt back my reasons for not delivering it. I dare not venture to rely upon my memory, how I expressed these reasons : and should be glad you would be pleasd to copy for me ye words of that, and of a following letter, in which I think I askd leave to burn yours to Bishop Williams. Be this as it will, I could not say less than yt I apprehended danger from ye deliverance of your Letter. Whereas it is certain yt a person upon ye spott observes many things that do not appear so lively at a distance; yt I could have no other view in detaining your Letter than ye Interest[1] I am concerned for; yt I could not be judged to seek an occasion to offend you, without being judged a madman; yt I never had ye least grudge against Fra Williams in all my life; much less against ye Order, for which I ever had a particular veneration, and for several good reasons : Whereas, in a word, I could not reasonably be suspected of any secondary sinister intention, I must also reasonably have expected to gain credit when I judged it was not expedient for ye Interest of ye Clergy to deliver any letter that contained a congratulation to Bishop Williams from any Clergyman,—and much more from one in that post, intrusted with ye education of ye best part of ye Clergy concerned.

It happened otherwise and I was not believed : and receivd by yours of April 25 a second repeated order to deliver your Letter with ye address,—Vic. Apo. in partibus Angliae Septibus (a title His Holiness has not yet given him) *whether he be Vicar Apostolic in ye North or not.* You cannot imagine into what anguish of mind this order cast me. On one side I saw evidently yt I should displease you to a very great degree if I did not obey ye order you gave me : on ye other side I judged invincibly yt in ye present conjuncture I could not obey without danger of my own conscience, in ye danger I apprehended of ye Clergy interest. To extricate myself

---

[1] That of the secular clergy.

out of this perplexity I resolved to send back ye Letter. I do
suppose you think my fears very vain, and yt a compliment could
never be of that consequence, as I imagine and magnify to
myself. But what could I do! I could not overcome them: they
appeared to me grounded upon experience in this very case, upon
ye sentiment of ye Congregation, and I will add (if I may be
believed without setting down something yt I know, but do not
think proper to speak of at present) upon ye conduct of a person
of distinction here, where in relation to this very affair I have
observd greater reservedness and nicety than I myself should have
judged necessary, and in things that even to me appeared very
remote from ye business in hand. After all, ye case being fairly
stated, I cannot tell whether my fears will appear of so very little
consideration to our Bishops, and generally to ye Clergy in England.
I know you had your eye intent upon another concern of ye two
universities Douay and Louvain; which you say was chiefly ye
import of your Letter. I would not have you think yt I slighted
this consideration, or yt that I could be without concern about what
you take so much to heart with a view of some great advantage;
though I am ignorant of ye concern in particular. Yet there were
many things yt lessened to me ye weight of this consideration. These
are two Catholic universityes, in a free commerce with Rome; ye
well meaning men of both have, or may have, their Agents here,
even Dominicans, men I need not fear to say of greater capacity,
experience and credit in this Court than Bishop Williams cann be
supposd to be: and then I was not inclined to think yt this concern
could be of such nature as to depend upon one point of time without
redress: whereas our concern, I apprehended, if my fears were not
vain and idle, might be determined suddenly and irrevocably: and
I could not find in my heart to concurr in hastening this moment.
Whereas day after day something might fall out favourable, and of
all things would cast away hopes ye latest that is possible. But be
that concern of ye two Universityes what it will, I could not in my
opinion at that time and in ye circumstances hitherto expressed,
allow it to balance with ye English Clergy's concern and interest.

I know very well it is free and easy for anyone of the Clergy to
write what and when he pleases to Bishop Williams, but as it is
impossible for anyone at a distance to judge of ye circumstances of
any concern, and ye humour of persons upon whom it depends, as
well as one upon ye spot; as to all things committed to my care I
understand an epiekeia to be sometimes very necessary: otherwise
contrary to ye intention of those I serve I may instead of doing
good, concurr to an irreparable damage. This liberty has all along
been allowed me by ye Bishops, and never yt I know of taken ill.

Could I have foreseen this long delay of Bishop Williams' Vicariate, I should certainly have rather advisd ye Clergy to write Letters of just remonstrances to be represented by ye Congregation, than congratulations to Bishop Williams; but this was impossible to be foreseen, or to guess at any period of time about a thing that is every moment in His Holiness's power. Thus farr is meant for a supplement to my last letter, which after many contrasts of uneasy thoughts I own I writt under some disturbance of mind; and so judged it necessary still further to explain and justify myself. But this is not all. A farther trouble and perplexity followed, which surprized me still more, than yours of April 25.

Bishop Williams sent to me to require your Letter, of which he had receivd advice, and I think directions to demand it by a letter from their Provincial, who had transcribed your complaints against me from your own Letter to one Dr. Clarkson at Louvain[1] (one I do not know). All that I could answer was yt I had indeed receivd such a letter, and had detaind it, with intention to deliver it when ye supposition on which it had been writt came to be verifyed; but yt this happening to be deferrd, I had sent it back, with my reasons to you for doing so; yt as to any disappointment of business I was not privy to, I was sorry; but hoped ye Bishop was either otherwise informed, or yt you would find wayes and means to retrieve it.

Now, dear Sir, I begg leave to take my turn of complaining. It is certain, yt though we all mean one thing, yet there may be a difference of opinions and judgments among us about wayes and means of manageing our concerns. As long as this remains among ourselves, whoever happens to be in ye wrong is only accountable to his owne Superiors and Brethren, remains coverd with a fraternall compassion, and no handle is given to any other body of men with other views to make an advantage of it.[2] Since ever I came to know anything of ye Clergy concerns I seem to have feard nothing so much as disagreements and partyes among ourselves : and believe this apprehension to be obvious from ye experience of past times. I understand allwayes to be expected such things as cannot be rectifyed among ourselves; for then without regard to anyone, redress is to be sought where it is to be had. Now supposeing me to be in ye wrong by detaining your Letter to Bishop Williams, I cannot for my life persuade myselfe yt this fault of mine is so enormous as to deserve no cover of fraternal compassion, but I must immediately be made accountable for it to another Body,[3] to other

---

[1] A Dominican of the University there.

[2] An allusion to Witham's indiscretion in telling the Louvain Dominicans of his letter to Bishop Williams.

[3] I.e. to the Dominican Order.

Superiors, obliged to justify my conduct to them, and obnoxious to those who might have made a handle of it, not only to my confusion, but, as I still think, to ye disadvantage of ye Clergy : had I been by this means obliged to produce ye Letter. Had you found a way, as it is hard to think this impossible, by means of Fr. Provincial of ye Dominicans, or ye aforesaid Dr. Clarkson, or otherwise, to provide for ye concern of ye two Universityes, and then had complained to ye Bishops and chief men of ye Clergy in England yt I had refused to deliver ye Letter, and had no sufficient reasons for doing so; this is what I could never with any face have complained of; but as things are, or at least appear to me, I cannot think but I have reason to take my turn of a very just complaint. I pray God to give us all one mind and one heart, and to inspire His Holiness to determine what is best for ye Mission and Catholic Faith in England.[1]

[1] Westm. Archives, XXXVIII, 130.

THE ELECTION OF POPE BENEDICT XIII

The Pope referred to in Appendix IV was the Dominican Pope Benedict XIII, who was 75 when elected. In view of the subsequent attitude of a few of the clergy in England over the Pope's personal selection of the Dominican Bishop Williams for the Northern Province, it is interesting to see how Bishop Giffard welcomed the election. After sending an enthusiastic letter of congratulations to the new Pontiff, the bishop wrote to Mayes on July 2, 1724, in which he said :

I assure you that what I hear daily of this great Pope so enlivens and animates me that I could almost forget my great age,[1] and with new vigour exert all my poor abilityes in the service of our Lord and Master, Christ Jesus. Oh God ! How powerfull is example ! And how sweetly does it move, animate, and even allmost force us to the performance of our duty ! I never yet had a tempting thought of going to Rome ;[2] but were I not so old, the great sanctity, and exemplarity of this great Prelate would draw me thither to receive his blessing, and to hear the supreme Prince of Pastors speaking by his mouth. Were all Bishops possessed with the lyke spirit, what a glorious Church should we have ! I know not how my letter will relish with the wise men of that Court, but I am sure I have poured forth my heart with great sincerity : ex abundantia cordis. I was never much given to compliment, much less to flatter ; and now my age and near approach to Eternity puts me above such poor, mean, empty things.

This is the more striking in that it soon became known that the Pope had told a Dominican that none did anything on the English Mission but the Jesuits ; and this made the bishops anxious. They wanted to know whether the Pope was in the hands of the Jesuits, and they feared he might favour his own Order.

---

[1] Presumably alluding to the fact that the Pope was only six years younger than himself.

[2] It is curious to realize that none of the Vicars Apostolic ever went to Rome after their consecration in this century, except Bp. Prichard.

BISHOP GIFFARD'S WILL

In the Name of God Father Sonne and holy Ghost.

I Bonaventure Giffard of the Parish of St. James make my last will and testament (revoking all former wills) in manner following. As to my soul I beseech our Lord and Saviour Christ Jesus to receive it into his mercyfull hands. As to my body I desire it may be bury'd in the Churchyard of St. Pancratius, wher are interred my Brother Andrew and Sister Anne. I should be glad it may be near to them. Mr. Fell can inform you as to the place. As to my temporal means, I give fifty pounds to the poor Catholicks of London. I give twenty pounds to the poor Catholicks of Wolverhampton including the poor Catholicks that are in ye neighberhood of the said town.[1] To each of my Executors hereafter named, I give twenty guineas to each. To my servant Cooper I give fifty pounds and all my wearing clothes, wollen, lining or silk, allso the bed and furniture he made use of at Stafford House. Of this my will, I constitute Executors my good friends Mr. Benjman Petre and Mr. Thomas Berington. As to ye remainder of my personal estate, I order it to be disposed of by my Executors as I shall give directions by any writing, writt by my own hand or at least signed by me.

September ye 26, 1733.

Signed then seald and publishd for my will in presence of the underwritten wittnesses.

Bonaventure Giffard,

Mary Dalyson.
William Crathorne.

---

[1] This was his birthplace.

FESTIVALS AND FASTS IN THE PENAL TIMES

An aspect of Catholic life in the eighteenth century of which
mention should be made in such a volume as this is the matter of
the festivals which were observed, and the laws of fasting and
abstinence as they then stood. Whatever the political disturbances
in the country, or whatever dissensions there may have been
amongst Catholics themselves, the liturgical life of the Church went
calmly on, and the changes in the liturgy which occurred during
the period are a matter of interest and an essential factor in the
religious life of the day. Here attention will be confined to the
points concerning which documentary evidence of the period exists.

To take the festivals first : there is at the very beginning of our
period a decree on the subject which was issued by Bishop Leyburn
on December 31, 1685.[1] This declared that those holidays of
obligation which had been determined by Pope Urban VIII were to
be continued, and to them were to be added the feasts of St. George
and of St. Thomas of Canterbury (i.e. April 23 and December 29).
It does not appear to be known for how long these last two feasts
continued to be holidays of obligation, but the fact that two
additions were thus made to the list ran counter to the general
tendency of the time which was rather to try to cut down the
number. Nor is that surprising in view of the fact that at that time
the holidays of obligation were very much more numerous than
they are to-day. Thus as early as 1701 Bishop Smith of the Northern
District petitioned Rome for power to make rules for lessening the
number of holidays of obligation in his District, or of dispensing
from their observance, owing to the poverty of many of the
Catholics in the North,[2] the point being, of course, that they were
prevented from earning their livelihood on those days. At the same
time the bishop stated that those which could most easily be kept
were the Feasts of the Circumcision, the Epiphany, the Purification,
the Annunciation, the Ascension, the Nativity of St. John the
Baptist, SS. Peter and Paul, Corpus Christi, St. George, All Saints,
Christmas, St. Stephen, St. John Evangelist, St. Thomas of Canterbury, and St. Augustine of Canterbury. It will be noticed that that
selection from the total list numbers fifteen (twice the number in

---

[1] Westm. Archives, XXXIV, 245.
[2] This power had already been granted as regards Scotland.

force to-day), and includes no less than four in Christmas week, and two more in the next week. Similarly in 1715 Bishop Witham petitioned for a diminution in the number of holidays, and wanted the number to be the same as in Scotland (fifteen), or else a transference to various Sundays of those which fell on weekdays, because of the poverty of the people owing to the great taxation of Catholics, and owing to the decay of piety.[1] But dissatisfaction with this matter continued for a long time, and many years later a decree was issued by Pope Pius VI, dated March 9, 1777, confining the holidays of obligation to all Sundays, Easter Monday, Whit Monday, Christmas, the Circumcision, the Epiphany, the Ascension, Corpus Christi, the Annunciation, the Assumption of Our Lady, SS. Peter and Paul, All Saints, and the Patron of each individual place, i.e. (apart from Sundays) twelve in all. Comparison of that list with the fifteen recommended above by Bishop Smith is interesting. Of these fifteen, the Purification, the Nativity of St. John the Baptist, St. George, St. Stephen, St. John the Evangelist, St. Thomas of Canterbury, and St. Augustine are missing from the Pope's list; while on the other hand the latter includes four (Easter Monday, Whit Monday, the Assumption, and the particular Patron) which are not in the bishop's list. The Papal decree also stated that if the feasts of SS. Peter and Paul, and of the Assumption should fall in harvest-time, the Vicars Apostolic could dispense from the order to abstain from servile work, but Mass should be heard.[2]

On the other hand Bishop Giffard was anxious to obtain greater recognition of certain feasts. He was much concerned at the ignoring of the old English saints in the calendar of his day. As early as 1717 he wrote to Mayes in Rome :

I have long been much concerned that we seem to have forgot the Saints of our own nation. Not the least mention made even of St. Augustin. I am resolved to show more gratitude to their memory, that we may allso receive more assistance from their protection and prayers.

He added that he had proposed to the other Vicars Apostolic to have St. Augustine's feast kept as a *duplex major,* and that he had compiled proper lessons for it taken from St. Bede and the Sarum office. St. Alban should also be a double major, and St. Edward the Confessor ' whose body we have in Westminster Church '. He instructed Mayes to inform the Congregation of Rites of his intention and to ask whether they want the lessons sent to Rome, adding :

---

[1] Westm. Archives, XXXVIII, 78.
[2] *Idem*, XXXIX, 158.

Of all countreys wee have been the most negligent and ungrateful as to the veneration due to our Saints. And yet no place stands more in need of such powerful advocates. Wherefore I am resolved to exert my zeal in order to awaken the devotion of my people towards the saints of our countrey.

He went on to mention St. Joseph of Arimathea as

an early preacher of Christ to us, and yet we keep no commemoration of him. Our predecessors have been much to blame; but it shall not be my fault if our Saints are not honoured for the future.[1]

A sentiment that would have pleased Challoner. In September, 1721, he sent the Lessons and Mass of St. Augustine to Rome for approval, but three years later we find him writing to Mayes :

. . . As for St. Augustin, I find your great officers [in Rome] have too much business to think of what I desird for paying due honour to so great a saint, and our most special Patron; and therefore I shall trouble them no more on that account, but doe by my own authority, what they neglect. If this displeases, the fault is their's. If I have not their approbation by the end of October, I will order the keeping of this Feast, and signify the same in our Directory.[2]

To turn to the question of fasts and abstinence : the above decree by Bishop Leyburn in 1685 ordered that in addition to the Vigils in the Roman Calendar, those of the Purification and of the Nativity of Our Lady, which had of old been in force in England, were to be observed as days of fasting; while on Fridays (except between Christmas and the Epiphany, and from Easter to the Ascension) the custom of our forefathers was to be resumed, save that eggs would be allowed except in Lent. This meant that Fridays were to be fast days,[3] but on the other hand Leyburn ordered that the three Rogation Days were not to be fasts, but only days of abstinence. Finally, fish were not allowed on fast days at supper.

The Decree of 1777 by Pius VI, referred to above, added the Wednesdays and Fridays of Advent as fast days, in place of the Vigils of those holidays of obligation which he had suppressed. But the Friday fast decreed by Leyburn, age-old as it was, was not popular, and in 1781 Bishop James Talbot of the London District instructed Mgr. Stonor (the Agent in Rome) to petition for its abolition, although, as he said, ' it is [of] almost the same date as

[1] *Idem*, Ep. Var., VI, 181.

[2] Ep. Var., VIII, 177.

[3] It was an act of intercession for the conversion of England.

M*

ye conversion of our Saxon ancestors '.[1] This petition was granted in a Rescript of July 8, 1781, for all Fridays except those in Lent and Q.T. (i.e. Ember Days), but the fast on the Wednesdays and Fridays of Advent was to remain. The petition had also asked for release from abstinence on the Rogation Days and on the Feast of St. Mark, but this was not granted.

Another time-honoured law in England forbad meat throughout Lent, and in the eighteenth century this was felt to be a great hardship. Accordingly some of the bishops granted dispensations from time to time allowing meat three times a week in Lent, except during Passiontide. But Bishop James Talbot deplored the inevitable tendency to whittle down penitential practices by the granting of dispensations, and he tried to put a halt to the process by refusing to dispense from this law in the London District in 1782, though he allowed eggs and cheese save on Ash Wednesday and the last four days of Holy Week.[2] However, in one subsequent year, 1789, he again gave the dispensation for meat, but said it was only for that year. But as he died a few months later the dispensation became a permanent arrangement, as his successors always granted it.

The keeping of Saturdays as days of abstinence (as done in Rome) was another very old English custom, and its abolition was also sought at this time. This was proposed by Bishop Douglass (Talbot's successor), who had received a petition from the London clergy to that effect. Bishop Milner objected to this vehemently, holding that the abstinence ought to continue, but all the other bishops approved of the change, chiefly because in practice the abstinence was largely ignored. A petition to this effect was sent to Rome, but it became overlooked there owing to the disturbed condition of affairs due to the Napoleonic wars; and the matter next came up at a meeting of the bishops at Wolverhampton in 1829. As a result, another petition was sent, and this was granted.

It is curious to find that Northern England had had from time immemorial a custom of its own : that of abstaining from eggs on all Fridays of the year and on every day of Lent. This matter was discussed at the General Assembly of the Old Chapter away back in 1674, and the meeting resolved that ' since the Regulars generally allow eggs on Fridays (to their people), the Superiors of Regulars be moved to endeavour to promote a conformity to the ancient custom of abstaining from eggs on Fridays and in Lent in the northern parts of England beyond the Trent '. But ten years later, at the General Assembly of 1684, it was stated that

[1] Westm. Archives, XLII, 11.
[2] See Ward, *The Dawn of the Catholic Revival in England*, I, 32.

the practice of abstaining from eggs on Fridays in the parts north of the Trent was in a great measure laid by, that those few who observed it did it chiefly in compliance with the decree of the General Assembly of 1676, that from this variety of practice happened often very scandalous disputes, in fine that most of the gentry desired conformity to the rest of England, especially since of late years that plenty of fish that had made their abstaining from eggs more easy had much failed; and it was agreed by much the major part that the northern Catholics on the other side of the Trent, may take the same liberty as to eating eggs on Fridays which is practised in other parts of England, and that this decree also extended to those on the other side of Ribble.[1]

[1] Kirk, *Op. cit.*, p. 85.

BIBLIOGRAPHY

In addition to the manuscripts preserved in the various Archives attached to the seminaries and cathedrals of this country, and especially those at Westminster Cathedral and Ushaw College, the following works also contain information on some aspects of the subject matter of this volume :

BERINGTON, JOSEPH, *The State and Behaviour of English Catholics.*

BRADY, W. MAZIÈRE, *The Episcopal Succession in England, Scotland and Ireland, 1400-1875.* 3 vols.

BURTON, EDWIN H., *The Life and Times of Bishop Challoner, 1691-1781.* 2 vols.

BUTLER, CHARLES, *Historical Memoirs respecting the English, Irish and Scottish Catholics.* 4 vols.

GILLOW, JOSEPH, *Bibliographical Dictionary of the English Catholics.* 5 vols. *The Haydock Papers.*

GUILDAY, PETER, *The English Catholic Refugees on the Continent, 1558-1795.*

GWYNN, DENIS, *Bishop Challoner.*

HUGHES, PHILIP, *The Catholic Question, 1688-1829.*
Rome and the Counter-Reformation in England.

KIRK, JOHN, *Biographies of English Catholics.*

MATHEW, ABP. DAVID, *Catholicism in England.*

MILNER, JOHN, *Supplementary Memoirs of English Catholics.*

OLIVER, GEORGE, *Collections illustrating the History of the Catholic Religion.*

PAYNE, J. O., *Old English Catholic Missions.*

THADDAEUS, *The Franciscans in England.*

THURSTON, HERBERT, *The Darkness before the Dawn.*

WARD, MGR. BERNARD, *The Dawn of the Catholic Revival in England, 1781-1803.* 2 vols.

WHELAN, DOM BASIL, *Historic English Convents of To-day.*
The Dictionary of National Biography.
The Catholic Record Society's volumes.

INDEX

189